AMERICAN GOVERNMENT

Issues and Challenges of the 1980s

Second Edition

Robert M. Bigler
Michael W. Bowers
Steven Parker
Dina Titus
Andrew C. Tuttle

University of Nevada, Las Vegas

Kendall/Hunt
Publishing Company
Dubuque, Iowa

B   403936   01

Contents

Preface   v

Chapter 1   **Foundations of American Politics**   **1**

Chapter 2   **The Judicial System**   **19**

Chapter 3   **Freedom and Rights**   **37**

Chapter 4   **Congress**   **59**

Chapter 5   **The Presidency**   **71**

Chapter 6   **The Administrative Branch**   **93**

Chapter 7   **Interest Groups**   **109**

Chapter 8   **Political Parties**   **123**

Chapter 9   **Campaigns and Elections**   **139**

Chapter 10   **Voting Behavior**   **173**

Chapter 11   **The United States and the World**   **193**

Chapter 12   **State and Local Government**   **207**

Chapter 13   **Issues for the Eighties and Beyond**   **219**

Appendix A   **The Declaration of Independence**   **237**

Appendix B   **The Constitution of the United States of America**   **241**

Index   257

Preface

The authors of this volume feel it is important to discuss American politics within the prescribed constitutional framework of government. However, they believe that analyses of the cultural, economic, and social context provides a better understanding of the issues and challenges of our times.

Consequently they have described and analyzed governmental institutions in the traditional manner while at the same time they have emphasized the many forces that have shaped, and continue to shape, American politics.

The authors wish to acknowledge the contributions of their colleagues, Professors Gary Jones and Jerry Simich, which include editing, suggestions, and writings. In addition, Miss Shari Brown should be credited for her patience and long hours of typing.

Chapter 1

Foundations of American Politics

The institutions which govern a society can best be understood as reflections of the beliefs, attitudes, and values of the people who make up the society. The framework of institutions which govern a society can, in the final analysis, be understood only through knowledge of the whole human environment. As Marc Bloch puts it: "social classification exists in the last analysis only by virtue of the ideas which men form of it."[1] Thus the actual character of a political system will be determined by the character of the men who make it up. Political institutions, like all institutions, are made up of the interactions of men. Those interactions are greatly influenced, even dictated, by the beliefs, attitudes, and values of the men who are engaged in them. What people do, and how they do it, is governed by what they believe. Politics begins, it may be said, in the minds of men. Political life among men begins when they have developed an intersubjective world (and only then may they be called "a people") in which each individual is recognized as a part of the group.

What this means is that the political behavior of a people, those interactions among them which constitute their political system, springs from, is influenced and determined by, their culture. What we shall be concerned with in this chapter is a description of American political culture, or what Thomas Jefferson once called the "American political mind." This mind is a substantive fact of life in America and is as tough and enduring as any other. If we are to come to an understanding of American political institutions we must first come to an understanding of the main ideas and values of the American people, and how they shape political, social, and economic life among them.

Culture

Before beginning our consideration of American political culture and its influence on the American political system it is important that we get clear about what we mean by "political culture." By *culture* is meant the habitual modes of thought and behavior characteristic of a given society; it is a way of thinking, of feeling, of believing. In other words, the culture of any society is its social heredity, the man-made part of the environment. It includes the ideas, habits, and traditions acquired by members of a group in the course of growing up in that group.

Edward B. Tylor, the first to use the term in its modern technical sense in English, defined "culture" as "that complex whole which includes knowledge, belief, art, morals, law, custom, and other capabilities acquired by man as a member of society."[2] It is, in a word, the social legacy the individual inherits from his group. Further, culture is abstract in the sense that it influences behavior but it is neither the behavior itself nor the tangible results. Culture does have a material

1

dimension in that "artifacts" or "culture objects" are cultural, but as concrete objects they are not a part of culture as that term is normally used. At its simplest, the term culture as used here refers to the common orientations toward action of two or more people.

These orientations toward action are composed of three elements:

1. *Ideas.* An important aspect of culture is its cognitive element, that is, the knowledge of the physical and social world possessed by those who share the same culture, the "cognitive map" of the members of society. It includes ideas about how a society works, how it is organized, about the nature of the cosmos, of man, etc. These ideas may be only partly true (if true at all) as demonstrated by logical and empirical methods, but they are, nonetheless, held to be true by the actors themselves.
2. *Belief.* Beliefs (or opinions) differ from ideas (or knowledge) in that they cannot be proven to be either true or false in logical or empirical terms. While belief and knowledge frequently get confused in the minds of the actors, they are, nevertheless, distinct phenomena.
3. *Values.* Values include the social principles, goals, and standards of a people. They are difficult to separate from attitudes with which they overlap. The values with which we shall be concerned here are those that are directly or indirectly involved in social relations, especially those that have been to a greater or lesser extent institutionalized.

In addition to ideas, beliefs, and values an important dimension of culture is the common sharing of certain signs, symbols, and rituals (e.g. flags, anthems, holidays) in terms of which the members of the society react toward one another.

Culture is important, then, in that it establishes a frame of reference within which action takes place. Culture not only shapes a group's orientation toward action; it helps define what is important among the multitudes of phenomena presenting themselves to the actors. It helps determine which *facts* they will notice and how they will interpret them. It literally programs them toward certain kinds of conclusions about the world. Culture is, in a sense, a grid a people imposes upon the world thereby making it intelligible. It determines the manner in which a people will define "reality."

Political Culture

Political Culture is not the same as general culture, though it is associated with and derived from it. In its simplest formulation, political culture is the political aspect of culture. It is a way of thinking, feeling, and believing about politics. Like culture in general, political culture is rooted in the cumulative historical experiences of particular groups of people. Indeed the origins of particular patterns of political culture are frequently lost in the mists of time. A people is, as is the case with individuals, a creature of its past.

All political systems are embedded in a set of political meanings and purposes. These include attitudes toward politics, political values, ideologies, national character, ethical standards, etc.—in other words, an orientation toward political action. Political culture is, then, the system of empirical or logical ideas, beliefs, values, and expressive signs, symbols, and rituals which defines the context in which political action takes place.

The cognitive element, that is, the *ideas,* of political culture are the ways people perceive and interpret the nature of political relationships. For example, the idea that America is a democracy. Political *beliefs* are those opinions about politics, etc. that can neither be proved nor disproved. For example, the belief that democracy is good. Political *values* provide the standards used to set the general goals of the political system, as well as the standards used to evaluate political demands, processes, and products. Expressive signs, symbols, and rituals express the way people feel about their political institutions and leaders, their patterns of loyalty, identification, and commitment to the political system. Additionally, signs, symbols, and rituals are an important means of reinforcing the people's loyalty, identification, and commitment to the political system.

Political culture, then, sets the stage for political action and that action has meaning only in that context. Political action, as a type of social action, takes place when people collectively embrace and share mutually understood forms of consciousness (or orientations for action) which authoritatively define relationships and allocate roles among them. The political institutions which make up a political system are one form of consciousness for action adopted by a people. This consciousness is the true, relatively stable and permanent "inner reality of the institutions." As Harry Jaffa once so aptly put it: "The political system that constitutes the United States exists mainly in the minds of the people of the United States."[3] Social and political institutions exist only in and through the orientations toward action current in society. The essence of a political institution is, then, that it is an expression of social agreement to act in accordance with certain established and accepted patterns.

While every political system is embedded and exists only within a political culture, a political culture does not necessarily coincide with one political system or society. It will frequently be the case that particular patterns of political culture will overlap several political systems and, alternatively, it is possible that two or more political cultures will be found to coexist within a single political system.

Impact of Political Culture

While little knowledge of the precise ways in which political culture exerts influence is available, it is possible to suggest some of the ways in which differences in political culture are likely to be significant. Political scientist Daniel J. Elazar suggests that there are three aspects of political culture that stand out as being particularly influential.[4]

1. The set of perceptions of what politics is and what can be expected from government, held both by the general public and the politicians.
2. The kinds of people who become active in government and politics, as holders of elective offices, members of the bureaucracy, and active political workers.
3. The actual way in which the art of government is practiced by citizens, politicians, and public officials in the light of their perceptions.

American Political Culture

While there are certainly local variations throughout the country, the United States as a whole shares a common political culture. There is now and traditionally has been a societal consensus on certain ideas, beliefs, and values in the United States and all political debate and action has taken place in their context. Therefore, if we hope to understand the American political system and the institutions which make it up, we must first identify and come to an understanding of the main ideas and values of American culture, and how it shapes the social, political, and economic behavior of the American people.

Perhaps the most important fact to be understood about American political culture is that it is decidedly modern. That is to say, it exhibits few of the pre-modern or feudal traits which are characteristic of European cultures. This is no doubt a consequence of the fact that those who migrated to the United States were those who were least attached to the prevailing ideas and values of European societies. But, it is not enough to say that American culture is modern, we must ask: in what does this modernity consist? "Modern" in this context does not refer to the facts of extensive industrialization, technological advancement, and unremitting urbanization. Rather, it is a set of attitudes about man and his possibilities in this world (and maybe the next) which underlies, accounts for, and, perhaps most importantly, permits those facts.

Liberalism

For the most part the ideas and values which animate the American political system have been derived from nearly three centuries of political thought and practice. They are derived especially from the contributions made by such writers as Adam Smith, David Ricardo, John Locke, Jeremy Bentham, and John Stuart Mill—all of whom built upon and extended the ideas of Thomas Hobbes. In actual political practice these ideas attained their fullest expression in the late nineteenth century. However, the roots of modernity are to be found in those two powerful movements involved in the shattering and breaking of the feudal system and the transformation of medieval Europe: Protestantism and capitalism. Taken together, these all constitute the cultural system of *liberalism*. What has been called the American liberal tradition is rooted, then, in the intellectual contributions of a few economists and political philosophers. This was accompanied by the simultaneous emergence of capitalism and the Protestant reformation tempered by the reality of the American frontier experience. It is the final basis of belief and action and is responsible for the whole structure of historical development of American society. It is, in a word, the ultimate root of American political conduct.

As a perception of what politics is and what can be expected from government, liberalism (or modernity) is the formulation most familiar to Americans. In fact, it is so familiar, with its stress on individualism, initiative, competition, private property, and the free marketplace, that most Americans see it as reality. It is, to them, natural, inevitable, nonproblematic—in a word, simply the way things are and not just one among many competing conceptions.

As a conception of the political order, liberalism has, in America, taken on two forms. That is, while the United States as a whole shares a general political culture, it is "rooted," as Elazar has noted, "in two contrasting conceptions of the American political order, both of which can be traced back to the earliest settlement of the country."[5]

In the first view, the political order is conceived as a *market-place* in which primary public, as well as private, relationships are the product of bargaining among self-interested groups and individuals. Under this view individuals are seen as possessing certain rights, and there are things no other person or group can do to them without violating those rights. People are, according to this view, ends, not means and therefore they may not be used for purposes to which they do not consent. For that matter, society itself is conceived in individualistic terms. Individuals, acting out of self-interest join together to create society in order to gain their private ends. Those who embrace this view say they are in favor of telling the government to leave the individual alone; that it ought to restrict its activities to those that foster and promote individual self-advancement. Out of the total universe of possible individual rights, the right to private property occupies a position of eminence. In fact, the right to private property is seen as *the* individual right; it is through the exercise of this right that the individual achieves his fulfillment. Private property is so cherished in this view, that there is a willingness to sacrifice human life in order to protect it. Those who accept this view believe that the just society is to be found in the free operations of the marketplace. Consequently they believe that most forms of societal intervention into human affairs must be resisted. In a word, they can best be described as those who embrace the ideology of "free enterprise." We can summarize this view by saying that those who follow it put their faith in individual self-achievement, in a sound business market, in respect for authority (especially moral authority), in a strong police force, in gut patriotism (i.e., "America: Love it or leave it"), and in American military superiority.

In the second view, the political order is seen as a *commonwealth*—an order in which the whole people are bound together in sharing a common interest. In such an order the citizens cooperate in an effort to establish and maintain the best government possible so as to achieve certain moral principles shared by all. While those who accept this view also place a premium on individualism, the institution of private property, and are committed to the free operation of the market place, they are also terribly disturbed by the severe inequalities which result from the free operation of the market place. They too, accept the basic structure and value system of the capitalist system, but their acceptance is tempered by a general commitment to utilize communal power to intervene in the private sphere whenever it is considered necessary to do so for the public good, or the well-being of the whole community. Government must at least try to rectify some of the damage wrought by the operation of the market place: poverty, unemployment, ill health, pollution, and so on. Government is seen, then, as a positive instrument charged with the respon-sibility of promoting the general welfare and of curbing the worst abuses of the economic system. In a word, it is charged with the responsibility of assuring that all members of society can attain the "good life." Those who hold to this view, then, are committed to attempting to incorporate some measure of equality into liberalism. In sum, like those who embrace the first view, they are committed to the market place and to the need to protect private property, that is, to capitalism. But that commitment is tempered by the belief that government is by right and necessity obliged to intervene in the economic and social life of the community to allay some of the sharp inequalities which emerge from the free operation of the market.

These two views were aptly summarized by Edward S. Corwin several years ago when he wrote:

> Under the democratic system there are two possible conceptions of what a government ought to be doing, provided neither is pressed to a logical extreme. One is that government ought to preserve an open field for talent and not disturb the rewards which free competition brings to individuals. The watch-word of such a government will, of course, be Liberty. The other theory is that govern-ment ought to intervene for the purpose of correcting at least the more pronounced inequalities which are apt to result from the struggle for advantage among private groups and individuals. The watchword of such a government will be Equality.[6]

The first of these two conceptions has been variously called the Individualistic, Libertarian, or *Laissez Faire* conception. In it government is perceived negatively, necessary only because of the perversity of men. Further, government is seen as something possessing interests alien to and almost at odds with those of citizens. The second view has been called the Collectivist, Reformist, Egalitarian, or the Interventionist view. Here government is perceived as a positive force with an important role to play in the social life of the citizens. It is not regarded as alien to those over whom it wields its power, rather it is their agent working for them.

Components of American Political Culture

American political culture is fundamentally rooted in two contrasting, even conflicting, values. The first of these is the aggressive assertion of equality in social relations. Since Alexis de Tocqueville, observers of the American polity have been impressed with its commitment to the principle of equality. Liberalism is, fundamentally, an egalitarian ideology, premised on the belief that all men are created equal and that all have the right to equality of opportunity and equality before the law. It was in the principle of equality that Thomas Jefferson and Abraham Lincoln found the inspiration for their great contributions to the American political testament, the Declaration of Independence and the Gettysburg Address. Jefferson claimed that in writing the Declaration in 1776 he intended it "to be an expression of the American mind." However, it must be noted, its affirmation of egalitarianism was neither a description of the facts, as any student of the era can see, nor a goal for political action. Likewise, Lincoln, in drafting the Gettysburg Address sought to give expression to American national self-understanding. In asserting that ours is a "government of the people, by the people, for the people," he gave expression to the American belief in democratic egalitarianism in all its fullness, with no trace of distortion. But, as was the case with the Jeffersonian statement, Lincoln's declaration is precisely that, mere declaration, an aspiration. It is, as H. Mark Roelofs has observed, "a myth, a whole myth, but essentially false in both its substantive and formal aspects."[7]

The belief in national egalitarianism is an essential ingredient in the American Dream. But, it is, and always has been, a dream. But it is not this that makes the Jeffersonian and Lincolnian aspiration a myth, rather it is the fact "that the American people have no realistic intention of turning the dream into reality."[8] The value of egalitarianism is one to which the American people only pay lip service. Put simply, Americans don't really want equality. In terms of the actual living of their lives, their commitment to egalitarianism is fundamentally ambiguous and ambivalent—whether in terms of specific issues such as race, sex, or the distribution of wealth or in terms of general principles. At bottom, the conception of equality Americans adhere to is that articulated by the English philosopher Thomas Hobbes; namely, that equality means simply that no man is by nature politically superior to any other man. At the operative level, the American commitment to equality is tempered by their insistence upon those rights enumerated by Jefferson in the Declaration: "Life, Liberty, and the Pursuit of Happiness." In the final analysis, the American people are libertarians, and because this is so, they not only tolerate, they actually encourage—we might even say, require—inequalities of every sort.

It is at this juncture that the second of the fundamental values of American culture comes to the fore. According to Roelofs "the fundamental tenet of modernity (and the one by which most it decisively turned against medieval thought) was anthropocentrism" and "this man-centeredness in general philosophical orientation was translated into radical individualism in practical ethics and politics."[9] To the medieval mind the social order came first, for it was prior to the individual. The individual comes into this comfortably articulated whole, with all its marvelously intricate traditional and legal order and finds his place—his identity, his status, and his life work—in it. In an important and real sense the individual has no existence, no identity apart from the social order. His identity, even, we might say, his humanity comes as a consequence of his participation in the social order. The liberal or modern mind, however, reverses this emphasis. In the beginning there is not order, but chaos. The world is not the world of the social, but of the self. Man is alone, self-motivating, self-defining, and self-reliant. He has an existence prior to and independent of society. In fact, society itself is his creation, a result of his conscious efforts to impose order upon a chaotic world. The social order which comes as a consequence of these acts of creativity is an aggregate of discrete, isolated individuals each in pursuit of his own private good. All who occupy it are basically alike, and are by nature egocentric, rational, competitive, and acquisitive.

An important aspect of this view is the notion that man is by nature an acquisitive being who must, of necessity (and hence should) act in accordance with that aspect of his nature. Man is, fundamentally, economic man, a being in whom the economic and spiritual aspects are inextricably intertwined. An important corollary of this conception of man is the belief that man can only find his fulfillment through the possession of property. To the liberal mind property rights are prior to and independent of society, that is, they are natural and it is the chief function of the state to protect those rights. This means that the liberal stress on individualism does not result in a belief in anarchy. Quite the contrary—as we shall see—it results in an insistence upon order. One need only read the first several of the essays of *The Federalist* and the Preamble to the Constitution of the United States to see this emphasis upon order.

The theoretical foundation for the idea of property is laid in the works of the English philosopher John Locke, especially his *Second Treatise of Government,* published in 1689. There Locke asserts the rights of the individual and uses every device he can to persuade his audience of the importance of the extra-social doctrine of natural rights, the foremost of which are "life, liberty and estate." The main thrust of Locke's argument is to demonstrate the proposition that property should be held privately, despite the fact the world was originally given to all men to hold in common. He is concerned to show that it is possible—if only by lines on a map or in words in a contract—to distinguish between what is "mine" and what is "yours." It never occurs to Locke—as it did to Jean Jacques Rousseau later—that criss-crossing society in this way might have some very serious consequences. Such distinctions shatter all sense of community and visit a sense of alienation upon the individuals affected by them. They come to view their interests as being different from, even at odds with, those of the other members of the society.

According to Locke, the right to private property is derived not from society or government, but from the labor of man in appropriating from nature what is necessary to his preservation. His argument rests upon two propositions:

1. Since man has a right to his preservation, he has also, by implication, a right to the means necessary to that preservation.
2. Man has an exclusive right to his own labor and whenever he mixes his labor with something he has mixed with it something which is exclusively his, thus removing the object from the common. According to this view, then, what is mine is purely a consequence of my own action.

The validity of the act of appropriation lies in the act itself and not in any social acknowledgment of it. That is, the individual's right to appropriate and possess what he can is prior to and independent of society. Regardless of how the argument is put, this is nothing other than the doctrine of might makes right.

In a world occupied by egocentric, acquisitive beings, the sole motive for human action is avarice. In such a world there is no room for duty and affection, there is no community because every man is isolated from all others. Human relationships in such a setting are nothing but bargains struck between isolated, self-interested individuals which endure only so long as the parties to them are mutually satisfied. One relates to another only to the extent that such a relationship will help him to attain his own private interests. Such relationships have been called relationships of "avaricious transactionism" by Roelofs. After having described economic and political relationships in such terms Roelofs goes on to say "Locke was assuming the ethics of business and political life were one thing and the ethics of family affection were another."[10] However, he doesn't go far enough. In a world of egocentric, acquisitive, and isolated individuals, *all* relationships (even familial relationships) have as their basis avaricious self-interest. This is, of course, why as liberal society pushes individualism to its logical culmination it experiences a breakdown even in the family unit.

Human Nature

Figuring prominently in the foregoing is a third component of American political culture—one that is not so much a value as an idea—a conception of human nature. While most Americans do not know who Thomas Hobbes was and those who do view his political theory with abhorrence, the conception of human nature they cling to found its most forceful expression in his *Leviathan,* first published in 1651. In *Leviathan* Hobbes is concerned with the development of a complete system of political science, or as he called it, civil philosophy, but he spells out a conception of human nature which serves as the foundation for the whole structure, and has become a most important ingredient of liberal culture.

The seeds of Hobbes' political science are sown in his theory of human knowledge and in his theory of happiness (or value). In the former his materialism is evident from the beginning. All human knowledge is reached, he argues, through the senses, and every idea is the result of an impression upon an organ of sense by the motion of some external object. Hobbes embraces the categories of space, mass, and motion which were utilized in the seventeenth century to explain the nature of physical phenomenon as adequate for understanding the whole of reality, the social and psychological dimensions as well as the physical. "Body" (or "matter") and "motion" are for Hobbes the ultimate phenomena, and all mental and moral concepts are derived from them—may even be reduced to them. Even those things which are normally regarded as non-material phenomena—such as desires, thoughts, hopes, fears, loves, and hates—are reduced by Hobbes to internal motions brought into play by the stimulus of some external body. The pressure on our sense organs of some external thing gives rise to these internal motions which we call sensations and it is sensations which form the core, the raw material of knowledge. Man himself is nothing but sensations, activity, constant motions; he is but a restless bearing in the world machine.

In his theory of value (or of happiness) Hobbes follows the earlier thinker Niccolo Machiavelli, in that he maintains that it is appetite, or passion (or desire) which defines the good for man. This conclusion is not reached simply through empirical observations of behavior, but is deduced from his general theory of reality—his materialistic metaphysics. At the root of all human passions, or emotions, is the antithesis of appetite and aversion, both of which he defines in terms of motion. If an object stimulates motion toward itself it is the object of an appetite and is therefore good. If, on the other hand, an object stimulates motion away from itself it is an object of an aversion and is therefore bad. And, it is important to note, there is, Hobbes tells us, no other distinction of good and evil than this. Furthermore, man's appetites and aversions are utterly and completely selfish. If in his efforts to gain his own goals or avoid his own evils a man finds it necessary to deprive another of a goal (or even of his life) he will do so and will, by nature, be guilty of no moral wrong.

Happiness, or "felicity" as Hobbes called it, is continual success in getting what one desires and is the goal of all human action. While happiness is the goal of all human action, there can be, however, no such thing as perpetual tranquility or happiness. In this regard Hobbes observes that happiness is "a continual progress of the desire from one object to another, the attaining of the former being still but the way to the latter."[11] The means by which men attain these never failing objects of desire Hobbes calls "power." Power is, then, the means of achieving happiness, it is the ability to secure a good and may consist in one or more of three things:

1. Superior faculties of body or mind;
2. riches, reputations, and friends, or
3. the secret workings of God which men call "good luck."[12]

In addition to the backdrop formed by his theory of human knowledge and his theory of happiness the shape of Hobbes' political science was determined by his scientific method. The scientific tradition of which Hobbes was a part was worked out in the Italian university city of Padua in the sixteenth century and came to Hobbes by way of Galileo and William Harvey. The basic idea which guides this methodological tradition is this: the way to understand something is to take it apart, either in deed or in thought, ascertain the nature of its parts, and then reassemble it. Hobbes' civil philosophy is shaped by this maxim. In the Preface to the English edition of *De Cive (The Citizen)* Hobbes provides an informal account of his application of his method to civil society.

> Concerning my method . . . I took my beginning from the very matter of civil government, and thence proceeded to its generation and form, and the first beginning of justice. For everything is best understood by its constitutive causes. For as in a watch, or some such small engine, the matter, figure, and motion of the wheels cannot well be known, except it be taken insunder and viewed in parts; so to make a more curious search into the rights of states and duties of subjects, it is necessary. I say, not to take them insunder, but yet that they be so considered as if they were dissolved.[13]

To consider society as if it were dissolved is to imagine its members in a state of nature, that is, to state what man's condition would be if there were no civil authority over him, and to go on to state what rational measures would be necessary in order to escape that condition. This is precisely how Hobbes begins his civil philosophy.

Before beginning a consideration of Hobbes' treatment of the state of nature it is important to note that his account is a logical or hypothetical one; it does not presuppose that such a state did in fact ever exist historically. The historical aspect is wholly disregarded and the natural state of man appears as an inevitable conclusion from the first principle of human nature: the proposition that all human action springs from the antithesis of appetite and aversion. The "general inclination of all mankind [is] a perpetual and restless desire of power after power that ceaseth only in death."[14] Furthermore, men in the state of nature are not primitive creatures, they are not neanderthals or what have you, but man. Man is man; his nature remains the same whether he is in society or not.

State of Nature

The first thing to be known about the state of nature is that it is a state of equality; whatever differences there may be in appetites, and in the ability to satisfy them—that is, in bodily constitution, education, experience—the differences are so inconsiderable "as that one man can thereupon claim to himself any benefit, to which another may not pretend, as well as he."[15] From this it is concluded that the actual state of mankind is one of unceasing strife; "From this equality of ability ariseth equality of hope in the attaining of our Ends, and therefore if any two men desire the same thing, which nevertheless they cannot both enjoy, they become enemies; and in the way to their End . . . endeavour to destroy, or subdue one another."[16] There are three causes of quarrel among men; competition, distrust, and love of glory. The competition between man and man for the means to satisfy identical appetites, the fear in each lest another exceed him in power, and, the craving for admiration and for recognition as superior. But, these are the characteristics of actual or potential war; and such is indeed the condition of man in the state of nature. The state of nature is a state of war. The hand of every man is raised against every man; and so long as there is no common power to hold them all in awe, every man is the enemy of every man; science, art, letters, and the other evidences of enlightenment remain unknown, and human life is "solitary, poore, nasty, brutish, and short."[17] All men are, in this condition, isolated, each has nothing to go by but his own needs and calculations, no one to rely on but himself. It is a condition in which man's egocentric emotions are given full, unfettered reign.

In addition to those cited above, the state of nature involves, logically, the following characteristics:[18]

1. There exists no distinction between right and wrong. There is in nature no common standard of good and bad, and where no such standard exists rightness and wrongness cannot be predicated. The establishment of a common standard can only be accomplished after a lawmaker is agreed upon and that agreement ends the state of nature.
2. Justice and injustice have no place in nature. "Where there is no common Power there is no law: where no Law, no Injustice." Prior to or independently of the formation of civil society there simply is no such thing as justice.
3. There is no such thing as private property. The state of nature is a state of equality and where each individual stands in precisely the same relationship to all external objects, might alone determines property right: as Hobbes says "only that to be every mans that he can get; and for so long as he can hold it."

Such is the condition in which man is placed by mere nature. It must be remarked once again that Hobbes never makes the argument that such a condition ever actually existed. He argued instead, that this is a fundamental, i.e., natural disposition in men. But man is not doomed to incessant internicine warfare, there is a possibility of getting out of it, "consisting partly in the Passions, and partly in his Reason."[19] Man's fear of death leads him to desire peace and his reason suggests Articles of Peace, or Laws of Nature, which will lead him to it.

Natural Law

In dealing with natural law, Hobbes makes a distinction between it and natural right.[20] *Jus Naturale,* or natural right is purely descriptive in Hobbes' eyes, it is the central axiom, or rule which describes human behavior in the state of nature. It denotes simply the liberty each man possesses to do what *he* deems best "for the preservation of his own Nature." And by liberty he means simply the absence of impediments. By right of nature then, man may do whatever is necessary to preserve his own life.

Lex naturalis, or natural law, on the other hand, is prescriptive and implies primarily restraint rather than liberty. It designates a precept, or general rule, found out by reason, forbidding any act or omission that is unfavorable to preservation.

It is the equal natural rights of all men which make their natural state a state of war, with a maximum of uncertainty with respect to life, the foremost of human desires, and so long as every man's natural right to everything endures there can be no security. Natural law is a body of precepts, or general rules, found out by reason which make life secure.

Hobbes, in his treatment of natural law, identifies nineteen precepts conducive to making life secure. However, only the first three need to be discussed here. The first law of nature is that which requires man to seek peace and observe it, for only then can his natural state, the state of war, be escaped. In order to accomplish this, men must follow yet a second rule: that which requires that each renounce his right to everything, for it is the equal claim of all men to all things that is a primary source of the strife that characterizes the state of nature. In order to insure this, it is necessary to follow a third rule, that which Hobbes calls *justice,* vis, "That men perform their Covenants made."[21]

It is at this point that need for a sovereign authority with awesome power comes to the fore, for the making of a promise is, Hobbes maintains, no guarantee that it will be kept. A promise, just like any other human act, is made on the basis of self-interest. There is in the nature of the act, therefore, no assurance that the thing promised will be performed. The performance or non-performance is also a question of self-interest. The only guarantee for the keeping of faith is, then, the certainty that the greater good lies in the keeping. This certainty only exists, however, when a superior power stands ready to impose some evil for failing to keep the promise. Such a power does not exist in the state of nature and, consequently, convenants and contracts are of no significance in that state.

Thus the laws of nature play an important, a crucial, role in Hobbes' civil philosophy. It is they which require men, in an otherwise lawless state, to establish a sovereign authority over themselves. It is they which lead men out of the chaos which is their natural plight. They are not, in Hobbes' sense of the term, really laws at all, rather "they are but conclusions, or theoremes concerning what conduceth to the conservation and defence of themselves, whereas law, properly is the word of him, that by right hath command over others."[22] But they are binding upon men. They are not binding in the sense that everyone should under all circumstances actually observe them, but that everyone should desire their observance—they oblige, that is *in foro interno*. The laws of nature are the result of calculations concerning what is necessary for one's preservation and are the necessary preconditions of civil or social life.

The conception of human nature, the state of nature, natural law, and the creation of civil society spelled out in Hobbes' *Leviathan* has become a most important ingredient in liberal political culture in that it provides the basis for conceiving the nature and character of society and the interactions that make it up. It is in light of these notions that those who partake of liberal culture interpret and judge the actions of others, and in turn, behave themselves. They form the matrix within which political and social action takes place.

With this recounting of the American view of human nature we have completed our identification of the main components of liberal culture. Boiled down to its essentials we may say that the ideas, beliefs, and values governing American political life are: *competitive individualism; equality; materialism;* the right to *private property;* the efficacy of the *market* as a coordinating device in social, economic, and political life; and *limited,* or *constitutional, government.*

Competitive Individualism and Materialism

When translated into the concrete, everyday life of the American people, liberal culture takes on a variety of observable forms. The first of these is the stress on individual achievement and social mobility. This results in a concern with personal problems, not public or political problems and a tendency to rely upon oneself rather than the government. One of the more important political ramifications of this is the unusually low level of political participation of the American people.

This stress on individual achievement finds expression in the belief that people are meant to stand on their own two feet, that nobody owes them anything (and, conversely, that they do not owe anything to others). This belief in individual self-reliance is never more clearly expressed than it is in the recurring complaints about people on welfare and the emphasis upon "welfare cheats." Those who must rely upon the government for support (whether it be in the form of welfare or, interestingly, employment) are viewed as being somehow inferior to the rugged individualist.

Closely allied with this image of the self-reliant individualist, standing on his own two feet, owing nothing to anybody, nor being owed, is the commonly held belief that people are naturally competitive, that thay are perpetually striving to better themselves in relation to others. This leads to our emphasis upon getting more and getting ahead, or as it is so frequently put, "keeping up with the Jones'." This is most clearly manifested in the American view of success. Observers of American society, going as far back as Alexis de Tocqueville[23] in the 1830's, have noted the primacy and tenacity of liberal values and self-definitions in the form of the "success ethic," the belief in "getting ahead," of "making it," of "striving and achievement." The principle aspiration or goal of the American people can be summed up in the single word "success" and success has generally been equated with making money.[24]

An outgrowth of this stress upon, and view of, success is a strong emphasis on materialism in American life, the preoccupation with accumulating as many goods as possible—preferably money and property. The practical result of this is an emphasis upon consumption and the development of what is known as consumerism. What Thorstein Veblen called "conspicuous consumption"[25] is one of the most prominent features of American society and has become one of the most important ingredients in defining the "good life" or happiness. But this consumerisn is more than just a habit—one which is fostered by advertisers who spend many billions of dollars every year to persuade people to consume as much as they can and even more than they can afford—it is a way of life. It goes to the very core of one's being, for it is a measure of his accomplishments and a proof of his worth, to put it simply, one is what one consumes. To the extent that one's status and his self-image are determined by his ability to consume, both are a constant cause for concern in American life. Loss of income and hence the ability to consume, results in a loss of esteem and a sense of despair.

Yet another dimension of the individualistic bias of liberal culture is to be seen in the peculiar sense of loneliness to which it gives rise. This is only logical, for a society which stresses individual self-reliance and aggressive competition is not likely to be characterized by feelings of fellowship and community. Even though the most important decisions controlling the realities of their lives are made by others than themselves, Americans persist in thinking of themselves as self-reliant individualists. In actuality what they seem to be referring to is the privatization of their lives and the atomization of their social relations. Individualism in the United States seems really to refer to the absence of cooperative forms of behavior in production, consumption and recreation.[26]

Finally, individualism in American life should not be construed as meaning the freedom to choose moral, political, and cultural alternatives of one's own design. One of the most important social traits dictated by liberal culture is that of conformity. While each person is expected to operate individually, he is expected to do so in socially accepted ways—that is, in more or less similar ways and directions. The tolerance for eccentricity is, in fact, surprisingly low. Interestingly, this social trait of conformity finds expression not only in the demand that others abide by the majority will but also in the readiness to abide by the majority will. That this is so is demonstrated clearly by the character and success of advertising in the United States.

Property

A second form in which liberal culture gets translated into concrete everyday life in the United States is observed in the centrality of property in the minds and actions of the people and the government. Property is, among the American people, one of those facts of life seldom needing either explanation or justification. Americans are firm in their conviction that the right to property is inalienable and that the primary function of government is to protect the individual in his use and enjoyment of it. Indeed, property has taken on a sacred character in liberal culture because individual property rights are seen as essential to personal liberty,[27] and individual self-fulfillment. Access to and control over productive resources are viewed as a primary right of citizenship, the sanctity of which is frequently maintained at the expense of human life, as the readiness to resort to violence (both on the part of individuals and the government) in its defense so dramatically demonstrates. Pushed to its extreme this frequently results in opposition to paying taxes of any sort when the money thus raised is used for "welfare" programs.[28]

The Market

Closely associated with the institution of private property is the belief that the free market is an impersonal, objective, and efficient device for regulating social, economic, and political affairs. Early liberals, and today, many neoclassical economists, have insisted that it is absolutely essential that an open field for private initiative be maintained. "The absence of imposed purpose (or order)," we are told, "allows free play to creative initiative, while maintaining an effective filtering system to sort out beneficial innovations."[29] It is through the private, creative acts of individuals solving problems through experimentation that the progress of civilization, and hence the good of all, is secured. However, what is frequently overlooked in this view of the market is the possibility that it is part of a larger power system and the cultural matrix attached to it rather than as an "objective" device for the regulation of social, economic, and political affairs. It is not an autonomous or independent apparatus but is, instead, a creature of those who control the power system and its subservient cultural and socialization processes.

Constitutionalism

Finally, liberal culture gets translated into the concrete everyday life of the American people in the form of an insistence on constitutional or limited government. The American desire for a "government of laws, not of men," is rooted in the suspicion of power harbored by the vast majority of the American people, regardless of who exercises it. This fear of power has had a long history among the American people, as Henry Adams has observed:

> The great object of terror and suspicion to the people of the thirteen provinces was power; not merely power in the hands of a president or a prince, of one assembly or several, of many citizens or a few, but power in the abstract, wherever it existed and under whatever form it was known.[30]

Power has, then, always been feared in America, whether it is will power or political power, and Americans have never been at ease until they felt there were some constraints on power.

This fear of power seems to find its source in the conviction that he who possesses power will most certainly abuse it—a conviction that finds expression in the readiness to quote Lord Action: "Power corrupts . . . absolute power corrupts absolutely."[31] Furthermore, the presence of power is seen as a threat to equality and/or as a bar to one's gaining recognition as a superior.

Whatever its source, this fear of power has resulted in the demand for constitutional government. That is, government founded on the premise that the supreme authority is not possessed of unlimited sovereignty and that it is therefore possible to talk of the abuse of governmental authority. In the United States this demand for constitutional government has also involved the demand for a written constitution which explains the nature and the limits of the power of the government. It is to this that the following chapters are devoted.

Notes

1. Marc Bloch, *Feudal Society,* Vol. I, trans. L. A. Manyan. Chicago: University of Chicago Press, 1964, p. 268.
2. Quoted in A. L. Kroeber and Clyde Kluckholn, *Culture.* New York: Vintage Books, 1952, p. 81.
3. Harry V. Jaffa, *Equality and Liberty.* New York: Oxford University Press, 1965, p. 210.
4. Daniel Elazar, *American Federalism.* New York: Thomas Y. Crowell, 1966, pp. 84–85.
5. Ibid., p. 85.

6. Edward S. Corwin, *Constitutional Revolution, Ltd.* Claremont, California: The Friends of the Claremont Colleges, 1941, p. 3.
7. H. Mark Roelofs, *Ideology and Myth in American Politics.* Boston: Little, Brown and Company, 1976, p. 147.
8. Ibid., p. 148.
9. Ibid., p. 50.
10. Ibid., p. 65.
11. Thomas Hobbes, *Leviathan.* Baltimore: Penguin Books, 1968, p. 160.
12. Ibid., p. 150.
13. Thomas Hobbes, *Man and Citizen.* New York: Anchor Books, 1972, pp. 98–99.
14. *Leviathan,* p. 161.
15. Ibid., p. 183.
16. Ibid., p. 184.
17. Ibid., p. 186.
18. Ibid., p. 188.
19. Ibid.
20. Ibid., p. 189.
21. Ibid., p. 201.
22. Ibid., pp. 216–217.
23. See Alexis de Tocqueville, *Democracy in America,* 2 Vols. Vintage Books, 1945.
24. Irvin G. Wyllie, *The Self-Made Man in America.* New York: The Free Press, 1954, pp. 3–4.
25. Thorstein Veblen, *The Theory of the Leisure Class.* New York: Penguin Books, 1979.
26. *cf.* Roelofs, *op cit.;* Thorstein Veblen, *Absentee Ownership: The Case of America.* Boston: Beacon Press, 1967.
27. *cf.* Justice Potter Stewart, *Lynch v. Household Finance Corp.,* 405 U.S. 552 (1972).
28. See, for example, Robert Nozick, *Anarchy, State and Utopia,* New York: Basic Books, 1974, p. 30.
29. Thomas E. Flanagan, "F. D. Hayek on Property and Justice" in Anthony Parel and Thomas Flanagan (eds), *Theories of Property: Aristotle to the Present.* Waterloo; Ontario, Canada: Wilfrid Faurier University Press, 1979, p. 339.
30. Quoted in Grant McConnell, *Private Power and American Democracy,* New York: Alfred A. Knopf, 1966, p. 33.
31. Quoted in Hans J. Morgenthau, *Scientific Man Versus Power Politics.* Chicago: University of Chicago Press, 1965, p. 196.

For Further Reading

Adler, Mortimer J. and William Gorman, *The American Testament.* New York: Praeger Publishers, 1975.
Elazar, Daniel, *American Federalism.* New York: Thomas Y. Crowell, 1966.
Kroeber, A. L. and Clyde Kluckholn, *Culture.* New York: Vintage Books, 1952.
Roelofs, H. Mark, *Ideology and Myth in American Politics.* Boston: Little, Brown and Company, 1976.
Slater, Philip, *In Pursuit of Loneliness.* Boston: Beacon Press, 1970.
Tocqueville, Alexis de, *Democracy in America,* 2 vols. Vintage Books, 1945.

Name _____

Section _____

Date _____

Review Questions for Chapter 1: Foundations of American Politics

1. Culture _____
   _____
   _____
   _____
   _____

2. Political culture _____
   _____
   _____
   _____
   _____

3. Liberalism _____
   _____
   _____
   _____
   _____

4. Market-place _____
   _____
   _____
   _____
   _____

5. Commonwealth _____
   _____
   _____
   _____
   _____

6. Egalitarianism _____

_____

_____

_____

_____

7. Competitive individualism _____

_____

_____

_____

8. State of nature _____

_____

_____

_____

_____

9. Natural law _____

_____

_____

_____

_____

10. Constitutionalism _____

_____

_____

_____

_____

Essay Study Questions

1. What are the major components of American political culture?
2. Discuss the concepts of human nature, individualism, egalitarianism, materialism, and constitutionalism. Then show how they impact our thinking about American Politics.

Chapter 2

The Judicial System

The American judiciary has again become the focus of a heated controversy. The issues are: have judges become too powerful, too "activist" in making new rules for society, and have judges abandoned the ideals of neutrality and detachment to become mere politicians, deciding important cases on the basis of personal whim and political favoritism? There can be no doubt that many critics of the judiciary, and especially of the United States Supreme Court, believe this to be true. Whether the charges can be made to stick or not, it certainly is the case that judges have involved themselves in a significant number of new and controversial areas of social policy. Judges have made it possible for women to obtain abortions (within limits), they have ordered far-reaching prison reforms in various states, they have personally supervised the racial integration of schools, judges have been instrumental in expanding the rights of those accused of crime, and minorities seeking educational and employment benefits, and judges themselves were overwhelmingly responsible for initiating and supervising the movement toward greater numerical equality in electoral districts.

Critics of many different persuasions simply do not think that the courts should be so active in the policy-making arena. They would leave controversial social issues to the "popularly" elected branches of government. Many of these critics view judges as a tiny elite, often electorally unaccountable, who substitute their personal biases and preferences for the majority will. The result of this judicial activism, claim the critics, distorts the separation of powers and often leads to the formation of disastrous public policy. Judges, they charge, no longer merely adjudicate legal disputes, they have taken the role of supervisors, managers and administrators—in short, they have become our new bureaucrats.

On the other hand, "activist" judges reply in defense that American history is replete with examples of judicial involvement in policy-making and that judges have a unique role to play in protecting not only the rights of minority interests, but in safeguarding the fundamental values contained within the language of the Constitution itself.

One early commentator on American government, Alexander Hamilton, argues the case for broad judicial power in *The Federalist* number 78. The judiciary, wrote Hamilton, is "the least dangerous branch" of government—the judiciary has neither the power of the "sword or the purse"; its main task is to resolve legal disputes and to interpret the Constitution. Hamilton's ideas actually anticipated Chief Justice Marshall's decision in the case of *Marbury v. Madison* (1803) which held that courts could invalidate legislation which went beyond the language of the Constitution. This practice, known as judicial review, has evolved into a powerful tool and places the courts squarely in the middle of the political process. As long as courts enjoy the power to invalidate actions undertaken by the other branches of government, one may reasonably assume that they will actually use that power to promote some interest they perceive as deserving constitutional protection.

Court Structure

The American legal system is actually a mixture of one national or "federal" system plus separate court structures for the states. The basis for this complex system can be found in the United States Constitution which, in broad terms, establishes the federal court system and allows each state to establish its own court structure.

State Courts

The state court systems vary from state to state but it is still possible to render a general picture of a typical court structure. While the names of the various state courts may differ, the functions they perform are quite similar in the different states. At the lowest level, one usually finds either a Justice or Justice of the Peace court and a municipal court. These courts normally deal with the less serious matters in both criminal and civil proceedings. At the next level exist what are commonly called county and in some states, superior courts. These bodies are equipped to deal with the more serious criminal offenses and civil matters of a more important nature than would normally be heard in justice or municipal courts. County or superior courts are also known as "trial" courts and many cases at this level are trial before a jury. Some states have an intermediate level of appellate courts which try cases appealed from lower courts. At this level the function is that of deciding points of law.

Finally, each state provides a highest court of appeal and this body is usually designated the "Supreme Court." This court represents the last word on state judicial matters and its decisions are usually final unless they are modified or extinguished in some form by legislative or state constitutional change. The only appeal that can be had beyond a state Supreme Court must involve a "substantial federal question," or some fairly serious matter involving the breach of some federal law. It should be emphasized that not every case in a state court system can be appealed to the federal court system. When and if there is a substantial federal question involved in state litigation, appeal might, but not necessarily, be made to federal courts.

Selection of Judges

There are various methods of staffing employed by the states concerning their judiciaries. Some, like Nevada, insist that judges be accountable to the electorate. In such states, all judgeships are subject to periodic competitive elections. Such elections may take two forms. Partisan elections are those in which a judicial candidate is identified with one or the other of the political parties (or as an independent) on the ballot. In a nonpartisan election, however, the judicial candidates are simply listed without party identification. Other states (e.g., Missouri) have adopted a compromise between the elective and appointive systems. The "merit system"—as this compromise method is called—consists of a blue ribbon panel of judges, lawyers and laymen which presents a slate of two or three prospective judges to the governor. The governor in turn selects a person from the list who will then fill the judicial vacancy. When the judge's term of office expires, he will then face the voters in a noncompetitive election. That is, the ballot will simply read, "Should Judge X be retained in office?" The voters are allowed to vote "yes" or "no" but cannot suggest who they would like to replace Judge X. Should the judge not be retained in office—a rare event—

State Court Structure

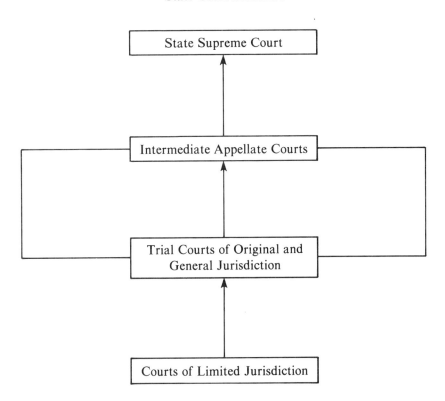

the blue ribbon panel would be required to present a slate of potential judges to the governor in order to fill the vacancy. States handle the removal and retirement of judges in accordance with their own individual statutes and customs.

State courts are, many of them, troubled by a sizeable backlog of cases resulting in long delays and public dissatisfaction. The vast majority of court cases, it should be noted, are heard in the state and not the federal courts. While state judges themselves are not usually blamed for this state of affairs, many observers believe that the cause lies in the proliferation of suits and the increased concern by members of the public in general with their legal rights.

Lower Federal Courts

There are at present ninety-five federal District Courts, with at least one in each state and territory. Larger states like California and New York have four and three, respectively. There are over 500 District Court judges currently handling the bulk of the federal case load. The District Courts, constitute the first or *trial* level of the federal court system. The District Courts, as do the United States Courts of Appeals and the United States Supreme Court, trace their origin to Article III of the Constitution.

The Federal Judicial Structure

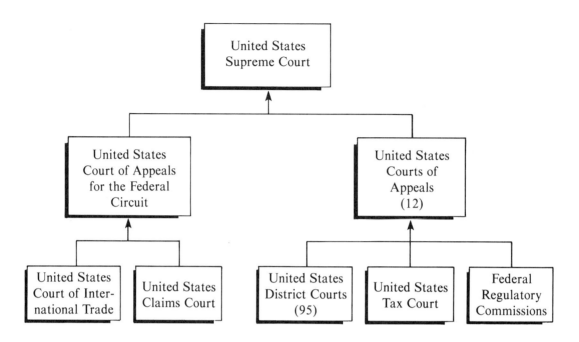

The United States Courts of Appeals, or "circuit" courts, form the next level and they consider cases only on appeal. They are composed of a panel, usually three judges, and there is no jury. This court is primarily concerned with procedural and constitutional issues of the proceedings below, rather than with matters of guilt, innocence or fact. Established by the Judiciary Act of 1789, circuit courts originally included a member of the Supreme Court. Each of these justices had a circuit and when the High Court was not in session, they would "ride the circuit" hearing appeals from the District Courts.

This requirement was subsequently changed in 1891 when Congress established ten circuits. There are currently thirteen Courts of Appeals in the federal system. There is one in Washington, D.C. and eleven others which are distributed regionally throughout the country. For example, the U.S. Court of Appeals for the Ninth Circuit hears appeals from the District Courts in Arizona, Nevada, Idaho, Montana, Washington, Oregon, California, Alaska and Hawaii. The thirteenth circuit court is also located in Washington, D.C. and is called the U.S. Court of Appeals for the Federal Circuit. This court hears only cases appealed from the International Trade Court and the Claims Court (see figure).

The so-called legislative or special courts include the U.S. Claims Court, the U.S. Tax Court and the U.S. Court of Military Appeals. These courts deal with special claims relating to affairs which Congress feels these courts are better equipped to handle. Unlike the District Courts, Courts of Appeals and the Supreme Court these courts are not Article III courts and the judges serve for a specified term of office. There are in addition a number of "independent regulatory commissions" such as the Federal Communications Commission and the Federal Trade Commission which perform quasi-judicial activities in the regulation of key sectors of the economy. Appeals from decisions handed down by these agencies can be made to the U.S. Court of Appeals.

Finally, there is the Supreme Court of the United States which consists of nine judges. The Supreme Court has both original and appellate jurisdiction and is the court of last resort in the American legal system.

Selection

All federal judges are nominated by the President. Before they are appointed however, they must be confirmed by a majority vote of the United States Senate. Nominees are investigated by the Judiciary Committee of the Senate. This group then makes a recommendation to the entire body. For the most part, a President's nomination is routinely accepted by the Senate. Occasionally, however, some of the senators may object to either the qualifications or the ideological persuasion of a nominee. An example of this occurred in 1969 and 1970 when the Senate refused to confirm two successive Nixon nominees to fill the seat vacated when Justice Abe Fortas resigned. However, the Senate found no reason to deny seating Sandra Day O'Connor, President Reagan's appointment to the high court. O'Connor is the first woman nominated to serve on the Court.

Federal judges are appointed to their positions for a period of good behavior. That is, they are virtually assured of a life-time job. There are only three ways that a person can be removed from the federal judiciary: (1) by death; (2) by resignation; and (3) by impeachment and conviction.

Lifetime Tenure

Some critics of the federal judiciary suggest that judges, like members of other professions, should be forced to retire at a reasonable age. It is believed that old judges are very likely to become physically or mentally incapacitated and that such disabilities could affect the quality of their decisions. Some people also believe that age produces ideological intransigency. On the other hand, it is desirable to have experienced and competent people on the federal bench. Health became an issue in 1974 and 1975, when Justice William O. Douglas suffered a stroke. His physical condition forced him to absent himself from proceedings on many occasions, thus late in 1975, Douglas ended the speculation and criticism by resigning. During the presidency of Franklin Roosevelt, Congress passed a law that was designed to make retirement a more desirable option for federal judges. It was decided that after age seventy they could retire at full salary.

Appointment for the period of good behavior is thought to be the very foundation of judicial independence. Ideally, it frees the judiciary from political pressures that could be exerted by a President, Congress, the bureaucracy, pressure groups, and public opinion. As such, it is argued, they can be objective about their interpretation of the Constitution and the application of justice.

The American Legal System

The United States has a mixed legal system. Its laws may be either statutory, common or both. Statutory laws are rules enacted by legislative bodies such as Congress, state legislatures, city councils and other units of government. Common law, sometimes referred to as "judge made" law, is a product of judicial decisions and custom. Precedent is extremely important to common law. In fact, the Supreme Court and other courts usually will follow the principle of *stare decisis,* that is, "let the decision stand." In this respect, statutory law can be more flexible. A legislative body may repeal or amend existing statutes, paying little or no regard to precedent.

Laws may be divided into an additional category, criminal and civil. The function of criminal law is to make society orderly, predictable and civilized. It establishes normative rules of behavior. Statutory penalties are prescribed for individuals who violate provisions of a criminal code. Usually a governmental unit will prosecute cases against alleged violators. For example, if a person is prosecuted for violating a federal statute the case will be the people of the United States versus the transgressor. The individual in this case constitutes a minority of one against the balance of society, a majority numbering some 240 million persons. Hence, procedural guarantees are most important. Civil law involves the concept of redress, which is to correct a wrong or to get relief from a wrong or an injury. Civil cases do not normally lend themselves to questions of guilt or innocence. Instead, the judge and jury are like umpires. They determine if a contract like marriage should be dissolved and then determine the conditions of dissolution. They also assess damages in matters such as medical malpractice, automobile accidents, and discriminatory treatment.

Supreme Court

The Supreme Court of the United States is at the apex of the American judicial system. These nine justices decide what the Constitution means from the perspective of the cases they adjudicate. It is, as Woodrow Wilson once observed, a kind of continuous constitutional convention.

The Supreme Court has original jurisdiction in matters involving foreign ambassadors and consuls and in disputes between two or more states, but cases of this sort do not constitute much of the Court's caseload. Diplomatic immunity protects members of the diplomatic corps and their families from criminal prosecution and civil suits, and there are few examples of interstate conflicts being resolved in this manner.

Appeals

There are a variety of cases that come from lower courts which the Court, in theory at least, must review. This method of getting a case before the Court is known as an appeal. If the highest court in a state declares a federal law or treaty provision unconstitutional or if it upholds a state law against a challenge that it conflicts with the federal Constitution or a federal law, then the Court will always adjudicate the conflict. Also, if a federal circuit court finds a state law or a provision of a state constitution in conflict with federal statutes or the federal Constitution then once again the Court will review the case.

Most cases which the Court is called upon to review reach the docket by having been granted a *writ of certiorari,* that is, a formal order wherein the Court agrees to hear the case. Members of the Court will give each request a preliminary review, and if four of the judges agree that the case has substantial merit, a writ will be issued and the Court will review the case. Requests for

FRANK AND ERNEST   **by Bob Thaves**

Reprinted by permission. © 1978 Newspaper Enterprise Association, Inc.

certiorari can only be considered if relief was denied by either a U.S. Circuit Court of Appeals or by the highest state court having jurisdiction. Every year the Court is besieged by thousands of such requests, but *certiorari* is usually denied to over 90% of them.

The increasing workload of the federal courts in general can be seen in the figure below which lists the number of cases at each of the three levels for the years indicated. For instance, between 1960 and 1983 the workload of the U.S. Courts of Appeals rose by approximately 750 percent! Similarly, the workload of the U.S. District Courts jumped during that time by about 300 percent. Increasingly, there have been calls by the legal community to boost the number of federal judges to handle this staggering case load. In response to those demands, Congress passed the Omnibus Judgeship Act of 1978 which created 117 new District Court judgeships and 35 new Court of Appeals positions. However, this proved to be inadequate and in 1984 Congress added 61 new judges to the federal courts.

Although the increased number of cases appealed to the Supreme Court has not been as dramatic as that in the lower courts, it too is operating under an increased workload. Although the Court denies review to the vast majority of these cases, the justices must still read the petitions in each case in order to decide whether or not to grant review. And, in those relatively few cases which the justices do hear, they will often write full opinions which explain their decisions. Although several proposals have been forwarded to reduce this workload, none have been instituted and the Court continues to be burdened with an increasing caseload.

Workload of the U.S. District Courts and U.S. Courts of Appeals

Year	U.S. District Courts	U.S. Courts of Appeals
1960	87,421	3,899
1970	125,423	11,662
1980	196,757	23,200
1981	210,931	26,362
1982	237,816	27,946
1983	276,523	29,630
1984	298,330	31,490

SOURCE: *Annual Report of the Director of the Administrative Office of the United States Courts, 1984.*

Workload of the U.S. Supreme Court

Year	Total Cases on Docket	Number Decided on Merits	Held Over	Denied Review
1978	4,731	271	714	3,746
1979	4,781	283	892	3,606
1980	5,144	282	948	3,914
1981	5,311	313	878	4,120
1982	5,079	315	878	3,886
1983	5,100	266	960	3,874

SOURCE: *Annual Report of the Director of the Administrative Office of the United States Courts, 1984.*

Judicial Review

The American Constitution, with its twenty-six amendments is a relatively short document that one can read in an hour or so. However, to be familiar with the constitutional system one would need knowledge of the body of constitutional law. Supreme Court action is known as judicial review. This is the power whereby the Court determines which practices or laws are or are not consistent with the Constitution.

Supreme Court of the United States

Name	Appointed by	Year	President's Party	Justice's Party
Warren E. Burger (Chief Justice)	Nixon	1969	Repub.	Repub.
William J. Brennan, Jr.	Eisenhower	1956	Repub.	Demo.
Byron R. White	Kennedy	1962	Demo.	Demo.
Thurgood Marshall	Johnson	1967	Demo.	Demo.
Harry A. Blackmun	Nixon	1970	Repub.	Repub.
Lewis F. Powell, Jr.	Nixon	1972	Repub.	Repub.
William H. Rehnquist	Nixon	1972	Repub.	Repub.
John Paul Stevens	Ford	1975	Repub.	Repub.
Sandra D. O'Connor	Reagan	1981	Repub.	Repub.

Article III of the Constitution outlines the judicial power. It is noteworthy that judicial review is not specifically mentioned. Congress, in order to define judicial duties more specifically, passed a series of laws starting in 1789. These various acts deal mostly with administration, size, duties and jurisdiction of the federal courts.

Marbury v. Madison (1803) helped to establish the precedent for judicial review. The Court, under the leadership of Chief Justice John Marshall, invalidated Section 13 of the Judiciary Act of 1789. When this action was accepted by the President and Congress without challenge, it confirmed the principle of judicial review. Successive Courts have affirmed the concept which includes authority over acts of executives and state governments as well.

Theories of Judicial Behavior

Generally, there are two theories about how the Court should operate. The first may be labeled self-restraint. That is, the Court should not seek to expand the powers and prerogatives of the judicial branch. Proponents of this view would favor state's rights and oppose governmental regulation and control of the economy. Judges of this persuasion are labeled judicial self-restraint advocates. Representatives of this school of thought would include Chief Justice Salmon P. Chase, who was appointed by President Lincoln. The second approach to judicial behavior may be called expansionist. That is, the Court should perform a nationalizing function. According to this premise, the Court should be a watchdog over the various governments as well as the private sector of the economy. Judges who subscribe to this approach often believe that their function is to protect the rights of certain groups and individuals by invalidating both state and federal laws which they feel deny those rights. Individuals of this persuasion also are known as judicial activists. Representatives of this viewpoint would include Chief Justice Earl Warren, appointed by President Eisenhower and the late Justice William O. Douglas, appointed by President Franklin Roosevelt.

It is difficult to label any one Court as having been either liberal or conservative. There are nine individuals who at times defy simple categorization. Many people point to the Warren Court as having been the most "liberal." However, it is interesting to note that many of its decisions were made by a margin of five to four. Some judges, like the late Associate Justice Hugo L. Black, seem to fit into both camps. Black was often a proponent of expanding functions of the national government, yet on the other hand, he regarded himself as a "strict constructionist" as far as the Constitution was concerned. This view is generally regarded as the hallmark of judicial conservatism. Black carried a copy of the Constitution with him and when he was asked a question by journalists or newscasters about an issue involving the First Amendment he referred to the document. "Congress shall make no law," he read. Then he would repeat with emphasis, "that doesn't mean some or any, that means *no* law."

Decision Making: Inside the Supreme Court

The publication in 1979 of *The Brethren,* by Bob Woodward and Scott Armstrong, created an uproar by depicting the Supreme Court in what some felt to be a highly unfavorable light. Instead of reaching carefully thoughtout decisions in a detached and neutral manner, Supreme Court Justices were shown to engage in vote-trading, petty squabbles and partisan activity. For the first time, the Court's veil of secrecy had been ripped away, exposing it as just another "political" institution. Critics of the book protested vehemently that the public would lose respect for the Court, and accordingly, for the idea of law itself. Many critics were also upset with the picture painted of Chief Justice Warren Burger, who came off looking like a jealous partisan, lacking in leadership abilities, suspicious of a free press and incapable of drafting a coherent opinion. It is probably too early to assess the damage to the Court's image instigated by *The Brethren*. If only half of what was reported in the book is true, it should stand as a reminder that judges are only human beings like the rest of us, in spite of the high calling of their position.

In order to acquire an insight into judicial reasoning, one should, of course, read the opinions of the Court. Once the Court has agreed to review a case, it will then deliberate the legal merits of the issues. Generally, the Court will meet Monday through Thursday. Almost all business of the Court is conducted in private, behind closed doors. The cloak of secrecy makes it possible for the justices to direct their attention to the merits of the cases, rather than to pander to reporters and television cameras. Indeed, secrecy of proceedings is another cornerstone of judicial independence. It shields judges from public view and enables them to perform their deliberations apart from the gossip and limelight that is part of the nation's capital. Members of the Court are among the most powerful people in Washington, D.C., yet they are usually the least visible.

There are two public sessions of the Court. The first is when oral arguments are heard on matters under review and the second is when the decisions are announced. After the justices have conduced a preliminary review of a case, they listen to counsel present the arguments of their respective clients. Members of the Court sit on a long bench in a rather impressive hall. The attorneys stand at a lectern facing the justices. Generally, they are allowed an hour to present their views and much of their time is usually spent responding to questions from the justices. There is no jury at the Supreme Court level and little drama. The justices have presumably read all of the legal briefs prior to argument by counsel and are therefore familiar with the case at hand. Hence, for the most part, interest is focused on specific details or technicalities. Many observers are firmly convinced that the judges have their minds made up prior to hearing oral arguments and contend further that they know how a particular justice will vote on an issue by the intensity of his questions or remarks he might utter.

Court Opinions

After the attorneys are heard the judges retire and again in secret decide the constitutionality of a case. The Chief Justice presents each case to his colleagues along with his own views and comments. After the Chief Justice is finished, then the associate judges, in order of seniority, discuss the particular case. When deliberation is finished, voting begins. The most junior judge votes first, the most senior last. A majority is needed to decide all issues. If for some reason there is a tie vote[1] it means that the Court cannot make a decision and the decision of the lower court is automatically affirmed. After the voting, the Chief Justice assigns the writing of opinions. If he is with the majority, then he often will write the Court's opinion. Drafts of the opinion are circulated among the members for their comments and then it is printed.

Opinions are what the Court has decided and why. They may contain references to the Constitution, other cases, various laws, legal scholarship, expert studies, and anything else that the judges deem necessary to substantiate their points of view. An opinion may be very specific in nature or it can be general. Usually, it will contain a court order wherein governmental agencies are ordered to embark upon a certain course of action, or they are ordered to discontinue practices that the Court has found to be unconstitutional.

Any given case also may include concurring and dissenting opinions. A concurring opinion is written by a justice who agrees with the majority decision but for different reasons. A dissenting opinion is written by a justice or justices in the minority who feel compelled to express their views and explain why they believe the majority is in error. The most well-known dissents have been written by Justices Oliver W. Holmes and Louis D. Brandeis, both of whom served on the Court during the first one-third of the twentieth century. More often than not their protests were concerned with denials of civil rights and liberties.

Opinion day is the other time the Court has a public session. On these days the Court, without the benefit of press agents and drama, briefly announces decisions that can be so profound as to affect the lives of generations of Americans. Yet, for the most part, Americans give the Court very little attention.

The Supreme Court is the least bureaucratized of the three branches and also the least expensive to operate. The Court's work load has increased tremendously since World War II. But the justices have not deemed it necessary to compartmentalize the institution. Together with its clerks and secretaries the Court is living proof that public affairs can be administered without the enormous machinery that has become characteristic of modern governments.

The Chief Justice

The post of Chief Justice of the United States is not a position one attains by seniority or by promotion. When a Chief Justice vacates his seat, the next person appointed automatically becomes the new chief judge. Occasionally, a President may seek to elevate an associate justice to lead the Court. Four Chief Justices, Rutledge, White, Hughes, and Stone, were recruited and appointed in this manner. In recent times, President Lyndon Johnson nominated Associate Justice Abe Fortas to be Chief Justice when Earl Warren announced his decision to retire. During the Senate investigation of Mr. Fortas, it was revealed that he had received and held for eleven months $20,000 from the family foundation of Lewis E. Watson who was later imprisoned for illegal stock manipulation. Stung by allegation of conflict of interest, and under the threat of impeachment, Fortas' name was withdrawn from consideration and he subsequently resigned from the Court. Mr. Warren remained on duty until his successor, Warren Burger, was appointed by President Nixon.

The Chief Justice has no more formal power than each of his colleagues. He naturally receives greater attention than the other justices because he is the spokesman for the Court. He also has a symbolic role to perform in that he represents the Court and in the chambers of the Supreme Court his only powers are his leadership and persuasive abilities. He cannot bully his colleagues into agreement by making threats or by promising them something they do not already have. The force of some personalities have dominated and shaped the Supreme Court. Men like John Marshall, Roger Taney, and Earl Warren were dynamic and creative and they left their stamp firmly upon the Court and its decisions. However, some Chief Justices, like Oliver Ellsworth and Edward White probably viewed their respective roles as that of dutiful managers rather than as innovative leaders. As a result, their courts are generally remembered, if at all, as having been dreadfully dull rather than controversially different.

Access to the Courts

Washington, D.C. is probably the most political city in the world. It has experienced and somehow survived an onslaught of people seeking to protect and promote private interests by whatever means that might work. This kind of pressure activity and influence peddling is as old as man's social history. Yet, in a city so jaded that it seems to react to only the most spectacular venality, one institution, the Court, appears outwardly to remain curiously aloof. Obviously, interest groups have stakes in the outcome of any given issue. But, the means of attempting to influence those nine votes have almost become part of the legal system itself.

Chief Justices of the United States

Name	Appointing President	Service Dates
John Jay	Washington	1789–1795
John Rutledge*	Washington	1795–1795
Oliver Ellsworth	Washington	1796–1800
John Marshall	J. Adams	1801–1835
Roger Taney	Jackson	1836–1864
Salmon Chase	Lincoln	1864–1873
Morrison Waite	Grant	1874–1888
Melville Fuller	Cleveland	1888–1910
Edward White	Taft	1910–1921
Charles E. Hughes	Hoover	1930–1941
Harlan F. Stone	F. Roosevelt	1941–1946
Frederick Vinson	Truman	1946–1953
Earl Warren	Eisenhower	1953–1969
Warren E. Burger	Nixon	1969–

*Rutledge was rejected by the Senate and only served as chief justice for four months

Individuals or groups seeking access to a court generally have to satisfy two requirements—"standing to sue" and they must see to it that the court in which they seek to litigate must have jurisdiction. One has standing to sue if she or he is a proper plaintiff. Broadly speaking, this means that the case is bonafide, not moot or feigned. Courts normally will not rule on hypothetical issues; in other words, the case must arise out of a concrete dispute between parties, one of whom at least has suffered some legal injury. Presumably courts will entertain a suit only if they are capable of supplying a remedy.

In addition to satisfying standing requirements, it must be demonstrated that the case falls within a particular court's jurisdiction. The jurisdiction of a court is determined either in a constitution or legislation and specifies what types of cases that court will hear. Jurisdiction is further subdivided with respect to geography, subject matter and hierarchy. Georgraphy refers to the territorial limits of a court's activity, be it, for example, a municipality, a county, a district, state, or the United States as a whole. Subject matter limits a court to the kinds of cases it can rightfully entertain; for example, misdemeanors only or a small civil matter, a divorce, while hierarchy refers to the fact that some courts are triers of fact or courts of original jursidiction while others are purely appellate courts, or courts that hear only those cases which are appealed from lower courts. Some courts, normally the highest courts in the states and the national government may have both original and appellate jurisdiction.

Access to the court system can also be understood in a broader sense as the ability of interest groups to influence judicial decision making in a variety of ways. These methods include court watching, letter writing, appeals to the media, attempts to influence appointments and elections of judges, demonstrations and the like. Often interest groups will seek to influence policy by instituting litigation themselves, as the history of the NAACP amply demonstrates. Groups may utilize legal devices such as class action suits wherein an individual sues for himself and others "similarly situated." Thus, for example, a single minority claiming racial discrimination may sue for himself and all other minorities falling within the same category. The effect of the decision applies to all the persons in that class, not just one person, as in a typical law suit. Interest groups have for some time now filed "amicus curiae" or "friends of the court" briefs which usually contain interpretations of the disputed legal issue and factual information by which the interested parties attempt to persuade the judges to their side.

If, for example, a municipality attempts to limit its growth by restricting construction of new homes, in all likelihood it would be taken to court by some association of building contractors. Briefs could be expected to bolster the claims of each side; for example, city briefs might be submitted by environmental groups, and for the plantiffs, briefs might be submitted by various groups representing contractors or various business and labor organizations fearful of a decline in business and job opportunities. All of these attempts to influence judicial behavior vividly demonstrate the important political role which courts play in the American legal system. While judges are not supposed to be open to lobbying in the same fashion as are legislators, interest groups nonetheless are keenly aware of the fact that they must attempt to reach judges in some fashion in order to make their views and interests known.

Checks and Controls

Although the Supreme Court has the last word on constitutionality, it is not without control. There are checks that are imposed by the other two branches as well as those that are self-imposed. The President, with the cooperation of the Senate, determines the composition of the Court. Some presidents such as Roosevelt and Nixon have used the appointive power to try to shape the Court into an ideological mold of their liking. However, several presidents have been very disappointed with appointees because they did not turn out as expected. Once confirmed, the justices are beyond executive control. President Eisenhower was reported to have observed that his biggest mistake was the appointment of Earl Warren; President Truman was equally disappointed with his choice of Tom Clark.

Another executive check is that of enforcement. The Court can make decisions and pronounce commandments, but for compliance it must rely upon good will and the executive branch. President Jackson, unhappy with a Court verdict, was said to comment, "John Marshall has made his decision, now let him enforce it."[2] Sometimes judicial pronouncements are enforced immediately. As soon as the Court in *U.S. v. Nixon* ruled that presidential tapes must be relinquished, Mr. Nixon turned over the recordings to the special prosecutor. On other occasions, a Court ruling may take years before it is universally accepted. In 1954, the Court, in *Brown v. the Board of Education of Topeka* ordered desegregation of public school facilities with "all deliberate speed." Thirty-two years later, desegregation is being realized in many states but continues to arouse deep-seated resentments. The major bone of contention is the use of court-ordered busing to achieve integrated schools.

Congress also checks the judicial branch. Impeachment and removal from office are Congressional functions. The size of the Court and judicial salaries are also determined by legislative initiatives. However, as a means of guaranteeing some degree of judicial independence the salary of a federal judge cannot be reduced while he is in office (Article III). And, in cooperation with three-fourths of the states, Congress can amend the Constitution and further control the courts.

Congress may also restrict the judiciary, as they have in the past, by passing a law. The tightest controls are imposed by the justices themselves by means of what has become known as judicial self-restraint. This is a code of behavior that has evolved, mostly through Court decisions, over the years.

Self-Restraint

The precepts of self-restraint prevent the Court from rendering advisory opinions. It will not advise the President or Congress or anyone else how it views action or legislation before there is a case. When there is a case, it must deal with specific constitutional issues. The Court does not entertain generalities. Furthermore, the "federal question" or constitutional issue must be substantial rather than trivial and it must be the pivotal point of the case. The case or controversy must directly concern the party asking for review. Finally, in this respect, the Court will not entertain a case unless relief has been denied in all lower courts.

With respect to legislative bodies, the Court will not ordinarily impute illegal motives to law makers. A law may be unjust, undemocratic, or outrageous, but still legal from a constitutional point of view. The Court, as the saying goes, is not a check against incompetent, unwise, or immoral legislation. Relief from these sorts of abuses must be sought at the ballot box.

If the Court decides to hold a law unconstitutional, it will always try to confine its ruling to a particular section or sections of the law. That is, it will attempt to separate out parts of the law that are in harmony with the Constitution rather than invalidate the entire statute. Rarely does the Court make broad sweeping pronouncements. Often judges will defer to legislative judgment by classifying a sensitive issue as "political," rather than as judicial, and therefore beyond the jurisdiction of the Court.

These precepts of self-restraint have enabled the Court to maintain its independence and integrity. Without an independent and at times courageous Court, the status of civil liberties would be in the Dark Ages, and there would be very little in the way of social progress that has greatly enhanced the dignity of human life in America.

Notes

1. Death, resignation or absence for one reason or another would leave the Court understaffed and raise the likelihood of a tie. Also, because of prior affiliation with a case, a judge may absent himself from a decision. This is likely with new appointees especially if they come from lower courts.
2. C. Herman Pritchett, *The American Constitution* 2nd ed. (New York: McGraw-Hill, 1968), p. 54.

For Further Reading

Abraham, Henry J. *The Judicial Process* 3rd ed. (New York: Oxford University Press, 1975).

———. *The Judiciary: The Supreme Court in the Governmental Process* 6th ed. (Boston: Allyn and Bacon, Inc., 1983).

Baum, Lawrence. *The Supreme Court* (Washington, D.C.: Congressional Quarterly Press, 1981).

Berger, Raoul. *Government by Judiciary: The Transformation of the Fourteenth Amendment* (Cambridge: Harvard University Press, 1977).

Bickel, Alexander M. *The Least Dangerous Branch: The Supreme Court at the Bar of Politics* (Indianapolis, Indiana: Bobbs-Merril, 1962).

Danelski, David J. *A Supreme Court Justice is Appointed* (New York: Random House, 1964).

Goulden, Joseph C. *The Benchwarmers: The Private World of the Powerful Federal Judges* (New York: Ballantine Books, 1974).

Horowitz, Donald L. *The Courts and Social Policy* (Washington, D.C.: The Brookings Institution, 1977).

Jacob, Herbert. *Justice in America: Courts, Lawyers, and the Judicial Process* 4th ed. (Boston: Little, Brown and Co., 1984).

Lewis, Anthony. *Gideon's Trumpet* (New York: Random House, 1964).

Pritchett, C. Herman. *The American Constitution* 3rd ed. (New York: McGraw-Hill, 1975).

Schmidhauser, John R. *Judges and Justices: The Federal Appellate Judiciary* (Boston: Little, Brown and Co., 1979).

Schmidhauser, John R. and Larry L. Berg. *The Supreme Court and Congress: Conflict and Interaction, 1945–1968* (New York: The Free Press, 1972).

Scigliano, Robert. *The Supreme Court and the Presidency* (New York: The Free Press, 1971).

Woodward, Bob and Scott Armstrong. *The Brethren: Inside the Supreme Court* (New York: Simon and Schuster, 1979).

Name _____

Section _____

Date _____

Review Questions for Chapter 2: The Judicial System

1. *Marbury* v. *Madison* (1803) _____

_____

_____

_____

_____

2. Merit system _____

_____

_____

_____

_____

_____

3. U.S. Courts of Appeal _____

_____

_____

_____

_____

4. *Stare decisis* _____

_____

_____

_____

_____

5. Writ of certiorari _____

_____

_____

_____

_____

6. Judicial self-restraint _____

_____

_____

_____

_____

7. Concurring opinion _____

_____

_____

_____

_____

8. Standing to sue _____

_____

_____

_____

_____

9. Amicus curiae _____

_____

_____

_____

_____

10. Legislative courts _____

_____

_____

_____

_____

Essay Study Questions

1. Given what you have read in the chapter and your own knowledge of the courts, do you believe the proper role of the courts is to be activist or restraintist in their approach to the interpretation of the laws and the Constitution? Justify your answer.
2. Discuss the structure of the federal courts in terms of the number and the duties of each.
3. One of the perennial questions concerning the courts is their exercise of judicial review. Using the Constitution, the *Federalist Papers* and *Marbury* as reference points, do you think that the exercise of judicial review by the courts is legitimate? Why or why not? If not, who would you select to determine the constitutionality of acts of government? Why?
4. Discuss the powers of and the limitations imposed on the courts. Ultimately, do you believe that the courts are accountable to the public and/or the other branches of government? Why or why not?

Chapter 3

Freedom and Rights

The last few decades of American history have been characterized by tremendous demands for the extension of civil rights and liberties. Many diverse groups within American society have been successful in attaining and expanding rights and liberties. More often than not, the political institutions most responsive to these claims have been the courts. As noted in Chapter 2, the courts, and especially the U.S. Supreme Court, have handed down decisions which have been extremely controversial. The Supreme Court, for example, has been instrumental in striking down laws which helped to perpetuate racial segregation; it has protected the rights of religious minorities; and it has been chiefly responsible for enforcing the rights of women in many cases by striking down laws which many felt were adverse to women.

The fact that so many groups and individuals are pressing their claims for equal treatment before the law is one indication of the great changes that American society is experiencing. Many groups are no longer satisfied with what they feel to be second class status—they seek change and they want it now—and if the "traditional" methods of politics do not give them satisfaction, they often turn to the courts.

Americans, in spite of the fact that they pay homage to the values of freedom, justice and equality, are aware of the fact that these values are not fully enjoyed by all members of our society. It is perhaps ironic that from the beginning of our nation certain groups found themselves at a distinct disadvantage—politically, legally, economically and socially. America, in its early development, witnessed the massive importation of Africans to be exploited as slaves; the indigenous native-Americans (Indians) were pushed out of the way for purposes of economic expansion, and even many lower-class whites were discriminated against in many cases. The history of American rights and freedoms is a fascinating story of a bitter and intense struggle to extend to all the rights and freedoms formerly enjoyed only by a select few. All men are, or ought to be, equal before the law, and no person is above the law according to the American creed. Political equality, with the opportunity for social and economic equality, are goals that are endorsed by almost all segments of American society. Is America a perfectly just society? Certainly not, and it probably never will achieve such a status. Nevertheless, the struggle to achieve a more just society continues.

It has been traditionally felt that citizens should be free from oppression in any form. Man, it was argued by Thomas Jefferson, has certain inalienable rights.

Americans have viewed alien ideologies and dictatorial governments as unnatural. Indeed, at times, part of the American mission, especially in the late nineteenth and early twentieth centuries, was to spread the word and to liberate victims of oppression all over the world. The irony of the ambitious design was that a good many Americans, Blacks in the South, Chinese in the West, and Mexicans in the Southwest, were being forced to live under some of the most oppressive of circumstances.

Americans have also usually associated freedom with the concept of limited government. It has been believed that government should be limited in terms of its functions, though not necessarily on the basis of its size. It has long been believed that governance should be a public, not a private and secretive enterprise. What outraged so many Americans about the Watergate affair were the cover-ups, misrepresentations, and "dirty tricks." Subsequently, congressional investigating committees have turned up evidence that the Central Intelligence Agency, the Federal Bureau of Investigation, and the Internal Revenue Service have harrassed American citizens by engaging in alleged illegal activities such as opening mail, infiltrating organizations, and administering drugs to unsuspecting citizens. Activities of this sort are beyond that which is considered acceptable and legitimate. Furthermore, such deeds appear to violate a fundamental trust that is supposed to exist between citizens and government.

It has been felt that freedom can only flourish if minority rights and views are protected. Throughout American history, the federal courts have been active in protecting and expanding liberties. State governments, on the other hand, have often had a record of being lax and oppressive. There are, however, some major exceptions to the above generalization. During the administration of John Adams, for example, Congress passed the Alien and Sedition Acts which made it unlawful to criticize any member of the administration. This law proved to be exceedingly unpopular and was allowed to expire. After the attack on Pearl Harbor, President Franklin Roosevelt ordered that all Japanese-Americans living on the West Coast be transported inland and placed in concentration camps. It was assumed that the allegiance of these people, many of whom were second and third generation Americans, would be to their nation of origin rather than to their country of birth. The Supreme Court upheld this action, which caused a great deal of misery and untold economic loss, because it was thought that as a class, Japanese-Americans constituted a possible threat to national security during wartime.

The Bill of Rights

Interestingly, when the Constitution was written in 1787 it did not contain a Bill of Rights. The Founders believed that a Bill of Rights was both unnecessary and dangerous. It was unnecessary, they argued, because nothing in the Constitution gave the federal government the power to infringe on freedom of speech, press, etc., and it was, therefore, unnecessary to explicity add such provisions. A Bill of Rights would be dangerous, they believed, in that a listing of the rights of Americans would necessarily be less than comprehensive and would, therefore, leave some out. However, in order to gain ratification of the Constitution, the Federalists agreed to add a Bill of Rights when the first Congress convened.

The first Congress proposed twelve new amendments to the Constitution and sent them to the states for ratification. Ten of these were adopted in 1791 and the first eight are generally referred to as the Bill of Rights. The major question after 1791 was whether the Bill of Rights protected Americans from action by the federal government only or whether these protections also limited the state governments. In 1833, the U.S. Supreme Court answered this question in *Barron* v. *Baltimore*. In that case, the Court's opinion by Chief Justice John Marshall held that the Bill of Rights had originally been added to the Constitution for the purpose of protecting Americans from the federal government and not the states. Therefore, such protections as right to counsel, freedom of speech and press and freedom of religion did not restrict the state governments in any way.

In 1868, however, an event occurred which was to change the course of American constitutional law. The Fourteenth Amendment was added to the Constitution in that year. The Due Process Clause of that Amendment prohibited the states from depriving "any person of life, liberty, or property, without due process of law." Some justices, such as the first John Marshall Harlan and Hugo Black, believed that the Due Process Clause intended to apply the entire Bill of Rights to the states. These justices were referred to as total incorporationists. The selective incorporationists, such as Chief Justice Warren and Justice Brennan, believed that only those provisions in the Bill of Rights which were "fundamental rights" were applied to the states by the Due Process Clause.

In any case, between 1897 and 1969 virtually every provision of the Bill of Rights was applied to the states. Of twenty-two provisions in the first eight amendments, only five have not been applied to the states. They are the Second Amendment, the Third Amendment, the Fifth Amendment Grand Jury Clause, the Seventh Amendment and the Eighth Amendment Excessive Fines and Bail Clause. The significance of this nationalization of the Bill of Rights is that, with the five exceptions noted, the state governments are prohibited from infringing on these civil liberties in the same way as the federal government has always been.

First Amendment

Rights protected by the First Amendment, such as freedom of religion, freedom from establishment of religion, freedom of speech, press, assembly, and petition are considered to be fundamental in the American system of government. Yet, as important as these rights may be, they are not unconditionally protected or absolute. The agency of government most responsible for defining the character of these rights has been the United States Supreme Court. Interestingly enough, almost all of the litigation surrounding the First Amendment has taken place since the First World War. The approach taken by the Court in resolving issues regarding First Amendment rights has been one of a pragmatic series of case by case adjustment. Although the Court has certainly recognized the value of these freedoms it has helped to limit them from time to time by upholding statutes thought to be necessary to protect order, peace, decency and national security. Much of the controversy surrounding freedom of speech, association, and the press has centered around the topics of subversion and obscenity.

Subversion

After the fascist forces were defeated, the Smith Act was applied to members of the Communist Party who were advocating revolution. At first, in *Dennis v. United States,* the Supreme Court upheld the constitutionality of the act. Perhaps, in this instance, the Court reflected the temper of the times. The late Senator Joseph McCarthy gained a great deal of notoriety and power by claiming that the country was heavily infiltrated by communist agents who were going to "sovietize" America. Furthermore, Americans were fighting communism in Korea and were shocked at the "loss" of China and the detonation of the Soviet Union's first atomic bomb in 1949. There was a genuine concern and fear about the progress of communist movements. Later, in 1957, when the times and the composition of the Court had changed, the *Dennis* ruling was amended. In *Yates v. United States,* the Court decided that there was an important difference between advocacy and

Interlandi, from the Los Angeles Times. Copyright © 1980. Reprinted by permission.

action. Stated differently, the Court deemed that one could, as a matter of political conviction, teach or advocate the violent overthrow of the government for whatever reason. Such utterances in and of themselves do not, it was reasoned, constitute any clear and present danger to the republic. But, activities that are designed to bring about that end, such as bombings, assassinations, and espionage, are clearly not protected and therefore, remain illegal. This decision and subsequent rulings bestowed upon the Communist Party and other militant and dissident groups such as the American Nazi Party, full legal status. In fact, the Communist Party had a convention in 1976 and nominated a candidate for the presidency. Members of the Communist Party are no longer required to register with the Justice Department as agents of a foreign government.

Obscenity

Obscenity has been a thorny issue that has plagued the Court since the 1950s. Originally, it was felt that government's role as the protector of public morals included the duty of censoring what appeared to be lewd and lascivious materials. Customs inspected the luggage of tourists for French postcards. Books by novelists such as Henry Miller were outlawed. The post office routinely inspected the mails for forbidden fruits. In reviewing books such as *Ulysses* by James Joyce, censors were confronted with the conflict between art and pornography. At first it was decided that such works would be sold only after certain portions had been deleted. Later it was determined that such practices mutilated a work of art. Hence, novels that were considered to be works of art could then be sold to the general public even though some aspects might be considered obscene.

In 1957, the Court, in the case of *Roth* v. *United States,* attempted to define what was obscene. When applying contemporary community standards, obscenity was deemed to be anything that was utterly without redeeming social value. The definition was extended in 1964 in *Jacobellis* v. *Ohio* to include prurient interest and patent offensiveness. In *Jacobellis* the justices also decided that contemporary community standards should be applied on the national, not the local, level. Thus, for a work to be judged obscene it had to appeal to a prurient interest *and* be patently offensive *and* be utterly without redeeming social value. Many publishers then began to hire "sociologists" and "psychologists" to write prefaces for their publications. The object was to demonstrate, by means of a professional opinion, that the books were patently inoffensive, had redeeming social value and did not pander to prurient interests. But, the Court was not finished with obscenity. After a series of minor cases involving books and films, the Court, in *Miller* v. *California* (1973), decided that the three-pronged test of *Roth* and *Jacobellis* was too broad. The Court held in *Miller* that the contemporary community standards to be used in the test were to be state or local and not national. Also, the Court eliminated the "utterly without redeeming social value" prong of the test and replaced it with what is known as the "LAPS test." This test requires only that the work be seriously lacking any literary, artistic, political or scientific value. In 1974 a local jury in Georgia decided that the R-rated film *Carnal Knowledge* was obscene. The Court came up with a rather curious decision in *Jenkins* v. *Georgia.* It was held that local juries could apply community standards, but then the justices turned around and ruled the film not to be obscene. The Court obviously wants to retain the final say on what is and what is not obscene, which, incidentally, seems to elude any tight definition.

Some communities have sought to regulate the availability of such literature by means of restrictive licensing and/or zoning regulations. In June of 1976 the Court, in the case of *Young v. American Mini-Theatres,* sanctioned this practice as a means of controlling obscenity. But, unless the Court reverses itself, X-rated materials will continue to be conveniently available for most Americans.

Religion

Religion, another aspect of the First Amendment, has also created some controversy. The old common law concept of sanctuary does not apply in the United States. In *Reynolds v. United States* the Court, in 1879, agreed that one cannot, under the guise of religious freedom, commit criminal acts and escape prosecution. In the 1960's, however, the Supreme Court held that some acts, ordinarily illegal, were protected by the First Amendment. In *Sherbert v. Verner* (1964), for example, the Court held that Ms. Sherbert was entitled to unemployment compensation even though she had quit her job. The Court reasoned that Sherbert's actions were protected by the First Amendment since she had quit for religious reasons; her schedule had been changed to require Saturday work which violated her Seventh Day Adventist religion. Likewise, in *Woody* v. *People* (1964), the California Supreme Court held that the use of peyote in Navajo religious ceremonies were protected by the First Amendment even though such use for non-religious purposes could be punished. These two cases and many others are based on the Court's interpretation of the free exercise clause. In defining that clause, the Court has had to depend upon a delicate balancing of the competing interests on each side.

The free exercise clause is only one of the religion clauses in the First Amendment. In order to ensure that religious freedom would flourish, the Founders added the establishment clause. They were convinced that there should be, in the words of Thomas Jefferson, a "wall of separation" between church and state. Separation has produced several problems but the two most emotional seem to have been prayer in public schools and tax exemption.

During World War II and the 1950s, a great wave of religious fervor swept the country. Children in public schools were asked to pray for victory during wartime as well as for the defeat of godless movements such as communism. Convinced that the religious experience was an important part of a child's education, most states required a daily recitation of a non-sectarian prayer. In 1962, the Court ruled in *Engel v. Vitale* that such required prayers composed by governmental officials was a patent violation of the establishment clause. Later, in *Murray v. Curlett* the Court ruled that even moments of silence where children were invited to pray in whatever fashion they wished constituted a religious exercise and was therefore unconstitutional. The reaction to these decisions was explosive. Earl Warren was accused of trying to dechristianize America. Critics felt that the Court was driving God out of the classroom and encouraging atheism. Actually, the justices merely insisted that governmental neutrality with respect to religion was the only way to guarantee free exercise. No one should be intimidated by the religious beliefs of others. Besides Christians, America's population includes Moslems, Jews, Buddhists, atheists, agnostics, and others. Their right of free exercise is equally important as that of the majority who happen to be Christians of one denomination or another. Of course, parents can send their children to parochial schools if they desire. In addition, there is released time for children attending public schools so that they may receive religious instruction off-campus during school hours. Nevertheless, there is a movement in Congress to reinstate prayer in the public schools which is strongly supported by various elements in American society.

Because they claim charitable institutional status whose income is primarily derived from voluntary contributions, religious organizations have been granted special tax privileges. They are exempt from federal taxation as well as state and local property taxes. Perhaps more important, they are immune from disclosing their assets and holdings. Most religious organizations have therefore maintained a cloak of secrecy about financial matters. Even members of some sects are usually not allowed access to such information. Madeline Murray O'Hare, a self-proclaimed atheist, felt that this privileged status was unjust. She instituted a civil suit against the Archdiocese of Baltimore, Maryland claiming that exemption of the vast land holdings of the Archdiocese was a violation of the establishment clause. Furthermore, she argued that because the Archdiocese was exempt everyone else had to pay higher taxes to make up the difference. This, she claimed, constituted a forced subsidy and was contrary to the equal protection of the laws guaranteed by the Fourteenth Amendment. Perhaps because the case was too touchy, review by the Supreme Court was refused.

The secrecy with which religious institutions have surrounded their fiscal affairs has produced all sorts of speculation about their true wealth. Some have erected front organizations and dummy corporations to further ensure protection from scrutiny. How much of America is owned by religious organizations? No one knows. This bastion of privilege and secrecy has remained, for the most part, undisturbed and unquestioned.

The entrance of Jerry Falwell's Moral Majority organization and other groups commonly referred to as the "religious right" has raised new issues in the area of the establishment clause. Under the Constitution, what is the proper relationship between religion and government? Undoubtedly, such groups are allowed by the First Amendment's free speech provisions to campaign for office holders and lobby for the passage of legislation which they favor. Opponents, however, fear that the influence of these groups could lead to a kind of "religious McCarthyism" whereby those who do not agree with these groups may be ostracized. Lending credence to such fears is the platform of the Republican Party in 1984 which proposed that any individual wishing to be appointed as a federal judge must publicly state his or her opposition to abortion. The issues presented by this new political-religious combination are complex and will not be resolved soon.

Fourth Amendment

Individuals who are suspected of committing a crime are protected by the procedural guarantees of the fifth and sixth amendments. The right to privacy and protection against unreasonable search and seizure are guaranteed by the fourth amendment. A search warrant is a document issued by a judicial officer which permits the police to conduct a search in cases where probable cause has been demonstrated. Each document must be specific as to the premises to be searched and the evidence that is sought. Once presented with a warrant, an individual cannot legally prevent a search.

What if the police present a warrant to search for one thing and discover something else which is illegal? Can that evidence be used in court? It depends on the circumstances surrounding the search. Dolly Mapp was a prostitute in the state of Ohio. One evening, the police came to her residence with an arrest warrant for a fugitive, who was believed to be seeking refuge at Mapp's home. During the search for the fugitive, the police uncovered a small box which contained illegal pornographic literature and pictures. Mapp was arrested, tried and convicted for possession of "lewd and lascivious" books, pictures and photographs. Mapp's conviction was overturned by the Supreme Court in 1961. The court took the decisive step and held that the "exclusionary rule" should be applied to state criminal proceedings. Evidence illegally obtained could not be used in any criminal trial. (*Mapp v. Ohio,* 1961)

It is in the area of searches and seizures where the Supreme Court under Chief Justice Burger has probably made the most inroads into the decisions of the earlier Warren Court. For example, in 1984 the Court held that evidence seized illegally did not have to be excluded from a trial if the police had acted in "good faith" in executing a search warrant. That is, if a magistrate has

improperly issued a search warrant the evidence seized under this warrant can still be used in court so long as it was the magistrate and not the police who made the constitutional error (*U.S.* v. *Leon* and *Massachusetts* v. *Shepherd*).

Fifth Amendment

When charged with a crime, an individual is protected by the Fifth Amendment privilege against self incrimination. A person may not be forced to confess, testify or otherwise provide evidence which could lead to a conviction of him or herself. The privilege is not an absolute right to silence. It is a right considered waived if the defendent does not claim it.

A series of Supreme Court decisions in the 1950s and 1960s have established the precise guidelines for procedure where the Fifth Amendment is applicable. The most significant and perhaps the most controversial of these decisions was *Miranda v. Arizona.* In March of 1963, a young woman was kidnapped and forcibly raped near Phoenix, Arizona. Ten days later, Miranda, an indigent with less than a ninth grade education, was arrested, picked out of a lineup by the victim, and interrogated. After a brief period of time he admitted guilt and signed a confession. The Court, however, ruled that the confession was inadmissible because he was unaware that he had the right not to incriminate himself. A storm of protest and criticism was set off by this decision. It was argued that the Court was making it easier for those accused of crimes to get off the hook. Actually, these guidelines were followed by federal officers prior to these decisions. In effect, the Court merely applied federal standards to the states. There appears to be no hard evidence that decisions such as *Miranda* have "handcuffed" the police or have contributed to an increase in crime.

Double Jeopardy

In addition to protection against self-incrimination, the Fifth Amendment protects individuals from repeatedly being prosecuted for the same offense. The Supreme Court has held that the guarantee against double jeopardy protects an individual both against multiple prosecutions for the same offense and against multiple punishments for the same crime.

In 1969, the Court ruled in *Benton v. Maryland* that the Double Jeopardy clause was applicable to state prosecutions as well as federal prosecutions as a protection afforded by the due process guarantee of the 14th Amendment. In the case of a mistrial or a split jury the double jeopardy clause does not forbid a defendant's retrial. Furthermore, if a defendant is convicted, he may waive immunity and seek a new trial or appeal the verdict to a higher court. In the case, however, that a defendant is acquitted, the Double Jeopardy clause absolutely forbids further prosecution for that crime.

The Fifth Amendment guarantee against Double Jeopardy applies only to multiple prosecution within a single sovereign government. Therefore, it is not violated when an individual is tried on both federal and state or tribal charges arising from a single offense.

Bail and Trial

Once arrested, an individual according to the Eighth Amendment, is entitled to be released after having posted bail. Sometimes bail is established by a judge at a pretrial hearing and other times it is predetermined by a legislative body. An alternative to bail is allowing the individual to be freed on his own recognizance. That is, a written or verbal promise that the accused will be present on the date of his trial. An example of self-recognizance is one's signature on a traffic ticket. Of course, if the individual is deemed a poor risk or if the crime is of great magnitude, bail may be denied and the accused person must await trial in jail.

The Sixth Amendment established procedural guarantees for a person tried for criminal acts. It guarantees a speedy and public jury trial where the crime was committed. Furthermore, the individual has the right to confront witnesses, present witnesses on his behalf, and to be assisted by legal counsel. Until Congress passed the Speedy Trial Act of 1974, this right was somewhat ambiguous. The provisions of the law indicate that by 1980 an individual who has been accused of a crime must be tried within 100 days. In the interim, the act established a 175 day requirement. Judges, defense attorneys and prosecutors have all expressed reservations about the time constraint. Judges, especially in urban areas where the volume is high, have expressed concern about their ability to handle both civil and criminal litigation. In early 1978, the U.S. Judicial Conference, in a special report to Congress, labelled the 100 day period as simply too short and asked that the time span be extended to 180 days. Defense attorneys have suggested that the effect of the new law is to rush defendants to trial. They argue that the time constraints, particularly in complex cases, seriously hamper their investigative opportunities. Prosecutors are of the opinion that the act may frequently result in the dismissal of charges against defendants who might otherwise be convicted. It appears that if Congress does not amend the act that there will have to be a sizable increase in the numbers of judges and prosecutors. The guarantee of a speedy trial does not apply to civil cases. Often people must wait years before their attempts to seek redress through litigation come to trial.

Trial by jury is a right that may be waived, in which case the presiding judge will establish guilt or innocence. If not waived, then every effort must be made to acquire an impartial jury. Prospective jurors, who are usually randomly selected from voter registration or property tax lists, are examined by both prosecutors and defense attorneys. If one is found to be prejudiced about the case then the attorneys can ask that he be excused. Once the jury is impaneled, it may be sequestered by the judge in order that their decision will not be unduly influenced by outside sources.

If defense attorneys are convinced that their client cannot receive a fair trial in the area where the crime was perpetrated, they can petition the judge for a change of venue. That is, they may change the locale of the trial in an attempt to acquire an impartial jury.

If an individual is accused of violating a state or local law, his trial may take place anywhere within the state. Venue in a federal offense can be anywhere in the United States or its possessions. Had Lee Harvey Oswald, the alleged assassin of President John Kennedy, not been shot and killed while in the custody of the Dallas police, he might very well not have been convicted. Almost every detail of that event was generously covered by the news media because the Dallas, Texas Police Department allowed an unprecedented amount of postarrest publicity. Venue could not have been outside of Texas because at that time the crime of presidential assassination was not a federal offense.

The guarantee of an impartial jury also means that there are, of necessity, constraints placed upon freedom of the press. Dr. Sam Sheppard, an Ohio osteopath, was tried and convicted, amid a carnival-like atmosphere, of murdering his wife. Sheppard's case was damaged by pretrial publicity which made it difficult to select a jury. Furthermore, once a jury was impaneled, the media made every attempt to influence its members. In *Sheppard v. Maxwell* the Supreme Court threw out the conviction and strongly criticized the trial judge for not taking measures to ensure an impartial jury.

In October, 1975, Irwin C. Simant was tried and convicted of mass murder and rape by a Nebraska jury. The details of the crime were so sensational that the trial judge ordered an almost complete news blackout. His action prohibited the media from reporting on the trial which, according to a 1976 court opinion, constituted prior restraint, a practice that had previously been found to be unconstitutional in *Near v. Minnesota* (1931). Nevertheless, the conflict between a fair trial and the right of the press to provide the public with information will continue to provide judicial fireworks, especially in sensational cases.

Right to Counsel

The Sixth Amendment right to counsel is a guarantee that until the early 1960s was not enjoyed by all Americans. In 1942, in *Betts v. Brady,* the Court ruled that states need not provide counsel for indigent defendants unless special circumstances, such as possible imposition of the death penalty, exist.

In 1963, Clarence Gideon, a penniless itinerant was convicted of a felony in a Florida court without the benefit of legal counsel. Gideon requested the court to appoint an attorney, citing the Sixth Amendment guarantee. His request was denied by the trial judge, who cited the Betts precedent, and Gideon was sentenced to spend five years in prison. Upon his conviction Clarence Gideon began petitioning the federal courts to declare his conviction invalid because it was obtained in violation of his constitutional right to counsel, and to order his release. The Supreme Court accepted Gideon's petition and the result of *Gideon v. Wainright* is that states are required to provide counsel for all defendants charged with felonies who are unable to pay a lawyer. Later the court extended this policy to include misdemeanors.

Eighth Amendment

After an individual has been tried and convicted of a crime, he or she is protected by the Eighth Amendment which stipulates that there shall be no excessive fines and no cruel and unusual punishment. Fines are usually statutorily prescribed and these have not posed much of an issue. The issue of cruel and unusual punishment, however, has caused considerable controversy. Specifically, is the death penalty a violation of the Eighth Amendment? Are conditions in American prisons so dehumanizing that they make incarceration cruel and unusual punishment?

Traditionally, the death penalty has been looked upon as a deterrent to certain types of offenses. Some feel that it is justified by the Biblical dictate of an "eye for an eye," and by society's right to retribution. Since World War II there has been a great deal of questioning about the death penalty. Some consider it to be legal murder and unquestionably within the scope of cruel punishment. In the 1972 case of *Furman v. Georgia,* the Court found the state provisions for the death penalty vague and arbitrary; thereby violative of the due process and equal protection clauses of the Fourteenth Amendment. After this decision, many of the states rewrote their statutes to conform to the new guidelines. On July 2, 1976, in *Gregg v. Georgia,* and four other related cases, the Court decided that death is not a cruel and unusual punishment. A person may be executed if the judge and jury were not given unfettered discretion over who lives and who dies. Furthermore, all factors that might call for leniency must be considered by juries. State legislatures, however, cannot impose death across-the-board on whole categories of offenders with no allowance for mercy or individual differences. In 1976, Gary Gilmore was convicted by a jury in Provo, Utah, of first degree murder and sentenced to death. Gilmore accepted the decision and demanded that the penalty be invoked. Organizations, such as the American Civil Liberties Union, against Gilmore's wishes, appealed imposition of the death penalty, and they lost. Utah law permits condemned prisoners to choose between a firing squad and the gallows. Gilmore chose the former, and on January 17, 1977, he was executed. Gilmore's execution marked the end of a capital punishment moratorium that had lasted for ten years.

In the early part of this century, liberal reformers felt that convicted criminals should be rehabilitated rather than punished. Overcrowded institutions are the setting for murder, homosexual rape, narcotics traffic and gang warfare. Indeed the situation is so bad in the state of Alabama that a federal district judge in 1976 ruled that confinement in that state's prisons constituted a violation of the Eighth Amendment. In 1978, the Supreme Court affirmed that ruling.

The Right to Vote

Voting, it has been said, is the cornerstone of democracy. Initially, voting was a privilege reserved for white male property owners. It was felt that they had the highest stake in society and therefore should determine its direction. An early nineteenth century trend toward egalitarianism, that is generally characterized by the administration of Andrew Jackson, extended the suffrage to all adult males. After the Civil War, the Fifteenth Amendment was adopted and extended the right to vote to all adult males, regardless of race.

In 1920, Congress and the states responded to the suffragette movement and extended voting rights to all adults regardless of sex, by means of the Nineteenth Amendment. The District of Columbia, since it is not a state, had no electors, hence residents could not vote in presidential elections. This situation was remedied by the Twenty-Third Amendment which gave the district three electoral votes. A more recent extension of the franchise is included in the Twenty-Sixth Amendment which granted the right to vote to those adults who are eighteen years or over.

Despite these constitutional guarantees, access to the polls has not always been easy for some Americans. Most of the discriminatory practices have been aimed at nonwhites. It was generally assumed that literacy should be a voting prerequisite. After all, it was reasoned, an illiterate would probably not cast an intelligent vote because he would be unaware of most of the issues and could be easily exploited by the unscrupulous. Hence, many states adopted literacy tests. A citizen was asked to read and interpret a part of a constitution or to answer a series of questions. If he or she failed such a test, and in the southern states all blacks were routinely flunked, then the right to vote was lost. Such blatantly discriminatory practices were declared illegal when Congress passed the Voting Rights Act in 1965.

Other discriminatory practices included the white primary, which allowed nonwhites to vote in general elections only. This practice was declared unconstitutional by the Supreme Court because in the then one-party southern states crucial decisions were made in primary elections. Registrars of voters often made registration very difficult if not impossible for nonwhite voters in most southern states. This inequity was also remedied by the Voting Rights Act which provided for federal registrars in those areas. A grandfather clause inserted into some state statutes after the Civil War excluded citizens from voting if their fathers or grandfathers were slaves. This practice was also declared unconstitutional by the Court. Some states required citizens to pay a tax before they could vote. Poll taxes clearly discriminated against the poor and were subsequently declared illegal in all federal elections by the Twenty-Fourth Amendment. Finally, terror tactics were used in some communities to prevent certain citizens from voting. In 1975, when Congress renewed the Voting Rights Act for another ten years, an amendment was attached to the bill that extended the franchise to non-English speaking citizens. Bilingual, and in some cases, tri-lingual, ballots must be printed in communities that have large non-English speaking minority groups.

Voting rights and the access to the political arena have been extended to virtually all adult Americans. Some, such as prisoners, ex-felons, and non-citizens will probably never be included.

Racial Equality

After the Civil War, Congress passed the 13th, 14th, and 15th Amendments to the Constitution. Since that time, the 14th Amendment has been the vehicle through which many reforms have been achieved. The 14th Amendment forbids any state to "deny any person within its jurisdiction the equal protection of the laws."

In 1875, Congress passed a civil rights act which contained a public accommodation clause. That is, accommodations such as bus stations, coffee shops and hotels that were serving the general public could not be discriminatory toward nonwhites. It was declared unconstitutional by the Supreme Court in 1883 because the judges reasoned that the Fourteenth Amendment did not proscribe discrimination when practiced by private entities. Segregation then became a way of life in Southern states with respect to blacks and in some Western states with respect to Orientals. This practice was reinforced in 1898 when the Supreme Court, in the case of *Plessy v. Ferguson,* declared that separate facilities were constitutional as long as they were equal. However, seldom were the facilities equal.

In 1954, the Supreme Court reversed the *Plessy* rule and found in *Brown v. Board of Education of Topeka,* that the practice of separation in public schools was inherently unequal and ordered the practice ended with all deliberate speed. Next, Congress passed a series of laws, the most significant of which was the Civil Rights Act of 1964. This law contained a public accommodation section which prohibited discrimination in the economic and social areas of life with respect to race, religion and sex. The aim of this law was not only to promote integration but also to provide equal opportunity. Subsequent action was initiated in the areas of open housing, and an issue that has been somewhat controversial, affirmative action. Employers who receive federal monies are required to make special efforts to recruit members of minority races and women to fill vacancies. This practice has led to charges of reverse discrimination. Many universities and professional schools began to adopt quotas for admission to various programs. Quotas were based upon the idea that representatives of minority groups were entitled to special consideration because they had been held back by society for so long. Affirmative action was challenged in *Regents of the University of California v. Bakke* (1978). Allan Bakke, a white male, was denied admission to the medical school at the Davis campus of the University of California. The medical school had a quota system wherein 16 out of 100 places were allotted to minority students. Bakke claimed that this system amounted to discrimination against better qualified whites, in violation of the Fourteenth Amendment. Bakke sued and won on appeal to the California Supreme Court. The United States Supreme Court was at last forced to address the controversial legal aspects of Affirmative Action. By a 5–4 vote, the Court upheld the California decision ordering that Bakke be admitted to the medical school. The Court held that Davis' numerical quota was in violation of the 1964 Civil Rights Act in that it discriminated on the basis of race. While the Court decided that quotas are illegal, it did affirm the notion that race *can* be taken into account by an agency when devising plans for Affirmative Action. The full impact of this decision is yet to be felt.

In 1979, another important decision involving Affirmative Action was handed down by the Supreme Court. In *United Steelworkers v. Weber,* a private corporation's voluntary plan which gave preference to black employees over more senior white employees in admissions to training programs, was upheld by the Court. The decision held that the Affirmative Action program was not violative of either the Equal Protection Clause of the Fourteenth Amendment or Title VII of the 1964 Civil Rights Act. Thus, the prospects with regard to Affirmative Action are unclear. The Court continues to steer a pragmatic course in this area.

Busing

In recent years, the most controversial issue with respect to the Fourteenth Amendment has been integration of public schools by means of busing. During the 1960s, many whites fled the inner cities for homes in the suburbs. The result was that certain sections of many large cities were primarily inhabited by poor urban blacks. It was reasoned by the Department of Health, Education and Welfare, and the courts, that equal access to educational and employment opportunities would only be achieved through a greater degree of integration. It was reasoned that the only functional means of achieving this end was to bus youngsters from their neighborhoods to other schools. Busing has generated many arguments and considerable violence. For the most part, it appears that busing has been an unsuccessful means of producing a greater degree of racial harmony and understanding. Indeed, the founding father of this mode of integration, James Coleman, a University of Chicago sociologist, admitted in 1975 that, for the most part, busing was counterproductive.

In 1976, the city of Boston, Massachusetts appealed to the Supreme Court for relief from a federal judge's busing order. The city claimed that court-ordered busing was oppressively expensive and that it was also causing social unrest and violence. Nevertheless, the justices decided to let the precedent stand and refused to grant a writ of certiorari. The politics of busing is likely to be the most emotional issue of the future. Many feel that the new Congress, along with the Reagan administration, will attempt to curb busing by disallowing the Justice Department to litigate busing cases.

The general trend toward equal opportunity is not without its critics however. Nathan Glazer, a Harvard University sociologist, claims that many of the guidelines produced by the liberal consensus in the 1960s has made ethnic identity more important than nationality. In the 1960s it was hoped that the great American "melting pot," which incorporated many of Europe's dispossessed, would also produce a situation wherein domestic disadvantaged groups would be able to share in the "American Dream." The "melting pot" and the "American Dream" are both myths. Many Americans have traditionally sought to live in ethnic neighborhoods. Indeed, some sections of large cities are exclusively Black, Oriental, Latin, Greek, Croatian, Polish, and so forth. In some of these areas English is almost a foreign language. Jimmy Carter, appealing to this reality, stated during his 1976 campaign for the presidency, that Americans had the right to ethnically pure neighborhoods. The stress on ethnicity and absolute equality could, as Glazer suggests, produce a situation wherein American society will become much more divisive and fragmented.

Women's Rights

The first Woman's Right convention was held in Seneca Falls, New York in July of 1848. The convention produced a declaration of Sentiments and Resolutions. Since that first convention in New York, women have sought to be recognized as equal citizens in the eyes of American jurisprudence.

Prior to the adoption of the 19th Amendment in 1920, the court held that the 14th Amendment did not compel the states to allow women to vote. The Court reasoned in *Minor v. Happersett* (1875) that although women were citizens, the right to vote was not a privilege or immunity of national citizenship prior to adoption of the 14th Amendment, nor did the amendment add suffrage to the privileges and immunities of national citizenship.

For some time the Court had engaged in what is commonly referred to as "romantic paternalism" in the area of women's rights. In cases involving working women the protectionist judicial attitude is most evident. In *Muller v. Oregon* (1908) the Court held that differences in legislation for men and women were justifiable on the grounds that woman's inferior physical capacities require legislation which will compensate for some of the burdens put upon her.

The feminist movement gained momentum as political and social awareness increased in the late 1960s and 1970s. "Women's Liberation" as it is generally labeled, has sought to create a climate of equality of opportunity for women.

Until 1971, in the case of *Reed v. Reed,* the Supreme Court had yet to hold a state law invalid because it discriminated against women. In an opinion written by Chief Justice Burger, the Court struck down an Idaho statute which gave preference to males in designating those eligible to administer estates. The Court reasoned that gender based classifications "must rest upon some ground of difference having a fair and substantial relation to the object of legislation so that all persons similarly circumstanced shall be treated alike." In 1973, the Court went even further to secure the fair and equal administration of the law where women are concerned. In *Frontiero v. Richardson* a female Air Force officer sought increased benefits for her husband and her dependent child. Her request was denied because the law stipulated that wives of servicemen were assumed to be dependents in need of additional benefits whereas husbands must prove dependency in order to be eligible. Justice Brennan argued that gender based classifications, like racial classifications, were inherently suspect, and that they could be justified only by a compelling governmental interest. Though the Court struck down the Idaho statute by an 8 to 1 vote, Justices Powell, Burger, and Blackmun were of the opinion that the Idaho statute did in fact violate the due process clause, but the classification could not be considered inherently suspect, thereby invoking "strict scrutiny" and an almost certain invalidation.

In the area of gender equality, the Supreme Court has tended to adopt something of a middle path. As noted above, it has not agreed to treat gender classifications in the same way as racial ones. Racial classifications are "inherently suspect" and can be upheld only if the government's interest is compelling and if the means used is narrowly tailored to achieving that interest. Neither has the Court decided to accept such gender distinctions if they are merely "reasonable." Instead, the Court when reviewing gender classifications requires that the distinction between males and females "must serve important governmental objectives and must be substantially related to achievement of those objectives" [*Craig* v. *Boren* (1976)]. Using this test the Court held in *Craig* that a state may not distinguish between men and women in the legal age at which they may purchase alcoholic beverages. However, in *Rostker* v. *Goldberg* (1981) the Court upheld the constitutionality of draft registration limited to males.

The feminist movement also produced the so-called Equal Rights Amendment, the proposed Twenty-Seventh Amendment to the Constitution. Its purpose is to eliminate all social, legal and economic distinctions between the sexes. Some critics of the ERA suggest that a constitutional amendment is unnecessary because great strides for women's rights have been made through the courts and legislative bodies.

The 1964 Civil Rights Act and programs such as Affirmative Action are designed to facilitate woman's ability to acquire professional employment at pay equal to their male counterparts. Women have gained access to what were previously all male bastions such as the Army, Navy and Air Force academies. Single and married women are more able to acquire consumer credit today than prior to recent series of Supreme Court decisions regarding these topics. In 1973, the Supreme Court in the case of *Roe v. Wade* further advanced women's rights by determining that abortion was a legal operation and could be made available to most American women. The Court ruled that a Texas statute prohibiting abortion was a violation of the right of privacy. The Supreme Court did, however, uphold a Congressional ban on Medicaid abortion (Hyde Amendment) in the case of *McRae v. Harris* (1980). This legislation prohibits federal funding of abortions, and was vigorously promoted in many parts of the country.

Nevertheless, ERA advocates believe that true equality can only be achieved by adding the constitutional guarantee. In the spring of 1978, supporters of the proposed amendment asked Congress for a time extension. As originally proposed, the deadline set for ratification was March 22,

1979. The proposed amendment, at that time, needed but three more ratifications to achieve the constitutional requirement of thirty-eight states. In the autumn of 1978, Congress, by a majority vote in both houses, granted an extension until June 30, 1982. No amendment has been so hotly contested and this marks the first time that a time extension for ratification has been granted. The Constitution requires that an amendment be proposed by a two-thirds majority vote in both houses. However, it is silent on time limits and extensions. Opponents suggest that a two-thirds vote is required for both proposals and extensions. Proponents, however, argue that since the time limit of seven years was not included in the *body* of the amendment but merely in the enabling legislation used to send it out for ratification that the time limit could be changed by a simple majority vote. It is unlikely that the Supreme Court will adjudicate this interesting constitutional question. On the one hand, the extension has also expired and the amendment is dead unless Congress decides to repropose it. And, it is possible that the Court will declare such an issue to be a "political question" to be resolved by the voters and the Congress and not a legal question for the courts to decide.

In the late 1970s homosexual groups were also actively seeking relief from alleged discriminatory practices. During the 1960s and early 1970s many cities and counties passed "gay rights" ordinances. "Gay rights" came under attack when the 1970s approached middle age. The first battlefield was Dade County, Florida. Anita Bryant was the primary spokesperson against the local ordinance. Her arguments were religious. She contended homosexuality is a sin and that homosexual teachers set a bad example for their students. Dade County voters sided with Mrs. Bryant and overwhelmingly repealed the ordinance. Thereafter, homosexual groups lost similar battles in Eugene, Oregon, St. Paul, Minnesota, and Wichita, Kansas. To date, the Supreme Court has been circumspect on the issue. Apparently, the justices have not been convinced that homosexuals have been denied due process. It is also possible, however, that the Court is once again being reflective of public sentiment.

Right to Die

Another important issue of late concerns the right to die. Medical technology has produced machines that are capable of sustaining life for long periods of time. The question created by these advances is how long should life be prolonged? This became a public issue in 1975 when a young New Jersey woman, Karen Ann Quinlan, took a near lethal dose of alcohol and tranquilizers. Physicians reported that her brain was so badly damaged that she could not survive without the aid of various machines that kept her living, but in a vegetative state. Her parents wanted the machines shut off so that Karen could die with grace and dignity. After losing their case in lower state courts, the Quinlans won the right to determine their daughter's future from the state Supreme Court.

Karen's plight called attention to a fear that plagues many senior citizens. How long should life be prolonged and how long should the agony and expense be endured? A bill was adopted by the California legislature in 1976 that would give an individual the right, by prior consent, to have life-saving measures discontinued in what might be a hopeless situation. Perhaps other law-making bodies will come to grips with this problem in the future.

Most of the great battles in this area were fought and won in the 1960s. To be sure, many groups believe that there is a long way to go before the ideal has been achieved, while others think that the expansion of freedom has produced more license than liberty. The mood in 1981 seems to be one of pause and reelection. Perhaps the transitional phase in this area is from that of drama and emotion to one in which the issues will become more thoughtful and well-considered. In the 1980s reason may replace passion in such matters.

For Further Reading

Abraham, Henry J. *Freedom and the Court: Civil Rights and Liberties in the United States* 4th ed. (New York: Oxford University Press, 1982).

Cortner, Richard C. *The Supreme Court and Civil Liberties Policy* (Palo Alto: Mayfield Publishing Co., 1975).

————. *The Supreme Court and the Second Bill of Rights: The Fourteenth Amendment and the Nationalization of Civil Liberties* (Madison: University of Wisconsin Press, 1981).

Emerson, Thomas I. *Toward a General Theory of the First Amendment* (New York: Vintage Books, 1966).

Kluger, Richard. *Simple Justice* (New York: Vintage Books, 1975).

Morgan, Richard E. *The Politics of Religious Conflict: Church and State in America* (New York: Pegasus, 1968).

Pritchett, C. Herman. *The American Constitution* 3rd ed. (New York: McGraw-Hill, 1975).

Sigler, Jay A. *American Rights Policies* (Homewood, IL: The Dorsey Press, 1975).

Sindler, Allan P. *Bakke, DeFunis, and Minority Admissions* (New York: Longman, 1978).

Way, H. Frank, Jr. *Liberty in the Balance: Current Issues in Civil Liberties* 5th ed. (New York: McGraw-Hill, 1980).

Name _____

Section _____

Date _____

Review Questions for Chapter 3: Freedom and Rights

1. *Barron* v. *Baltimore* (1833) _____

_____

_____

_____

_____

2. Total incorporation _____

_____

_____

_____

_____

3. *Yates* v. *U.S.* (1957) _____

_____

_____

_____

_____

4. *Miller* v. *California* _____

_____

_____

_____

_____

5. Free Exercise Clause _____

_____

_____

_____

_____

6. *Engel* v. *Vitale* (1962) _____

_____

_____

_____

_____

7. Exclusionary rule _____

_____

_____

_____

_____

8. *Miranda* v. *Arizona* (1766) _____

_____

_____

_____

_____

9. Double jeopardy _____

_____

_____

_____

_____

10. Speedy Trial Act of 1974 _____

_____

_____

_____

_____

11. *Gideon* v. *Wainwright* (1963) _____

_____

_____

_____

_____

12. *Furman* v. *Georgia* (1972) and *Gregg* v. *Georgia* (1976) _____

_____

_____

_____

_____

13. Voting Rights Act of 1965 _____

_____

_____

_____

_____

14. "Separate but equal" doctrine _____

_____

_____

_____

_____

15. *Regents of the University of California* v. *Bakke* (1978) _____

_____

_____

_____

_____

16. *Craig* v. *Boren* (1976) _____

_____

_____

_____

_____

17. Abortion rights _____

_____

_____

_____

_____

18. *Jacobellis* v. *Ohio* (1964) _____

_____

_____

_____

_____

19. "Wall of separation" _____

_____

_____

_____

_____

20. Change of venue _____

_____

_____

_____

_____

Essay Study Questions

1. Discuss the "nationalization" of the Bill of Rights. What constitutional provision was used to do this? What were the opposing theories of the Court? Are any provisions of the Bill of Rights *not* applicable to the states?

2. Obscenity has long been a problem for the courts. Justice William O. Douglas argued that the state had no business telling people what they could or could not read. However, the majority of the Court has rejected this view and has attempted to draw the line between the obscene and the protected. Discuss how their definition has changed. Do you think the current test is a workable one? If so, how do you handle cases like *Jenkins*? If not, what do you believe would be the proper standard?

3. The question of search and seizure has long troubled judges, lawyers and the public. The prohibition against unreasonable searches and seizures and the exclusionary rule sometimes work to protect the guilty as well as the innocent. Do you believe that the exclusionary rule is the price we must pay to protect ourselves from governmental intrusion or do you think that the exclusionary rule should be abolished even if it would allow the police to violate privacy of the innocent? Justify your answer.

4. In the area of racial equality the courts use a "strict scrutiny" standard which requires a *compelling* governmental interest. In gender equality cases, however, the courts use the standard of an *important* governmental objective. What factors would suggest that race and gender should be treated the same? What factors would suggest that they be treated differently? What do you think should be the proper standard in gender discrimination cases? Why?

Chapter 4

Congress

Congress is considered by many today as an outdated institution characterized by incompetence, inefficiency, impropriety and impotence. Not only has it lost considerable power to the executive branch, but it has also grown so large and cumbersome that it cannot seem to manage its own affairs. Furthermore, it has been rocked by scandals in recent years, ranging from sexual pecadilloes to criminal activities, which have cost its members the confidence of the American public. Such was not the attitude toward the Congress in 1789, however, when the founding fathers placed it first in the Constitution as a reflection of its deemed significance.

Congressional Structure

The creation of Congress resulted from a compromise reached at the Constitutional Convention between the small states and the large states, both of which sought to protect their interests under the newly centralized system of government. In the New Jersey or Patterson Plan presented at the convention, the small states proposed that the new legislature operate similarly to the way the United Nations works today, with each state having one vote. The large states, on the other hand, in the Virginia or Randolph Plan, called for a legislature in which representation would be based on population. After considerable debate, the Connecticut or Great Compromise was reached which created a bicameral or two house Congress. In one house, called the House of Representatives, population would provide the basis for representation with each state having at least one representative; and in the other, called the Senate, the states would be equally represented by two Senators from each state.

Over the next century and a half, as the population of the country grew, so did the size of the Congress. This proved to be a problem for the House of Representatives, so in 1910 Congress froze the number of members in the House at 435. Since that time, every ten years when the national census is taken, rather than adding more representatives, the 435 seats are simply reapportioned to reflect any changes in population patterns. The recent trend has been an increase in the number of representatives from the Sunbelt states of the southwest and a decline in the number from the northeast, reflecting the move of many people to and from those areas.

The founding fathers also included in the Constitution certain requirements which must be met before a person may become a member of Congress. In order to qualify as a Representative, a person must be 25 years old, must have been a U.S. citizen for 7 years, and must be a resident of the state from which he or she was elected. The requirements for a Senator are a bit stricter. In addition to being a resident of the state from which elected, a person must also be 30 years old and a 9 year U.S. citizen. Related to the difference in requirements is a difference in terms of office for the two houses. Representatives serve two year terms while Senators serve for six years.

Finally, under the original Constitution, the selection of legislators also varied. Members of the House were chosen through direct election by the people; Senators, however, were chosen by the state legislatures. It was not until 1913 when the 17th amendment was added to the Constitution that we began to have direct election of Senators as well.

In addition to membership terms, requirements, and selection, there are several other structural characteristics of Congress which must be addressed before one can understand how and why Congress functions as it does. Within each house there are certain administrative officers who preside over operations within the chamber. In the House, the presiding officer is called the Speaker of the House. Elected by the membership, he is always a representative of the party which holds a majority of the seats in the House. He is a very powerful figure who controls committee assignments, serves as a liaison to the White House, and appears to the public as the voice of the House. Unlike the Speaker, the presiding officer in the Senate is not a member of that body but rather is the Vice President of the United States; called the President of the Senate, he lacks the power of the Speaker of the House and can vote only to break a tie. There are two additional administrative officers in the Senate, the President Pro Tem who is the senator of the majority party who has the most seniority and the Assistant President Pro Tem who is any senator who has previously served as President or Vice President. The President Pro Tem presides when the Vice President is absent which is most of the time, whereas the Assistant President Pro Tem is primarily an honorary position.

In addition to these administrative officers, both houses have party officers who direct the party business in each chamber. There are majority and minority leaders, also called floor leaders, who are elected by their respective parties; and majority and minority party "whips" who assist the floor leaders by informing party members of important issues and insuring that they are present when the issues come up for a vote.

Committees

Finally, a basic structural characteristic of Congress which has great significance for the legislative process is the existence of committees. These committees, often referred to as "little legislatures," are not mentioned in the Constitution, but have evolved over the past 200 years out of necessity. As the issues facing Congress have increased in both number and complexity, the ability to deal with them all has become more and more difficult; consequently, committees have been created to improve efficiency and develop specialized expertise in different policy areas. Basically, there are four kinds of committees in Congress. Standing committees are permanent committees created by acts of law; they consider legislation on various kinds of issues which roughly parallel the executive departments, such as agriculture, commerce, foreign relations, etc. There are currently 22 standing committees in the House and 15 in the Senate with all members of Congress serving on at least one. The membership of these committees is drawn to reflect the party distribution in the house and the chairman is always a member of the majority party. Second, ad hoc committees are temporary committees set up to investigate some specific question; once the investigation is finished and a report is filed, these committees go out of existence. Third, joint committees are composed of members of both houses; they generally deal with nonlegislative, noncontroversial matters such as the U.S. Printing Office. Fourth, conference committees are joint committees created when a bill is passed in different forms by the two houses; their purpose is to draw up a compromise version of the bill.

Congressional Functions

In addition to describing structural characteristics of the Congress, the founding fathers also included provisions for the various powers or functions Congress has to perform. Some of these are enumerated or spelled out in specific detail in Section 8 of Article I, while others are more elastic and subject to interpretation. Some of the enumerated powers include the power to lay and collect taxes, to borrow money, to coin money, to establish a post office, and to punish counterfeiters.

Legislative Functions—Of all the powers described, however, the primary function of Congress is to make laws. As stated in the last paragraph of Section 8, Congress shall "make all laws which shall be necessary and proper for carrying into execution the . . . powers vested by this Constitution." The process by which Congress carries out this legislative function is a cumbersome one. A bill, which is a proposed law, can begin in either house, with the exception of appropriations bills which must start in the House of Representatives. Bills may be written by anyone—staff members, Congressmen themselves, lobbyists, private citizens, executive departments—but they must be introduced by a member of the Congress.

Let us follow a fictitious appropriations bill through the legislative process. Once introduced in the House, the bill is "placed in the hopper." The "hopper', is the clerk's desk. There, it is given a number, printed and distributed to the membership. The Speaker of the House, currently Mr. "Tip" O'Neill from Massachusetts, will decide to which of the standing committees he will assign the bill for hearings. Next, the chairman of that committee will assign the bill to one of its subcommittees. Here, the bill receives its first consideration. At the hearing, lobbyists, other members of congress and anyone else who is interested in the bill may testify for or against its passage. Also, the bill is "marked-up," that is, amendments may be added, passages deleted or riders attached.

If a majority of the subcommittee recommends passage, then the bill is referred back to the standing committee. There, the merits may once again be debated. If a majority of the standing committee recommends passage, the bill is then sent to the powerful Rules Committee. Sometimes called the "traffic cop of the House, " the Rules Committee will fix a time limit for debate when the bill reaches the floor of the House for a vote and it will also assign the bill to a legislative calendar. Appropriations bills are placed on the union calendar. Other bills of a general nature that do not involve major expenditure of monies are placed on the house calendar and bills that are primarily concerned with a member's district are placed on the private calendar. When the bill's time comes up, it is sent to the floor for debate and a vote. Before a vote is taken, the entire House may convert itself into a committee of the whole, where last minute amendments or changes may be made. Finally, the bill is voted on, a simple majority being necessary for passage. The Speaker will then sign the measure and it is sent to the secretary of the Senate.

There, the process is similar, but there are some significant differences. In the Senate there are but two legislative calendars, business and executive. The executive calendar is for treaties and presidential appointments to public office. Every other bill is assigned to the business calendar. In the Senate, the assignment of bills to one of the 15 standing committees is done by the leadership. The Rules Committee in the Senate takes care of such general business as recommending changes in procedural rules, but it does not have the power of its counterpart in the House.

When bills come before the Senate for consideration there is an opportunity for a filibuster, which is an unlimited attempt to talk the bill to death. Senators resort to a filibuster as a last ditch attempt to kill or modify a bill. A filibustering senator may read the newspaper, the Bible or a phone book. Since this is official business, a quorum of Senators must be present and all of the utterances are duly recorded and published in the Congressional Record. Senator Strom Thurmond of South Carolina holds the all-time record for individual effort. He droned on for 24 hours in a filibuster against the 1957 Civil Rights Act. Filibusters can be stopped by the Senate invoking cloture, which now requires a ⅗ vote. The Senate can then consider the bill and a majority is required for passage.

If the bill is not passed in identical form by both houses then it must go to a conference committee. A conference is a joint committee and usually consists of members of the standing committees that considered the bill in the House and Senate. The purpose of the committee is to reach agreement, through compromise, on those portions of the bill that are in conflict. After the conference finishes its work, the revised bill is sent to the floors of the House and Senate for the approval of the membership. If no compromise is reached, then the bill dies.

Once a bill is passed by both houses in identical form it is sent to the President for his consideration. He has ten days in which to act. He can sign the bill and it immediately becomes law. Or, he can wait for ten days and if Congress is still in session the measure becomes law without his signature. If during the ten days Congress adjourns then the bill is dead and this is called a pocket veto. Finally, the President can veto the bill and send it back to Congress with a message about what that branch can do to make the bill less objectionable. Congress can then either rewrite the bill or override the presidential veto. An override requires a ⅔ vote in each house, which is difficult to achieve. A persistent criticism of the presidential veto is that the President must accept or reject the entire bill with all of its amendments and riders. He cannot go through a bill and cancel out specific items. This power of "item veto" is available, however, to the governors in some states.

Finally, it should be noted that a bill lasts only as long as the session of Congress in which it was introduced, or a maximum of two years. If a bill has not been passed by the time the session ends, it must be reintroduced in the next session and start the process all over again. For that reason and because there are so many pitfalls along the way, only a small percentage of the bills introduced in Congress ever become law.

Budgetary and Appropriations Function—Spending perogatives are supposed to be the function of the Congress; however, this power has largely been preempted by the President. Up until ten years ago, the President simply sent to Congress a budget reflecting his own priorities which was then used as a guide for funding programs during the upcoming year. Then in 1975, in an attempt to reassert itself, Congress created a standing budgetary committee in both houses to draw up an independent budget which could then be used in addition to the President's proposal as an allocation guide. Nonetheless, Congress continues to follow the President's lead in most cases; occasionally it may add more than was requested or reduce the amount desired by the executive branch, but generally it goes along with President's recommendations.

Amending the Constitution—Congress also participates in amending the Constitution. There are two ways to amend the constitution, only one of which has ever been followed. First, a proposed amendment is introduced in Congress and must be approved by two/thirds of both houses. Once Congress approves the amendment, it must be ratified by three/fourths of the states before it can become part of the Constitution. Congress also sets the time that will be allowed for the ratification

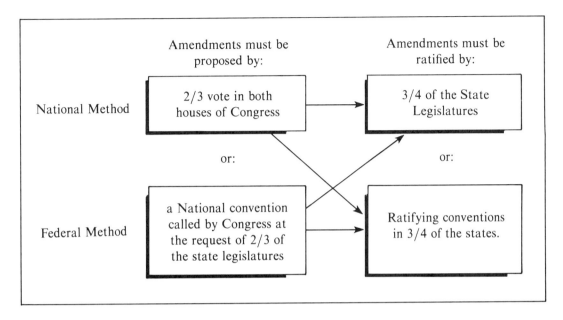

process; this is generally seven years. For the recent 27th or so-called Equal Rights Amendment, Congress granted a three year extension. Even so, the amendment was not ratified and must now start the process all over again.

A second way to amend the Constitution is for ⅔ of the states to petition Congress to call a convention. Amendments will then be introduced and approved by delegates to the convention before going to the states for ratification. Efforts are currently underway to call for a convention to attempt to add an amendment which will require the federal government to have a balanced budget. Many politicians are hesitant to take this action in light of the fact that at the last constitutional convention, held in 1789, rather than amending the existing Articles of Confederation, they threw the whole thing out and started all over.

Checking the Other Two Branches—The three branches of government were originally set up in such a way that power would be divided among them and they could check the activities of one another. Consequently, many of Congress's functions deal directly with checking the powers of the executive and judicial branches.

Congress's first check on the President is the confirmation of many of his appointments. This is primarily a function of the Senate which according to Article II, Section 2 of the Constitution has the power of "advice and consent" over appointment of ambassadors, federal judges, cabinet secretaries, and various other public officers such as members of regulatory commissions. Presidential appointees require a majority vote in the Senate for confirmation. Most appointees are noncontroversial and are routinely confirmed. However, President Nixon had trouble when he attempted to appoint Clement F. Haynsworth and G. Harold Carswell to the Supreme Court, for the Senate refused to confirm their nominations. The exception to this exclusion of House involvement is in the case of a vacancy in the vice presidency. The 25th Amendment provides that in such an eventuality, the President can appoint a new Vice-President who must be confirmed by a majority vote of both houses. Since the amendment was added in 1967, its provisions have been invoked twice. Spiro Agnew, one of President Nixon's Vice-Presidents, resigned from his post after he was convicted of not having paid income taxes on bribes that he took when he was Governor of Maryland. Nixon selected Gerald Ford, who was minority leader in the House to be Agnew's successor. Ford was investigated by both houses and confirmed. When Richard Nixon resigned from the presidency in the wake of the Watergate scandal, Ford became the first nonelected President. He chose Nelson Rockefeller for the Vice-Presidency, who was also confirmed by Congress.

The Congress also has the power to impeach and remove the President from office but this is a function that is rarely performed. In addition to the President, the members of the federal judiciary, as well as some presidential appointees may be removed from office by this process. The procedure starts in the House where any member or group of members can prefer charges against an offending or offensive member of the administration or judiciary. The Speaker of the House will refer the charges to a standing committee, usually the judiciary committee, for investigation and review. There, charges will be investigated and the committee will make its recommendations to the House. If a majority of the membership votes in favor of the charges the individual is impeached, which is similar to indictment in criminal matters. The Speaker then will appoint several members of the House to manage its case before the Senate where the trial takes place. If the President is being tried, the Chief Justice of the Supreme Court will preside over the proceedings. Otherwise, the President of the Senate, who is the Vice-President, will be the presiding officer. The accused is allowed to be represented by counsel and to have witnesses testify in his behalf; however, since this is not a criminal proceeding, the ordinary rules of evidence do not apply. After the testimony has been presented, the Senate goes into a secret session to debate the merits of the case. A ⅔ vote is necessary to convict the impeached individual, the penalty for which is immediate removal from office.

Only 13 individuals have been impeached in our history, one of whom was President Andrew Johnson who missed being convicted by a margin of one vote. All others were federal judges. Of those impeached, only four were convicted and removed from office. The Judiciary Committee in the House recommended that President Richard Nixon be impeached. However, Nixon resigned from office before the House could act on the charges and the matter was dropped.

Congress can also check the President's powers in foreign relations. Although the President is the Commander-in-Chief of the military and can send troops into battle, it is Congress who must actually declare war. However, war has been declared only five times over the last 200 years and yet many battles have been fought. This problem became especially critical during the Vietnam War which was never declared. In response to the dissatisfaction of the American public, Congress passed in 1973 the War Powers Act which limited the time that troops could be involved in an undeclared war to 60 days. President Nixon vetoed the act, and Congress responded by making it a resolution which expresses the sentiment of the Congress but may not be binding on the President should such an occasion arise. Indeed, Congress itself extended the original 60 day limitation to 18 months in 1983 when President Reagan sent the marines to Lebanon.

Also in foreign affairs, the Senate must approve international treaties which are negotiated by the executive. Ratification of treaties requires a ⅔ vote in the Senate. Treaties are referred to the Senate's Committee on Foreign Affairs for hearings. Usually the Senate will follow the President's lead; however, President Carter had to lobby very hard to obtain the ⅔ vote to ratify the treaties that returned the sovereignty of the canal to Panama.

Congressional checks against the judicial branch include the power to impeach and remove judges and the Senate's approval of judgeship appointments made by the President. There is a tradition in the Senate known as "senatorial courtesy" which comes into play over such appointments. Should a Senator not approve an appointment made to a federal judgeship in his own state, the rest of the Senate will generally honor the wishes of their fellow member and vote against the president's nominee. In addition, Congress can create lower courts, set the number of judges who serve on the Supreme Court, and limit the courts' appellate jurisdiction.

Power of Investigation—Although not stated specifically in the Constitution, Congress has also very broad powers of investigation. Usually, this function is carried out by committees or subcommittees. Investigation is different from hearings in that the purpose is to probe areas where legislation may be needed to cure ills or prevent abuses. At times, special or select committees are created to investigate specific areas. When the magnitude of the Watergate scandal began to emerge after the election of 1972, the leadership in the Senate appointed a special committee to investigate the affair. The committee subpoenaed witnesses and asked them to testify under oath, probed many aspects of the administration and investigated the campaign donations that flowed into the effort to re-elect Nixon. There is no doubt that the committee's work was instrumental in Nixon's resignation and the conviction of the Attorney General and several top aides for perjury. Other investigations have dealt with organized crime, assassinations, corruption and communism.

Limitations on Congressional Powers—Also written into the Constitution are a few things which Congress explicitly cannot do. For instance, Congress cannot pass ex post facto, that is, retroactive laws or bills of attainder which in effect deny a person his right to judicial process. Nor can Congress grant titles of nobility. Congress cannot suspend the writ of habeas corpus which is the right to be charged with a crime if arrested. Finally, Congress cannot tax articles exported from any state nor favor one state over another in the regulation of commerce.

Congressmen Themselves

So far this chapter has dealt with Congress as an institution, but, what about the men and women who serve in Congress? For the most part, Congress is dominated by well-educated white males who are middle-aged and older. As of today, over 90% of the members of Congress have attended college with 60% having educations beyond the college level, either in law school or graduate school. Over half of the members are attorneys, an occupation which accounts for only one tenth of one percent of the nation's work force; businessmen and educators are the next highest groups represented. In 1981, the average age of members in the House was 48.4 years and in the Senate was 52.5 years. Most members of Congress are Protestants with Episcopalians, Methodists, and Presbyterians found more frequently than other denominations. Most members are also white; in 1983 only 20 members of the House (4.6%) were black with no black members in the Senate. The numbers are similar for women: 21 in the House and an unprecedented 2 in the Senate. Finally, most members of Congress come to "the hill" with some previous political experience, having usually held state legislative offices.

Problems Facing the Congress

Seniority—One of the problems which plagues Congress is the influence of seniority in the policy-making process. The longer a person stays in office, the more seniority he or she accumulates, and the more power he or she is able to wield. Senior members serve as floor leaders, as committee chairmen, and as general power brokers in negotiations among members. The problem with this is that senior members tend to be more conservative and less innovative than the newer, younger members who are forced to "wait their turn."

Inefficiency—The number of domestic issues, the technical complexity of policies, and the increased involvement since WWII of the United States in international affairs have resulted in expanding the time and staff and expertise needed by Congressmen to effectively address the questions facing the nation at any given point. As a result, the apparatus of Congress, which now includes not only 535 members but thousands of personnel and committee staffers, has become so large, so expensive, and so cumbersome that the institution no longer seems able to operate economically and efficiently.

Representation—Does your Congressman or Senator really represent your interests or is he or she tied to special interest groups which can afford to contribute great sums to his/her reelection campaign? Should you ever write a letter to Washington, it will be answered and will bear the signature of the member of Congress. However, it is very likely that only a staff member saw the letter rather than the elected official. Is this real representation? One must also ask the question: Do you want your congressman to use his own judgement in your behalf, ie. to act like a trustee; or do you want him to simply be a straw in the wind, a delegate, who does only what his constituency demands?

Salary and Fringe Benefits—Many people feel that members of Congress are overpaid. But is $61,500 enough to cover living expenses in Washington and at home? Is it competitive enough with private enterprise to attract the "best and brightest" to serve in the government? On the other hand, it should be noted that members of Congress are allowed to earn outside money by giving speeches and publishing articles. They receive fringe benefits such as travel allowances, stationery, postage, telephone privileges, legal counsel, and health and life insurance packages. The prestige of the office and the corresponding respect afforded to members of Congress can also be advantages both while in office and after leaving the Congress.

Ethics—Congress has been faced with serious breaches of ethical conduct in recent years. In 1976, there was concern about Tongsun Park, a South Korean businessman, who, for over six years, hosted lavish parties for Congressmen and passed out large sums of money. It was discovered that Congressman Wayne Hays' "secretary" could not type or even file and then there was Congressman Wilbur Mills' celebrated affair with a stripper called the "Argentine Firecracker." And in 1980 evidence of the ABSCAM scandal, which involved taking bribes from undercover agents posing as Arab businessmen in return for votes on immigration policies, was made public and resulted in the expulsion of several members of Congress. There are ethics committees in both houses to deal with such cases. They can either censure a fellow member which is an official condemnation of that member and can result in loss of committee positions and the like or they can expel or throw out a member. Seven members of the Senate and nineteen members of the House have been censured and only 4 have ever been expelled. Despite these procedures for internal policing, such episodes have cost Congress the respect and credibility that it once had in the eyes of many American citizens.

Overview

If you visit your congressman in Washington, D.C. you will usually be met by a courteous receptionist who will offer a cup of coffee and ask you to sign the guest book. Most likely the office will contain pictures and memorabilia from your state or district. The staff member will provide you with passes to the galleries where you can observe the Senate or House in action or, more likely, inaction. If available, the Congressman will meet with you briefly in his inner office. Perhaps, and most likely, the Congressman will want to have his picture taken with you in front of his office where the seal of your state is obvious. A staff member will take several pictures and several weeks later you will receive a large, glossy autographed picture of you and the Congressman. All of this, of course, is official business. The Congressman obviously hopes that you will be impressed and support him with campaign contributions and your vote. Before you make that decision why not ask him or her some specific questions about his or her attitudes, motives, and positions on important issues?

For Further Reading

Congressional Quarterly Press, *Congressional Ethics,* 2nd ed., (Washington, D.C.: Congressional Quarterly Inc., 1980)

Barbara Hinckey, *Stability and Change in Congress,* 2nd ed. (New York: Harper & Row, 1978)

William J. Keefe & Morris S. Ogul, *The American Legislative Process: Congress and the States,* 5th ed. (Englewood Cliffs, N.J.: Prentice Hall, 1980)

John W. Kingdon, *Congressmen's Voting Decisions,* 2nd ed. (New York: Harper & Row, 1981)

Donald R. Matthews, *U.S. Senators and Their World* (Chapel Hill: University of North Carolina Press, 1960)

Name _____

Section _____

Date _____

Review Questions for Chapter 4: Congress

1. Great Compromise _____

_____

_____

_____

_____

2. Speaker of the House _____

_____

_____

_____

_____

3. Party Whip _____

_____

_____

_____

_____

4. standing committees _____

_____

_____

_____

_____

5. conference committees _____

_____

_____

_____

_____

6. necessary and proper clause _____

_____

_____

_____

_____

7. filibuster/cloture _____

_____

_____

_____

_____

8. advice and consent _____

_____

_____

_____

_____

9. War Powers Resolution _____

_____

_____

_____

_____

10. writ of habeas corpus _____

_____

_____

_____

_____

11. senatorial courtesy _____

_____

_____

_____

_____

12. seniority _____

_____

_____

_____

_____

13. censure _____

_____

_____

_____

_____

14. trustee/delegate _____

_____

_____

_____

_____

15. ABSCAM _____

_____

_____

_____

_____

Essay Study Questions

1. Compare and contrast the House and Senate in terms of structure, process, and function.
2. Discuss the various ways Congress can check the powers of the other two branches of government.
3. Describe the various problems facing Congress and suggest ways to deal with them.
4. Discuss the functions and importance of committees in the legislative process.

Chapter 5

The Presidency

As has been the case with all modern governments the United States has witnessed a marked tendency toward the concentration of political power in the hands of the executive. Throughout the greater part of our history the relative balance of power between Congress and the executive has ebbed and flowed, sometimes favoring the former, at other times the latter, depending upon circumstances and the stature and force of character of the individuals involved. In the twentieth century we have witnessed, however, the victory of the executive branch and, for better or worse, that victory appears to be irreversible and permanent.

What we are talking about is, in a very real and important sense, a fundamental transformation in the character of the American constitutional system. In the course of the twentieth century the presidency has increasingly taken over much of the function of policy initiation. While it is true that Congress may, and frequently does, amend or reject presidential policies, it is now the President who determines the legislative agenda and it is to him that the American people have come to look for leadership.

It is true that the sordidness of the Watergate affair did damage the presidency not inconsiderably and did bring about something of a reversal in the ever increasing trend toward an all-powerful presidency. In the post-Watergate era public opposition to and suspicion of the concentration of power and congressional attempts to reassert its power have served to check, at least momentarily, the growth of presidential power. Yet even in its tarnished and weakened form the power available to the presidency remains awesome. Indeed, it is so awesome that the presidency is frequently described as the single most powerful office in the world.

In spite of the awesomeness of presidential power there are occasions when a President, caught in the net of circumstances, finds himself reduced to utter helplessness and all the powers associated with the office serve him, and the people he would govern, to no avail, as was the case, for example, with President James E. Carter. This is so because power is not some concrete thing that can be neatly tied in a bundle and handed to successful candidates. It is, instead, a relationship and the extent of the power bequeathed to a successful candidate is conditioned by a variety of factors—not the least of which is the political skill of the individual attaining the office.

Regardless of the greatness or ineptitude of presidential office holders, it is the presidency which has become the focal point of American government and politics.

Qualifications and Selection

In all, forty men have served as President of the United States. In view of the awesomeness of its power the formal constitutional requirements for the nation's highest office are surprisingly modest. In order to be a candidate for the presidency one must be at least 35 years old, a "natural-born citizen," and must have resided within the United States for fourteen years. This seems a hardly adequate set of qualifications for our nation's most powerful office. Simply meeting the constitutional requirements does not, however, make one eligible for the presidency. In practice there are many additional *political* considerations which serve to govern the selection of presidential candidates.

What is it that makes a man eligible for candidacy? First, he must make his availability known, i.e. he must nominate himself. No President has ever been drafted. Every successful presidential candidate has actively sought the office and made his availability known to influential members of his party. Secondly, the aspiring candidate must secure his party's nomination. Thirdly, he must win more votes than any other candidate in enough states and the District of Columbia to give him a majority, i.e., 270 of the 538 votes in the electoral college.[1]

It is clear that the Framers of the Constitution were concerned with securing only the most qualified men for the office and consequently erected an electoral system that would function as a kind of filter, refining and extracting out of the masses of men otherwise eligible those who, in the words of writers of *The Federalist,* possessed "the most attractive merit and most diffusive and established characters."[2] It is no doubt the case that the practical considerations that determine the ultimate availability of candidates has undergone considerable change since 1789, but they are nonetheless still an important aspect of presidential selection.

What qualities make an individual a viable candidate? First, virtually all of our presidents have been professional politicians. They have served as members of Congress, governors of their states, and as presidential cabinet officers. (See Table 1). The U.S. Senate has been, at least until very recently, the most important supplier of candidates, for example, all the candidates of the two major parties in 1960, 1964, 1968, and 1972—John Kennedy, Richard Nixon, Lyndon Johnson, Barry Goldwater, Hubert Humphrey, and George McGovern—served their apprenticeship in the Senate. The two most recent Presidents, James Carter and Ronald Reagan, served their apprenticeship as governor of their respective states.

Secondly, a candidate has a greater chance of success if he comes from a pivotal state with a large population and one where the two major parties are roughly equal in strength in national elections. Of the successful presidential candidates since 1960 only President Carter came from a state that did not have a large bloc of votes. Conversely, the only unsuccessful candidates to come from large states were Richard Nixon in 1960 who was defeated by John Kennedy, a candidate from another large state, and Gerald Ford in 1976 whose association with the preceeding Nixon administration was no doubt a contributing factor.

Regional considerations are also important. Until very recently the primary regional source for presidential candidates was the Northeast and the Midwest. For example, from 1868 to 1972, of the thirty-eight presidential candidates put forward by the major parties, twenty-one were from three states—New York, Ohio, and Illinois. However, as a consequence of recent demographic trends this appears to be changing. In 1976 a candidate from a southern state narrowly defeated a candidate from a midwestern state and in 1980 both candidates were from so-called Sun Belt states: Ronald Reagan from California and James Carter from Georgia. With the reapportionment resulting from the 1980 census we can expect to see more candidates emerging from the Sun Belt, i.e., the South and the West.

Table 1. Presidents, Their Terms and Experience

			Prior Service			
		Party	VP	Cabinet	Cong.	Gov.
1. George Washington	1789–97	Fed.				
2. John Adams	1797–1801	Fed.	x			
3. Thomas Jefferson	1801–09	D/R	x	x	x	
4. James Madison	1809–17	D/R		x	x	
5. James Monroe	1817–25	D/R		x	x	x
6. John Quincy Adams	1825–29	D/R		x	x	
7. Andrew Jackson	1829–37	Dem.			x	x
8. Martin Van Buren	1837–41	Dem.	x	x	x	x
9. William Harrison	1841	Whig			x	x
10. John Tyler	1841–45	Whig	x		x	x
11. James Polk	1845–49	Dem.			x	x
12. Zachary Taylor	1849–50	Whig				
13. Millard Fillmore	1850–53	Whig	x		x	
14. Franklin Pierce	1853–57	Dem.			x	
15. James Buchanan	1857–61	Dem.		x	x	
16. Abraham Lincoln	1861–65	Rep.			x	
17. Andrew Johnson	1865–69	Union	x		x	x
18. U. S. Grant	1869–77	Rep.		x		
19. Rutherford Hayes	1877–81	Rep.			x	x
20. James Garfield	1881	Rep.			x	
21. Chester Arthur	1881–85	Rep.	x			
22. Grover Cleveland	1885–89	Dem.				x
23. Benjamin Harrison	1889–93	Rep.			x	
24. Grover Cleveland	1893–97	Dem.				x
25. William McKinley	1897–1901	Rep.			x	x
26. Theodore Roosevelt	1901–09	Rep.	x			x
27. William Taft	1909–13	Rep.		x		x
28. Woodrow Wilson	1913–21	Dem.				x
29. Warren Harding	1921–23	Rep.			x	
30. Calvin Coolidge	1923–29	Rep.	x		x	
31. Herbert Hoover	1929–33	Rep.		x		
32. Franklin Roosevelt	1933–45	Dem.				x
33. Harry Truman	1945–53	Dem.	x		x	
34. Dwight Eisenhower	1953–61	Rep.				
35. John Kennedy	1961–63	Dem.			x	
36. Lyndon Johnson	1963–69	Dem.	x		x	
37. Richard Nixon	1969–74	Rep.	x		x	
38. Gerald Ford	1974–77	Rep.	x		x	
39. Jimmy Carter	1977–81	Dem.				x
40. Ronald W. Reagan	1981–	Rep.				x

Wealth and social standing have also been an important factor in the selection of presidents. In spite of the American belief that "anyone can be President," less than a dozen presidents have risen from the ranks of the very poor. Most have grown up in the upper-middle classes (i.e., the business and professional classes) and some, like George Washington, Franklin D. Roosevelt and John F. Kennedy have been extremely wealthy.

Religion, sex, and race have also entered into presidential politics. With the exception of John Kennedy, whose victory was an extremely narrow one and who never stood for re-election, all our Presidents have been White Anglo-Saxon Protestant males. Only two presidential candidates, Alfred E. Smith and Kennedy, both Catholics, have been non-Protestants; none have been Jews. Likewise, custom has for the most part excluded women from candidacy for our nation's highest office and will probably do so for some time to come. Thus far, only Senator Margaret Chase Smith has made a serious bid for the nomination of one of the major parties but the virtue of her candidacy was not recognized by her party. A Negro candidacy has likewise been inconceivable due to the racial prejudice of the majority of Caucasians who make up the electorate. One would hope that the day will come when a candidate will not be barred because of religion, sex, and race, but recent reactionary trends suggest that it will be a long time in coming.

Finally, a successful candidate must possess the ability to project an image. If a candidate is to succeed in his quest for the White House he—and his family—must appear as a "man of the people." Paradoxically, he must at the same time appear to be more than Everyman, not too ordinary, not too pedestrian.[3] It is at this juncture that the advertising techniques of Madison Avenue become important, for it has become necessary to package and market presidential candidates in much the same way we do soap or toothpaste. Unfortunately, it takes more than marketability to be successful as a President, it takes character and this is something much more substantial and enduring than an image. It is becoming increasingly apparent that the qualities of character necessary to win nomination and the election may have nothing to do with and, perhaps, even be at odds with the temperament necessary to govern well.[4]

Theories of Presidential Power

Article II of the Constitution, which establishes and empowers the presidency, is brief and framed in very general terms. This fact alone allows room for development and change in (not to mention debate about) the character of the office to suit changing conditions; it provides scope for personal, political, social, and economic influences to affect the nature of the presidency.

Article II begins with the sentence: "The executive power shall be vested in a President of the United States of America." But what, precisely, does this mean? The debate over the power vested in the President was immediate and has persisted throughout our history. During the course of this debate there have emerged three basic views concerning the nature and extent of presidential power. The first of these is a restricted view, frequently referred to as the "Constitutional" theory and is commonly associated with the name of William Howard Taft. According to this view Article II contains an enumeration of executive powers and that the President must be prepared to justify all his actions on the basis of either a power enumerated or one reasonably implied from some specific power. As Taft wrote:

> The true view of the Executive functions, is, as I conceive it, that the President can exercise no power which cannot be fairly and reasonably traced to some specific grant of power or justly implied and included within such express grant as proper and necessary to its exercise.[5]

Additionally:

> Such specific grant must be either in the Federal Constitution or in an act of Congress passed in pursuance thereof.[6]

And, finally:

> The grants of Executive power are necessarily in general terms in order not to embarrass the Executive *within the field of his action plainly marked for him,* but his jurisdiction must be justified and vindicated by affirmative or constitutional or statutory provision, *or it does not exist.*[7]

This is, then, a narrow view based upon a strict construction of the Constitution; one which argues that the President may do only those things the Constitution and the laws say he can do.

A more expansive view is that put forward by Theodore Roosevelt and known as the "Stewardship" theory. This view calls for a more active President, for as Roosevelt put it:

> My view was that every executive officer, and above all every executive officer of high position, was a steward of the people bound actively and affirmatively to do all he could for the people, and not to content himself with the negative merit of keeping his talents undamaged in a napkin. I declined to adopt the view that what was imperatively necessary for the nation could not be done by the President unless he could find authorization to do it. My belief was that it was not only his right but his duty to do anything that the needs of the nation demanded unless such action was forbidden by the Constitution and the laws.[8]

According to this view the President is a steward of the people obligated to do whatever the needs of the people require. It does involve a broadening of executive power, but not the usurpation of power for there are limits. Again, as Roosevelt observed:

> I *acted for the public welfare,* I acted for the common well-being of all our people, whenever and in whatever manner was necessary, unless prevented by direct constitutional or legislative provision. . . .[9]

This is, then, a broader, more liberal view of Presidential power. One which holds that Presidents may do whatever they judge to be necessary and proper for the public well-being.

By far the most controversial view is that known as the "Prerogative" theory. This conception has its origins in Chapter XIV, "Of Prerogative" in John Locke's *Second Treatise of Government.* There prerogative is defined as "the power to act according to discretion for the public good, without prescription of the law and sometimes even against it."[10] According to this view, the President's most important obligation is to preserve the nation no matter what. As Abraham Lincoln put it:

> It was in the oath I took that I would, to the best of my ability, preserve, protect, and defend the Constitution of the United States.[11]

And:

> I did understand . . . that my oath to preserve the Constitution to the best of my ability imposed upon me the duty of preserving, by every indispensable means, that government—that nation, of which that Constitution was the organic law.[12]

This quite often means sacrificing constitutional and legal constraints on presidential behavior on the altar of "emergency" and "commanding public interest." And in Lincoln's mind this is precisely the case:

> By general law, life and limb must be protected, yet often a limb must be amputated to save a life; but a life is never wisely given to save a limb. I felt that measures otherwise unconstitutional might become lawful by becoming indispensable to the preservation of the Constitution through the preservation of the nation.[13]

Acceptance of this view by recent Presidents has been largely responsible for the tremendous growth in presidential power and has resulted in what some call the "imperial presidency."[14] Yet even this view does not assert that there are *no* limits on presidential power, for Presidents acting in accordance with this view are ultimately held accountable for their actions, both by the public at large and the other branches of government. This is perhaps the most important lesson to be learned from the Nixon experience, i.e., even under the prerogative view it is possible for a President to exceed his authority.

Styles of Presidential Leadership

In the course of our history Presidents have filled out the loose design of the office prescribed in the Constitution, and in doing so have exhibited differing styles of leadership. In his *Presidential Government*,[15] James MacGregor Burns identifies three basic models of presidential leadership, each of which lends a differing dimension to American government. The first of these models he names the Madisonian model after James Madison, the "father of the Constitution," who was primarily responsible for establishing it in theory and law, though he was not the first to try it out in practice. This model is premised on the need for government with countervailing powers and embraces four basic concepts:[16]

1. *Checks and Balances:* According to this view each of the three branches of the national government possesses powers of its own, but they each have, at the same time, some sort of veto power over the actions of the other two branches. Government is a marvelously contrived instrument balancing powers between the three branches. At the very least "each branch must protect its own independence arising from its unique constitutional powers and bolstered by its special constituency and method of recruitment." Even those Presidents generally regarded as weak have taken care that the other branches of government did not pre-empt their prerogatives.
2. *Minority Rights:* This view places a premium upon minority rights. Indeed the main purpose of the whole checks and balances system is the protection of minority rights—at least as understood in the context of *Federalist #*'s 10 and 51. It is important to note, however, that it was protection of minority rights *from* governmental power, not *through* it.
3. *Anti-majoritarianism:* Perhaps the most important aim of the Madisonian formula is that of thwarting majority tyranny. It quite deliberately attempts to keep popular majorities—or the majority—from gaining control of the government and turning it toward its own ends at the expense of the minority.

4. *Prudent, limited government:* Government, especially at the national level, must be, according to this view, carefully hedged-in. The main bugaboo of the Madisonian model is rash governmental action, for it is based upon an innate fear that government will succumb to the mob. This does not mean that it preaches government by stalemate, it does recognize the need to be governed. Rather it asserts that government wait and act only after a popular consensus, including all the various interests and constituencies in society, is reached. It places much credence in the observance of constitutional limitations and proprieties.

The second model embraces concepts and practices that are somewhat antithetical to those of the Madisonian. This model Burns calls the Jeffersonian, after Thomas Jefferson, who fashioned it in theory and practice. This model is predicated on a strong, coherent party system and it too embraces four basic concepts:[17]

1. *Unified political system:* This model requires a highly united group of political leaders and government officials who overcome the checks and balances (though leaving the Constitution intact) through party control of the government. This party control is exercised by a coherent and disciplined party which has won office in the preceding election on the basis of a meaningful and principled party platform and is therefore able to lay claim to a popular mandate.
2. *Collegial leadership:* Under such a scheme it is the party leader who becomes President and governs through his party. Because he and other party leaders were elected on the basis of a clearly articulated party platform, their main responsibility in policy and programs is to the party at large and the popular majority that elected them. The President, in this view, is a "team man," both in office and out. He governs with the passive consent of other party leaders, who themselves enjoy some independent power. While he enjoys considerable latitude as party leader, his policies and programs are ultimately governed by party purpose and limited as well as supported by other party leaders.
3. *Majority rule:* In direct contrast to the Madisonian model this model seeks not to stifle the majority but to give expression to it. Here government acts on the basis of a mandate endorsed by a majority of the voters, who have judged competing party platforms and candidates. Once granted power on this basis, party leaders are given free rein to govern subject to only two basic limitations: "free criticism protected by the Bill of Rights" and other constitutional safeguards and free elections within a limited span of time. Because it is the embodiment of majority rule this model envisions an energetic and productive government.
4. *Minority opposition:* Because this model results in an active, interventionist government it also requires a vigorous, vocal, and responsible opposition to scrutinize and criticize the policies and programs of the government.

The third model, called the Hamiltonian, "implies an active national government revolving around a vigorous, energetic, resourceful, inventive, and ruthlessly pragmatic executive officer. This model is more difficult to define than the others in that it has at its core large elements of opportunism and expediency. However, it is still possible to identify the key concepts embodied in this style:[18]

1. *Heroic leadership:* Under this approach the President is a national leader in the fullest sense of the word. He is not just an administrative chief or party leader. "He must exert great leadership in behalf of the whole nation. He must not be unduly restricted by his party; when

necessary (as he sees necessity) he can ignore it or even desert it." Hamiltonian presidents possess—or at least are thought to possess—some of the qualities of the hero in modern setting. They cut an impressive figure and have style. They speak movingly and even passionately and seem to establish a direct link with the public at large. They are invested by the press and public with superhuman qualities—they are physically inexhaustible, they can read with lightening speed, they have total recall, and so on.

2. *Personal organization:* The presidency is a much more personalized office under Hamiltonian leadership. The President depends less—and is committed less—to the party as a whole and relies more on the personal organization he has built up over the years. This organization is far more centralized, disciplined, and efficient than is the general party organization. Furthermore, it is bound directly to the leader by ties of intense personal—and frequently, ideological—loyalty and hope of reward and consequently has an ambiguous and fluid relationship with the regular party.

3. *Expedient use of power:* It is in the exercise of power that the Hamiltonian model differs most sharply from the first two. It differs from the Madisonian in that it involves an active and broad exercise of power regardless of constitutional theory and principle; and it differs from the Jeffersonian in that power is more personalized. "The Hamiltonian president has no . . . reservoir (of party) support; he must employ every weapon that he has—his own reputation, his prestige, his patronage power, his political friendships—to achieve the results he wants." Because he has attained office by means outside the party he must rely more on personal influence than on party influence and support and he must constantly draw on, and replenish his personal store of political credits.

4. *Disorganized opposition:* Because his power base is outside the framework of the party the Hamiltonian President is freed from party obligation and control and this in turn gives him much greater latitude in political tactics and governmental decision making. But the latitude he enjoys complicates the role of opposition party leadership. The "out" party, if we can speak of one in this context, needs a clear target to shoot at, but what it gets is a constantly moving and shifting one.

While Presidents throughout our history have attempted to govern in light of all three of these models—or variations on them—it appears that as a consequence of changes in the electoral system, future Presidents, as have Presidents Carter and Reagan, will be forced to embrace the Hamiltonian model.

Functions and Roles of the President

Just what tasks are Presidents expected to perform regardless of the approach to leadership they adopt and the theory of the office they embrace? Clinton Rossiter, in a classic study of the presidency, observed that "if there is any one thing about our highest office that strikes the eye immediately, it is the staggering number of duties we have laid upon its incumbent."[19] The President performs many different roles, and in doing so he exercises many different kinds of power. The President is: chief of state, chief executive, chief diplomat, commander-in-chief, chief legislator, chief of party, voice of all the people, protector of the peace, manager of prosperity, and world leader.

Chief of State

The first of the roles of the President is that of chief of state. From the time of George Washington the President has served as the ceremonial head of the government of the United States. "He is, or can be," as one political scientist has written, "the essence of the nation's personality."[20] As chief of state the President is the symbol of our sovereignty, continuity, and grandeur. As the official representative of our nation he must play many parts ranging from the most solemn to the downright silly. The performance of these parts may put a strain on the President's other duties, but their performance is absolutely necessary for the President who wishes to stay in touch. From the time he gets up in the morning until he goes to bed at night he is the object of public scrutiny.

In his capacity as the ceremonial head of the nation he is called upon to greet distinguished visitors from all parts of the world. He lays wreaths on the tomb of the Unknown Soldier and before the statue of Lincoln, etc. He makes speeches to a myriad of social, civic, religious, and ethnic groups. He throws out the first ball of the baseball season. He attends an endless series of social events, such as breakfasts with legislative leaders, luncheons and dinners at the White House with foreign dignitaries and religious leaders.

Moreover, the President is expected to not confine this sort of activity to the White House and the city surrounding it. "The people expect him to come to them from time to time, and the presidential grand tour, a precedent set conspicuously by George Washington, is an important aspect of the ceremonial function."[21]

The duties performed by the President as chief of state may often seem trivial, even foolish, yet the President who ignores them does so at his peril. It is through this role that the President is able to keep in touch, and to stay in favor with the people, the ultimate source of all his power.

Chief Executive

The second, and the most immediately obvious, of the President's roles is that of chief executive. Whether he is in fact able to do so or not, the President is perceived as being responsible for running the executive branch. In Rossiter's words: "He reigns, but he also rules; he symbolizes the people, but he also runs their government."[22] Ironically, while the Constitution charges the President with executive responsibility, the powers granted to him are imperfect and incomplete, i.e., his powers are simply not equal to his responsibilities. No matter how qualified he may be and how much he may enjoy the details of administration, all Presidents have had more difficulty carrying out this responsibility successfully than any other.

The Constitution places upon the President the primary responsibility—which no law or plan or circumstance can ever take away from him—to "take care that the laws be faithfully executed. Obviously, he cannot perform this task alone—he must have help in the form of assistants. In order to insure their responsibility to him, he receives from the Constitution, explicitly or implicitly, the twin powers of appointment and removal—though the latter is restricted only to "purely executive officers."[23] Furthermore, the President has received further acknowledgment of his administrative leadership from Congress through such legislative mandates as the Budget and Accounting Act of 1921 and the succession of Reorganization Acts.[24] It is the President's responsibility, then, to see that the laws of the United States are executed and the hundreds of laws implemented daily by government officers are executed in his name and under his general supervision—even though some independent regulatory agencies such as the National Labor Relations Board and the Interstate Commerce Commission operate, by design, outside his immediate area of responsibility.

It is in his need for assistants in carrying out his executive responsibilities that the President encounters difficulty in performing this role. For, as Louis W. Koeing has pointed out:

> Although the President appoints the heads of the great operating departments and agencies, the principal resources on which they depend—their legal powers, the programs they administer, and their annual funding—are derived from acts of Congress. Programs and policies, to the extent they are implemented, are carried out by tenured civil servants, who were on the job before the incumbent President arrived and will remain after he leaves.[25]

But, even if he were able to exert greater control over his subordinates, it may well be that viewing the President as the "general manager" of the executive branch is a misapprehension. Typically, Presidents assuming office lack knowledge of the intricate workings of the bureaucracy, and none, save Herbert Hoover, have shown much interest in—let alone capacity for—administrative management. The primary responsibility of the President is to sce that the laws are faithfully executed and this is more a question of political leadership than administrative skill.

Chief Diplomat

Nearly fifty years ago Justice George Sutherland of the Supreme Court observed of the President that he is "the sole organ of the federal government in the field of international relations."[26] This statement draws our attention to the third of the President's most important roles, that of chief diplomat. Even though the Constitution vests authority in the field of foreign relations in three organs of the national government—the President, Congress, and for two special purposes, the Senate—the President's role is paramount, if not indeed dominant. The growth of presidential authority and responsibility over foreign affairs seems to have been almost inevitable. The Constitution, laws, customs, the practice and perceptions of other nations, have all combined to place the President in a dominant position.

The practice of presidential dominance in foreign relations does indeed make good sense. Diplomacy is a sensitive activity and as Rossiter notes: 'Secrecy, dispatch, unity, continuity, and access to information—the ingredients of successful diplomacy—are properties of his office, and Congress, I need hardly add, possesses none of them."[27]

In so far as constitutional authority is concerned, the field of foreign relations may be roughly divided into two sectors: the formulation of general foreign policy and the conduct of affairs. "The first of these is a joint undertaking in which the President proposes, Congress disposes, and the wishes of the people (presumably) prevail in the end."[28] From Washington's Proclamation of Neutrality in 1793 to the present day, Presidents have repeatedly taken the lead in the formulation of broad policy, subject to Congressional acquiescence. Occasionally Congress has compelled the President to abandon a policy he has initiated, as it did when the Senate rejected the Versailles Treaty negotiated by Woodrow Wilson after World War I, or when it forced James Carter to withdraw the SALT II Treaty in 1980. While the House of Representatives is not specifically mentioned in connection with foreign policy, the House has on occasion been able to force Presidents to alter or abandon policies by threatening to not appropriate the funds necessary to carry that policy out; thus Presidents from Washington to the present have found it politic to at least consult with House leaders as well as with Senate leaders in the conduct of foreign policy. But in spite of occasional Congressional checks on presidential initiative in the foreign policy area, it has become increasingly difficult to restrain him even in this area.

The second sector of foreign affairs, that of their actual conduct, is the President's exclusive baliwick. "The transaction of business with foreign nations is, as Jefferson once wrote, 'executive altogether,' and Congress finds it difficult to exercise effective control or to deliver constructive criticism—not that Congress can be accused of lack of trying."[29] It is the President, or his appointees, who carry out the day to day conduct of foreign affairs, negotiating and conferring with and even threatening, other nations.

In recent years, the role of chief diplomat has become one of the most important and exacting of all those we ask the President to perform. Furthermore, it is this role that is the primary cause of the tremendous growth in presidential power in the 20th century.

Commander in Chief

The United States, like any other state, must provide for its defense and survival. Consequently, the Constitution pays considerable attention to the question of the common defense and to the war powers. It specifically designates the President as "Commander-in-Chief of the Army and Navy of the United States, and of the militia of the several States when called into the actual service of the United States." Thus, while the President shares the ultimate responsibility for national defense with the legislative branch, it is he, with the aid of the secretary of defense, the Joint Chiefs of Staff, the National Security Council, and his national security advisor (all of whom are his personal choices) who must look to the state of the nation's defenses. During times of peace he is charged with raising, training, supervising, and deploying the forces that Congress sees fit to provide. When the winds of war blow, the President's power to command the forces at his disposal swells out of all proportion to his other powers. During times of war all major decisions of policy and strategy, and many of tactics, are his and his alone to make or to approve. Presidents Lincoln, Wilson, Franklin Roosevelt, Truman, and Lyndon Johnson all involved themselves intimately, and forcefully, in the details of the military conduct of the wars fought during their terms of office.

But the power and the responsibility vested in the modern President by the commander-in-chief clause go far beyond the simple power to command the military forces of the United States. No doubt the Framers saw this power, as Hamilton did, "as nothing more than the supreme command and direction of the military and naval forces, as first General and Admiral of the Confederacy."[30] But the idea that the President's power under the commander-in-chief clause was something purely and merely military gave way under the harsh realities of modern war. As Rossiter observes:

> Faced by an overriding necessity for harsh, even dictatorial action, Lincoln used the commander-in-chief clause—at first gingerly, in the end boldly—to justify an unprecedented series of measures that cut deeply into the accepted liberties of the people and the routine pattern of government.[31]

Under subsequent wartime Presidents, particularly Wilson and Franklin Roosevelt, this clause carried the presidency to breathtaking heights in its control over the social and economic order. These wartime expansions of power have invariably been sustained by the Supreme Court because the military prosecution of the war becomes the first priority of the President and of the government.

Chief Legislator

The duties of the President are not all strictly executive in character. While the Constitution, as it was written, clearly intended to rest all legislative powers of the national government in Congress, it also sketches certain working relations between the President and Congress in this area. The President, is, then, also intimately associated, by the Constitution, reinforced by custom, with the legislative process. Today, as a consequence of two centuries of national growth, the President and his aides have come to have, in the normal course of events, more influence over national policy than any single congressman or group of congressmen; truly the President is the chief legislator.

True, Congress still has the paramount responsibility for legislation and has its strong men to carry it through, but the complexity of the problems facing modern society make imperative external leadership. This leadership role naturally falls upon the President, for as Rossiter writes:

> The president alone is in a political-constitutional, and practical position to provide such leadership, and he is therefore expected, within the limits of constitutional and political propriety, to guide Congress in much of its law-making activity.[32]

The President proposes legislation for Congress to consider and by doing so sets the legislative agenda. He makes legislative proposals either through his annual State of the Union message, or in the form of specific laws. Consequently, many of our most celebrated laws clearly bear the imprint of the President under whom they were enacted. Frequently, important legislation is "drafted in the President's office, introduced and supported (in Congress) by his friends, defended in committee by his aides, voted through by a party over which every form of discipline and persuasion was exerted, and then made law by his signature."[33]

The President who lacks a congressional majority finds the task of leading in this area difficult, but even those Presidents who possess a congressional majority must exercise leadership; and if, as in the case of Ronald Reagan, his majority position in the country outweighs his minority position in Congress, he will be expected by both the public and Congress to turn his programs and policies into law. The task of providing legislative leadership is formidable and delicate, but absolutely necessary. The President who does not attend prudently and steadily to this task will be judged, as was President Carter, a failure. However, the President's role as legislative leader has become so central and crucial that "the President who will not give his best thoughts to guiding Congress, more so the President who is temperamentally or politically unfitted to 'get along with Congress,' is now rightly considered [not only a failure, but] a national liability."[34]

The presidential roles thus far discussed—Chief of State, Chief Executive, Chief Diplomat, Commander-in-Chief, and Chief Legislator—comprise the strictly constitutional roles of the President. As broad as these powers are, they do not, however, exhaust the whole range of presidential responsibility. In addition to these roles, there are at least five more roles, not specified in the Constitution, which have assumed crucial importance.

Chief of Party

The first of these is the President's role as leader of his party. Every President since Thomas Jefferson has entered the office as a party man and consequently every President since then—especially if he wishes to be re-elected—has had to put his hand firmly to the task of politics. He must devote at least an hour or two of every day to being the leader of his party—mending fences, lending support, and in general furthering the aims and interests of the party. This seemingly endless dabbling in partisan political activity is as important in presidential performance as the exercise of his constitutional power. If the President wishes to attain a loyal, cohesive, and effective administration, and persuade the Congress to adopt his programs and policies the game of partisan politics cannot be avoided.

Voice of the People

In addition to being the titular head of his political party the President is also the voice of the people, the leading formulator and expounder of public opinion in the United States, he is, as President Harry Truman put it, "the lobbyist for all the people." While he is the partisan leader of some he is the moral spokesman of all.

The President is in a position to exercise political leadership of the nation at large for "his is," as Woodrow Wilson once said, "the only national voice in affairs." Once he is elected, the President must transcend the narrow confines of partisan politics and represent not simply the interests of his own party but those of the whole people. The President knows no special constituency, but is the representative of the whole people, even of those who voted against him and who still oppose him.

Protector of the Peace

Perhaps the least known of the President's functions is "the mandate the holds—from the Constitution and the laws, but even more positively from the people of the United States—to act as Protector of the Peace."[35] The President is the chief law enforcement officer in the United States and it is upon him that the responsibility for restoring domestic tranquility often falls. While it is normally true that state and local authorities deal with social and national calamities, it is also frequently the case that the scope of the calamity—a riot in Watts, a hurricane and flooding in Louisiana, a volcanic eruption in Washington, is beyond the capabilities of the state and local authorities. It is to the President that the people turn in such circumstances for aid and comfort.

The President is certainly the person who can give such aid and comfort. No one man or combination of men can supply the men and materials necessary to cope with a disaster. He can supply troops, experts, food, money, medical supplies, equipment, loans of a magnitude far beyond that of the state and local authorities.

Manager of Prosperity

While the Constitution does not expressly grant any economic powers to the President, he has come to play a central role in the management of the national economy. Originally it was believed that the responsibility for the public finance should be that of Congress alone. The Constitution rests the authority to raise revenue through taxation, to borrow money on the credit of the United States, to regulate commerce, and to appropriate money for governmental functions in the legislature. Yet, as the functions and complexity of the national government expanded it became increasingly apparent that Congress simply lacked the cohesion and competence to control the economic affairs of the nation. Finally, in 1921, Congress conceded its inability to control the finances of the sprawling and disorganized national government and enacted the Budget and Accounting Act which required that the President prepare and transmit an annual budget to guide Congress in carryong out its responsibilities. The act also created a Bureau of the Budget to be housed in the Treasury Department—but transferred to the Executive Office in 1939 and reorganized as the Office of Management and Budget during Richard Nixon's presidency—to aid him in the preparation of the budget.

Yet the President's role in economic affairs is not limited to the finances of the national government alone. While it is true that many people, including President Reagan, regard the very idea of the President as manager of the nation's economy as economic and political heresy, the American people in general now expect the government, and especially the President to prevent a depression or panic or curb inflation and not simply to let such disasters fall upon them unopposed. The President who is unwilling, as was President Herbert Hoover, or unable, as was President Carter, to actively involve himself in the economic life of the nation will simply not be re-elected.

The origin of the President's role in this area can be fixed with unusual clarity. In the Employment Act of 1946—which was the first clear acknowledgement on the part of the national government of a general responsibility for maintaining a stable and prosperous economy—the President is singled out as the official most responsible for securing these ends and is empowered to appoint a Council of Economic Advisers to aid him in accomplishing them.

But even if Congress had never enacted the Employment Act the President's duties and powers in this area would have been as extensive as they are with its enactment. As Rossiter writes:

> We have built some remarkable stabilizing devices into our political economy since 1929, and the men who control them—in the Federal Reserve System, the Securities and Exchange Commission, the Federal Security Agency, the countless credit organizations of which former President Hoover has complained so bitterly, the Federal Deposit Insurance Corporation—are wide open to suggestions from the White House.[36]

While the idea of the free operation of the market still claims the allegiance of many Americans, then, most have come to accept increased governmental intervention in the economy as both necessary and desirable.

World Leader

Finally, with the emergence of the United States as a world power, the President has had to assume the role of world leader. For better or worse, the President has been marked out as a leader of those nations united in support of capitalism. Modern Presidents, whether they like it or not, must concern themselves with a constituency much larger than the American electorate; their words and deeds have an impact far beyond the boundaries of the United States. The prominent, if no longer preeminent position of the United States, both militarily and economically, in world affairs requires that the President take a broader view and attempt to coordinate interests with those of the United States. Despite some considerable erosion of America's leadership role under President Carter, this will continue to be one of the most important roles played by the President.

Presidential Character

Having discussed the various roles performed, or hats worn, by the President it is necessary now to fit the pieces together into an organic whole. The President does not perform these roles in isolation from one another, he is not one kind of official during one part of the day and another kind during another part—i.e., he is not chief legislator in the morning, chief executive in the afternoon, and head of state in the evening. He is all of these roles rolled into one and each one influences and is influenced by all the others. Despite the immensity of the burden of performing these ten roles and the thousands of men and women who serve as his aides, the presidency is a one-man job filled by a single man. It is the President who is ultimately responsible under the Constitution and in the minds of the people. Consequently, the character or personality of the individual assumes a great deal of importance. In an interesting and provocative book first published in 1972,[37] James D. Barber attempted to develop a scheme by which we might assess this aspect of the presidency.

In assessing the impact of personality upon presidential performance, Barber clustered all Presidents since Theodore Roosevelt into four personality types. In developing his typology Barber used two baselines which he claimed stand for the two central features of anyone's orientation toward life. The first of these Barber calls the *activity-passivity* baseline and concerns the amount and intensity of energy the individual invests in the office. That is, how much energy does he expend in the performance of his duties. Some Presidents invest considerable energy, not to mention time, in performing the duties of office while others approach their obligations much more casually. Lyndon Johnson, Barber tells us, "went at his day like a human cyclone, coming to rest long after the sun went down," while "Calvin Coolidge, on the other hand, often slept eleven hours a night and still needed a nap in the middle of the day."

The second baseline Barber calls the *positive-negative affect* baseline and concerns the way the individual feels about what he does. "Relatively speaking, does he seem to experience his political life as happy or sad, enjoyable or discouraging, positive or negative in its main effect. Basically the idea is very simple: is the individual someone who, insofar as we can tell, exhibits the feeling that he takes pleasure in political life, or is he, on the contrary, one who is burdened. What the positive-negative affect baseline is intended to measure, then, is the "fit" between the individual and his experience, the satisfaction derived from his experience."

These two dimensions, Barber claims, can help us outline the main character types because they are crude clues to the orientations of everyone toward life and are easily reducible to four basic character types long familiar in psychological research. What Barber is arguing is that Presidents are just like other people in that they "try to cope with the roles they have won by using the equipment they have built up over a lifetime." Presidents are not shapeless organisms molded by the office but individual human beings with personal histories which shape their behavior. The belief that merely moving into the White House will turn a James Carter into a Thomas Jefferson or a Ronald Reagan into an Abraham Lincoln is a naive and dangerous one. Presidents assume office with a personality which is fully formed (and is often responsible for their election in the first place) and while it is the office which empowers them to do great things it is their personal character which enables them to do them.

In summary form the four main character configurations identified by Barber are:

1. *Active-Positive:* In this character there is a congruence, a consistency, between much activity and the enjoyment of it. These individuals work hard at politics (actually, at everything) and have fun at it. They exhibit relatively high self esteem and relative success in relating to their environment. Such individuals are oriented toward productivity as a value and exhibit the ability to use their styles flexibly, adapting their style to the needs of the moment. Additionally, they have an image of what they might yet become and see themselves as developing toward a well-defined goal. They also emphasize the rational mastery of their surroundings, a characteristic that occasionally gets them into trouble for not everyone will see things the way they do and they will have difficulty in understanding why. The Presidents Barber places in this category are Franklin D. Roosevelt, Harry S. Truman, John F. Kennedy, and, with less justification, James E. Carter. We might also place Ronald Reagan in this category.

2. *Active-Negative:* Here we have a character full of contradictions, not the least of which is the relatively intense effort they invest in their role and the relatively low emotional reward they receive for that effort. Active-negative types are hard workers, but theirs is the hard work of a workaholic—it has a compulsive quality about it, as if they are trying to make up for something or to escape anxiety. They seem ambitious, striving, upward, power-seeking. Their stance toward the environment is aggressive and pugnacious, and they have a persistent problem in managing their aggressive feelings toward others. Such individuals have a poor self-image, one that is vague and discontinuous. Life is for them a hard struggle to get and keep power, hampered by the condemnations of a perfectionist conscience and a sense of inadequacy. In sum, active-negative types invest much energy in their roles, but it is energy distorted from within. The Presidents Barber includes in this category are Woodrow Wilson, Herbert Hoover, Lyndon B. Johnson, and Richard M. Nixon.

3. *Passive-Positive:* Here we have the compliant, receptive, other directed individual whose life is a constant search for affection for being agreeable and cooperative rather than personally assertive. This character type also involves a fundamental contradiction—this time it is a contradiction between low self-esteem (because they feel they are unlovable) and a superficial optimism. Their hopeful outlook helps dispel doubt and elicits encouragement from others. The passive-positive types can perform an important function in the political system because they help soften the harsh edges of politics and provide an atmosphere of decency. But, unfortunately, the fragility of their hopes and enjoyments make disappointment in politics very likely. The Presidents Barber placed in this category are Theodore Roosevelt, William Howard Taft, and Warren G. Harding. While Barber views Gerald Ford as an active-positive, it is probably more appropriate to place him here.

4. *Passive-Negative:* In the passive-negative character we have a personality in which the two factors are consistent, but we are presented with another kind of contradiction: why does such an individual enter politics? That is, why is someone who does little in politics and enjoys it

even less, there at all? The answer, Barber claims, "lies in the passive-negative's character-rooted orientation toward doing dutiful service; this compensates for low self-esteem based on a sense of uselessness." In short, these individuals are in politics because they think they ought to be, it is their duty. They may be well adapted to certain non-political roles, but they lack the experience, the flexibility and the creativity to be effective political leaders. The passive-negative types, as might be expected, exhibit a tendency to withdraw, to escape from the conflict and uncertainty of the political arena by emphasizing vague principles—especially prohibitions—and complex social arrangements. They become, in a sense, guardians of the right and proper way and see themselves as being above the sordid politicing of lesser men. The Presidents falling into this category are, according to Barber, Calvin Coolidge and Dwight Eisenhower.

Notes

1. See Louis Koenig, *The Chief Executive.* New York: Harcourt, Brace and World, 1964, p. 35.
2. Alexander Hamilton, James Madison, and John Jay, *The Federalist.* New York: Mentor Books, 1961.
3. Thomas E. Cronin, *The State of the Presidency,* 2nd ed. Boston: Little, Brown and Company, 1980, pp. 13–14.
4. See Michael Krasner, "Why Great Presidents Will Become More Rare," *Presidential Studies Quarterly,* 9 (Fall, 1979), pp. 367–375.
5. *The President and His Powers.* New York: Columbia University Press, 1916, pp. 139–140.
6. Ibid., p. 140.
7. Ibid. Italics added.
8. *The Autobiography of Theodore Roosevelt,* Centennial Edition. New York: Charles Scribner's Sons, 1958, pp. 197–198.
9. Ibid., p. 198. Italics added.
10. New York: Mentor Books, 1963, p. 422.
11. Letter to A. G. Hodges, April 4, 1864 in *The Life and Writings of Abraham Lincoln,* Philip Van Doren Stern (ed.). New York: The Modern Library, 1940, p. 807.
12. Ibid.
13. Ibid., pp. 807–808.
14. Arthur Schlesinger, Jr., *The Imperial Presidency.* New York: Houghton Mifflin Company, 1973.
15. Boston: Houghton Mifflin Company, 1965.
16. Ibid., pp. 108–110.
17. Ibid., pp. 110–112.
18. Ibid., pp. 112–115.
19. *The American Presidency.* New York: Harcourt, Brace and Company, 1956, p. 4.
20. Sydney Hyman, *The American President.* New York: Harper Brothers, 1954, p. 13.
21. Rossiter, *op. cit.,* p. 5.
22. Ibid, p. 6.
23. *Humphrey's Executor vs United States,* 295 U.S. 602 (1935). *Myers vs Unites States,* 272 U.S. 52 (1926).
24. Rossiter, *op. cit.,* pp. 7–8.
25. *The Chief Executive,* Fourth Edition. New York: Harcourt Brace Jovanovich, Inc., 1981, p. 185.
26. *United States vs Curtiss-Wright Export Corp.,* 299 U.S. 304 (1936).
27. *Op. cit.,* pp. 9–10.
28. Ibid., p. 10.
29. Ibid.
30. *The Federalist,* p. 418.
31. *Op. cit.,* p. 13.

32. Ibid., p. 14.
33. Ibid., p. 15.
34. Ibid., pp. 15–16.
35. Ibid., p. 19.
36. Ibid., p. 22.
37. James D. Barber, *The Presidential Character,* 2nd ed. Englewood Cliffs, N.J.: Prentice-Hall, Inc., 1977. The following discussion is a summary of Chapter One of this work.

For Further Reading

Barber, James D. *The Presidential Character,* 2nd ed. Englewood Cliffs, N.J.: Prentice-Hall, Inc. 1977.
Koenig, Louis W. *The Chief Executive,* 4th ed. New York: Harcourt, Brace Jovanovich, Inc., 1981.
Neustadt, Richard E. *Presidential Power.* New York: John Wiley and Sons, Inc. 1980.
Pious, Richard M. *The American Presidency.* New York: Basic Books, 1979.
Rossiter, Clinton. *The American Presidency.* New York: Harcourt, Brace and Company, 1956.

Name _____

Section _____

Date _____

Review Questions for Chapter 5: The Presidency

1. presidential qualifications _____

_____

_____

_____

_____

2. styles of presidential leadership _____

_____

_____

_____

_____

3. chief of state _____

_____

_____

_____

_____

4. chief executive _____

_____

_____

_____

_____

5. chief diplomat _____

_____

_____

_____

_____

6. commander in chief _____

_____

_____

_____

_____

7. chief legislator _____

_____

_____

_____

_____

8. chief of party _____

_____

_____

_____

_____

9. voice of the people _____

_____

_____

_____

_____

10. protector of the peace _____

_____

_____

_____

_____

11. manager of prosperity _____

_____

_____

_____

_____

12. world leader _____

_____

_____

_____

_____

13. active-positive _____

_____

_____

_____

_____

14. active-negative _____

_____

_____

_____

_____

15. passive-positive _____

_____

_____

_____

_____

16. passive-negative _____

_____

_____

_____

_____

Essay Study Questions

1. Discuss the different styles of presidential leadership.
2. What are the different rules performed by the President? How can one person discharge all these duties?
3. Comment on Barber's 4-fold classification of presidential character. Where would you place President Reagan in this classification? Why?

Chapter 6

The Administrative Branch

For almost two hundred years our system of government has been devoted to the principle that those who govern must be responsible to those who are governed; that the people have the power. Of course implied in this is the idea that when the people are dissatisfied and lose confidence in their leaders they can remove them through the electoral process.

The officials whom we elect, however, are just the tip of the iceberg. Below them serve approximately three million civilian employees and officials whose jobs are focused on the day-to-day running of the government. This vast structure is directed primarily by the chief executive and is frequently referred to as the "administrative branch" of government. Its primary job is to enforce the laws of the land, and in carrying out this mission it touches our lives both directly and indirectly.

That's right. It touches *your* life. Today. Food you consumed within the last twenty-four hours was processed under supervision of the U.S. Department of Agriculture. Have you ever taken vitamins with your breakfast? The U.S. Food and Drug Administration took them first to insure their quality; it similarly tests hundreds of other dietary supplements. One of the main reasons why you can listen to your favorite music on the radio is the fact that the various frequencies are regulated by the Federal Communications Commission. Without its licensing activities the signal of one station would constantly be interfering with that of another; and it always seems that it's the music you like best that gets blocked out the most. The various synthetic fibers in the clothes you are wearing at this very moment, unless you're reading this chapter while taking a shower, have to conform to standards set by the Consumer Products Safety Commission. The pricing and quality of the books and other materials sold in your campus bookstore have been directly affected by actions of the Federal Trade Commission and the Interstate Commerce Commission. Have you received any mail in the last twenty-four hours? Who delivered or lost it? As a matter of fact the safety and quality of the very air you breathe and the water you drink, and thus of the beer you drink, are the responsibility of the U.S. Environmental Protection Agency.

In short the various agencies of the government's administrative branch virtually surround you. In some cases they restrict you; in others they may present you with benefits, such as student loans, and in still others their goal may be to protect you, or at least to make your life a little less hazardous or hassled.

There Are Different Types of Agencies

Within the executive branch of government there are numerous departments, agencies, commissions and boards. Such bodies have critical differences among them. Some of these differences have to do with their legal structure and accountability and others have to do with the type of work they perform. The most important types of administrative agencies are the cabinet-level departments and the independent regulatory commissions.

Departments

The primary government agencies are known as departments. They currently number thirteen, and each is headed by an individual directly appointed by the President. Each of these officials is called a "secretary," and thus we have such titles as Secretary of Defense, Secretary of State, Secretary of Commerce, etc. Together the thirteen secretaries make up the president's *Cabinet.* That is, individually each person is the head of one executive department, while collectively the members serve together as a group of advisors to the president.

Given our system of checks and balances, we must also consider the role of the Congress. The Senate must give its "advice and consent" on these presidential appointments in order for them to become finalized. Thus it is said that the president nominates and the Senate confirms. Furthermore, when a president leaves office virtually all of his department heads go with him.

The best way to answer the question, "what do these departments actually do?" is to look at them in terms of certain categories. Broadly speaking, there are *five types of departments,* five types of departments with five very distinct orientations:

foreign affairs
resource oversight
group accommodation
service provision
system maintenance

The first category takes in the two major departments whose mission has to do with representing and defending the nation abroad: The Department of State and the Department of Defense. It is the responsibility of the State Department to formulate and implement U.S. foreign policy. This broad authority covers such areas as economic and business affairs, trade promotion, the gathering and analysis of intelligence, representation of the U.S. at international forums such as the United Nations, consular services which protect U.S. citizens abroad, and consultation to the president on the diplomatic aspects of national security policy. Finally, the Department of State is responsible for the operation of the Foreign Service, which provides America's system of representatives abroad—at well over two hundred embassies, missions and branch offices.

The military side of the foreign-policy equation is covered by the Department of Defense (DOD) whose role is to deter war and protect the nation's security. DOD is the largest of all the departments, and it is appropriately housed in the Pentagon—"the world's largest office building."

The armed forces directed by the Pentagon include approximately two million individuals on active duty in the Army, Navy, Marines and Air Force. Should a crisis arise these forces are backed up by two and one half million members of the reserves. In addition, DOD employs approximately one million civilians.

Together these two departments are responsible for dealing with both our friends and our enemies, and thus they must cooperate closely with each other to determine the right mix of diplomatic and military strategy. For example, such a weighing and mixing of strategies was evident throughout the crisis caused by the Iranian capture of the United States embassy in 1979.

The second type of department focuses on resource oversight, and has as its goals the conservation and development of the nation's natural resources. Agencies of this type are the Departments of Interior, Energy and Agriculture.

The Department of the Interior is without a doubt the nation's most important conservation agency. Most publicly owned lands come under its jurisdiction including the national parks. The department does not exist solely for the sake of conservation, however. It also has responsibility to assess and develop our mineral resources. Thus its Bureau of Mines works as a fact-finding agency doing research in the technology of mineral-resource extraction. Perhaps this housing of a dual responsibility, conservation and resources extraction, in a single agency highlights a basic problem faced by the resource departments. The functions of conservation and development are often in conflict with each other since one urges a slow and steady path in order to stabilize and preserve our natural heritage while the other frequently counsels a "let's bring it on line as soon as possible" philosophy.

An example of this problem is provided by the U.S. Forest Service, a unit of the Department of Agriculture. The Forest Service is supposed to conserve one hundred eighty-three million acres of national forest lands for future generations and at the same time supply today's builders with the raw materials they need to meet existing housing demands. Can one (person) serve two masters? A similar situation is faced on the livestock grazing issue by the Bureau of Land Management, a unit of the Department of the Interior. An argument often made is that when the BLM allows its resources to be developed for the livestock industry today it is merely taking them away from "all the people" and turning them over to a few select beneficiaries.

The resource department least buffeted by the cross pressures of conservation and development is the Department of Energy (DOE) since development is its stated objective. Created by Congress in 1977, the department's purpose is to provide a comprehensive energy plan for the nation. Toward this end it is responsible for:

—energy technology research
—regulation of energy products and use
—pricing and allocation
—collection and analysis of energy data

DOE regulations directly affect not only the price you pay at the pump for gasoline but whether it is available at all. Thus far the department has pushed for development by allowing the price of energy to rise astronomically. It is clear, however, that this cannot go on indefinitely.

The third type of department is oriented toward group accommodation since its very direct purpose is to serve the interests of certain segments of the economy. The Departments of Commerce, Labor, Education and Health and Human Services fall under this heading, since each was created to serve the needs of a particular clientele. The Department of Health and Human Services deals primarily with the needy through such programs as Social Security, Medicare and Aid to Families with Dependent Children. The Departments of Labor and Commerce help to balance the power of unions and management. In this way they provide both sides with access to governmental leaders. It is instructive to note that all attempts to merge these two units into a single department concerned with economic affairs have failed. Each prefers to have its own separate spokesman in Washington.

In 1979 President Jimmy Carter fulfilled a long-standing campaign pledge to teacher-groups around the country by creating the Department of Education. In return he received a 1980 endorsement from most teacher unions. Why? The teachers, like most other special interest groups, believe that they can be better served by an agency devoted exclusively to them. The alternative?

Being lumped with several other groups in a Department of Health, Education and Welfare and having to face more competition for scarce federal dollars. Ronald Reagan was opposed by most teacher groups, and as President he vowed to abolish this department.

It is common among political analysts to refer to the group served by a particular department as its *clientele*. Just as an attorney or investment broker looks after the needs of his clients, so too do many federal departments take care of their own. For example the Census Bureau collects data on residential patterns, income, occupation, etc. Such information is worth literally billions of dollars to big business in decisions on such questions as the location of new manufacturing plants and the targeting of high-priced advertising campaigns.

Thus while many groups complain about "big government" they are certainly not complaining about that part of it which has been set up to serve them directly. And if so many actors in the play known as "American Politics" want their own guardian in Washington, can it be any wonder that the federal budget is so high?

A fourth type of executive department is known as the *service-provision* agency, and many of its functions are aimed at the nations' cities. The Department of Transportation (DOT) and the Department of Housing and Urban Development (HUD) both target billions of dollars each year for the solution of urban problems. Many of their programs are run directly by the departments themselves while others are administered primarily by state and local governments. In this latter situation the department makes a money grant to the locality and the locality then sets up and operates the program.

A good example of such a program is known as the Community Development Block Grant Program (CDBG). Begun in 1974, the program provides an automatic "entitlement" of money to America's cities so that they can provide services such as recreation, public safety, redevelopment, and housing-code enforcement. For example, in 1980 the authorization was three billion eight hundred million dollars and the monies were allocated to the cities by HUD automatically on the basis of their population size, degree of poverty and level of housing needs. Needless to say, the program is very popular among the country's mayors and city managers who see it as a source of "free funds" for serving and rebuilding their cities.

Not all service programs bring such positive results, however, since frequently they wind up working at cross-purposes with each other. And where HUD and DOT are concerned it has often been said that the "right hand doesn't know what the left hand is doing." Consider the case of America's interstate highway system, being completed by the DOT, and our on-going effort to revitalize our central cities, the responsibility of HUD. HUD spends billions of dollars each year attempting to wipe out urban blight and thereby keep the middle class and the affluent from moving to the suburbs. Such efforts are important to the cities since when the monied-classes leave the urban tax base declines.

At the same time that HUD is trying to promote the redevelopment of central-city areas, DOT is providing money for a thru-way system that encourages these same individuals to flee to suburbia's open spaces. Without thru-ways the time spent commuting back and forth to work would simply be too great and thus many affluent families would never leave the city. DOT's policies thus hasten the migration, or what has been called "white flight."

It should be obvious that other departments are also caught in this web of urban cross-purposes. The Department of Health and Human Services carries a major share of the responsibility for ending decades of racial segregation, but for years FHA loans, administered by HUD, made it possible for whites to simply pack up and move when a city neighborhood was "threatened" with integration. The same kind of paradox exists for the Department of Energy. Thruways made travel easier and safer for millions of Americans, and so we began using our cars more and more. As our gasoline consumption doubled every ten years we became more and more dependent on foreign sources of oil. The result was quite predictable, and DOE was left to pick up the pieces.

Thus a service orientation does not always work smoothly, especially when the scale of operation is as large as that of some departments. Still, the goals of housing our citizens adequately and moving them from place to place remain fundamental. Thus, the service departments will continue to play a significant role in the governmental decision making process.

The fifth, and final, type of high-level agency is the system-maintenance department. Devoted to providing a stable framework in which Americans can undertake both public and private activity, these departments focus on maintaining law and order and on providing a sound economy. The two departments that typify this category are Justice and the Treasury.

The Department of Justice has been known to call itself the "largest law firm in the nation." The clientele of this particular law firm is also the largest since it is composed of the general citizenry of the U.S. It is termed a system-maintenance department since its functions include general protection, for all citizens of the system, against criminal activity and subversion. It also carries some responsibility for the promotion of competition in the market place through its anti-trust procedures. In both of these areas the department's activities involve law enforcement, crime prevention, crime detection and prosecution. Some of the best-known units of the department include the Federal Bureau of Investigation, the Drug Enforcement Administration and the U.S. Bureau of Prisons.

Shoe

Reprinted by permission of the Chicago Tribune-New York News Syndicate, Inc.

The Justice Department is also the agency that argues the government's case in all Supreme Court suits involving the U.S. The cases may involve issues as diverse as the rights of the accused or the forcing of school busing to achieve racial integration. But if the U.S. is a party to the case the nation will be represented by its top "law firm."

Another aspect of system-maintenance involves the provision of a healthy economic system in which individuals can pursue their own goals. Such is the responsibility of the Department of the Treasury which manufactures our coins and currency. It is this provision of a stable medium of exchange that allows the economic system to operate. The department is also charged with helping to formulate fiscal policy—the government's set of decisions about how much it is going to tax and spend.

Independent Regulatory Agencies

In addition to the cabinet-level departments discussed above there is another "breed of cat" in Washington, the independent regulatory agency. The most important of these bodies include such well-known names as the Interstate Commerce Commission, the Federal Trade Commission, and the Federal Communications Commission. Their basic purpose is to regulate various sectors of the economy and society, as directed by Congress.

A key factor that makes these agencies distinct from the cabinet-level departments is their independence from the President. Department heads are appointed by the President and can be removed by him at any time. Such is not the case with the commissioners who sit on these independent boards. They are protected from presidential influence by the fact that they can be removed only for "cause." That is, a President cannot fire a commissioner simply because the appointee has been brave enough to disagree with him. He must show that the individual has broken some law or been guilty of gross negligence. This limitation on the power of dismissal means that the commissioners have more of a free hand in reaching decisions and do not have to "bend" to the President's wishes.

This, then is one reason why the term "independent" is used to describe these bodies. Another is the fact that the commissioners serve staggered terms. The result is that a president cannot simply "clean house" when he takes over even though he may wish to. One member's term may be ending, but the others will remain. Thus, for years a President may face a commission that is only lukewarm, or even hostile, to his priorities.

The government has a legitimate need to watch over various operations that affect the nation as a whole, yet Congress cannot provide this regulation on a day-to-day basis since it lacks both the know-how and the manpower. The solution is to rely upon the independent regulatory agencies. The operation of the stock market provides a good example of the problem . . . and the solution. The buying and selling of stocks and bonds on Wall Street and at other trading centers across the country is absolutely vital to the well-being of the economy. Wall Street helps generate the money necessary for business to expand and prosper . . . and hire more employees. Investors looking for the highest return on the dollar are brought together with businessmen looking for money with which to build or diversify.

However, the market can be as dangerous as it is beneficial, as the crash of 1929 proved. With millions of shares of stock being traded daily there is ample room for manipulation and shadey dealing . . . dealings and techniques which can change daily and which the Congress could never hope to keep up with. The solution was to create the Securities and Exchange Commission (SEC) and give it the authority to set regulations governing the buying and selling of stocks and bonds. It is staffed by experts in the field of finance who work constantly to give the investing public the most comprehensive disclosure possible and offer protection from the effects of malpractice.

To allow it to operate the Congress has provided the SEC and the other regulatory agencies, as well, with a powerful weapon known as *delegated authority.* Under the Constitution it is the Congress, and only the Congress, that has the authority to enact laws. However, under certain circumstances the Congress can turn this authority over to some other body and that body can actually enact laws. This concept is central to the functioning of the independent regulatory agencies since they deal with highly technical and ever-changing fields that are really beyond the ability of the Congress to handle. Thus Congress merely passes a broad statute empowering the agency to make law. An example closer to home may help illustrate the point. You own your own car and can exercise the exclusive right to drive it yourself. However, you can also give someone else permission to drive it if you so desire. That is, you can delegate to them the authority to drive your car. Well, in much the same way, Congress can put the administrator "in the driver's seat" by delegating rule-making authority to him.

The discussion of the concept of delegated authority brings up what is perhaps the most important consideration in any examination of the independent regulatory agencies, and what makes them different from all other government agencies. They violate the principle of *separation of powers.* This is so since they combine in one set of hands first, the power to make law; secondly, the power to administer that law and finally the power to decide whether a particular individual or firm has violated it. Many have argued that such an arrangement is unconstitutional but the courts have generally upheld it as long as strict limits are placed beforehand on just how far the agency can go.

Perhaps one of the best-known regulatory agencies is the Federal Trade Commission (FTC). Given responsibility to prohibit "unfair methods of competition" and "unfair and deceptive practices," it was for years a captive of the very industries it was supposed to regulate. . This situation began to change, however, when FTC action led to the current practice of displaying health warnings on cigarette packages. An activist role on the part of the agency brought on a major confrontation with the tobacco interests, including the U.S. Department of Agriculture which sided with the industry in its contention that such government meddling was inappropriate.

Frequently whether an agency takes a passive or an activist role is decided by the personality of the individual at the helm. Thus the FTC got a real jolt when Jimmy Carter appointed Mike Pertschuk as its chairman shortly after his inauguration. During his years on the staff of the U.S. Senate, Pertschuk had earned a reputation as a thoughtful critic of business, and it wasn't long before that reputation began to be felt. There was a flurry of anti-trust activity; various consumer

consumer protection measures were beefed up and others were proposed. Among the most controversial was a rule aimed at limiting advertising on children's television programs. Clearly "the little old lady of Pennsylvania Avenue," as the FTC was once called, had taken a dose of megavitamins. The end result, however, was a confrontation with Congress that nearly wiped out all previous consumer gains. Congress' message seemed clear: "We'll delegate you all the authority you need . . . as long as you don't step on any powerful toes." President Reagan, as well, has been very direct in instructing the FTC to "cool it."

Another good example of the fundamentally political nature of the regulatory agencies is provided by the Interstate Commerce Commission (ICC). It was created in 1887 in order to deal with monopolistic abuses by the railroad industry, but from the first it was controlled by those it sought to dominate. Originally it was those who ran the trains, but with the passing of time it became those who run the trucks. Today the main purpose of the ICC seems to be the limitation of competition between surface carriers, not its stimulation. This can be seen in a number of ways. First, the Commission has used its delegated authority to set rates in such a way as to keep those charged by the railroads artificially high. That is, the railroads are prohibited by regulation from lowering their prices for the hauling of various products and commodities. This is done under terms of a system called "value of service" pricing, which dictates that rates be based not on the cost of transporting some product but on the nature of the product. Thus even though something can be moved more cheaply by train, the railroads cannot necessarily offer a lower rate. Of course trucks move faster than trains and can offer door-to-door service. Now assume that you are a manufacturer trying to decide how to ship your load of valuable cassette recorders to market. You are quoted nearly identical rates by both types of carriers, even though the rail estimate would be considerably lower if free competition were allowed. If it is not, you select to go by truck.

Hopefully this raises some curiosity on your part. "Wait a minute" you say, "I thought that regulatory agencies were supposed to regulate, not protect." In this instance, however, the purpose of regulation is to provide stability for the transportation industry, and unfortunately stability may also mean the limitation of competition.

Furthermore, it is not just a vague body called the "trucking industry" that dominates the setting of ICC policy, but a relatively small number of existing common carriers. They have a stake not only in limiting competition with railroads and waterways but also in keeping the number of "competing" trucking firms as low as possible. Thus, the Commission's authority to control entry into the business of interstate trucking is of fundamental importance to them. Anyone wishing to go into business cannot simply do so "overnight." He must apply to the ICC for a "certificate of public convenience and necessity." In this application it must be shown, not that the proposed firm can carry the goods more efficiently or more safely, but that those currently in the field are actually incapable of doing so at all. Furthermore, even if the new firm is allowed to begin operations it will have to send its trucks over routes that are designated by the ICC and it will be able to haul only those goods for which it is licensed. Thus, the new fleet may be able to carry TV sets, but not engine parts; furniture but not appliances. The end result is that the trucking industry is kept stable . . . by the limitation of competition.

Controlling the Bureaucracy

It should be evident by this time that the administrative branch of the government possesses a great deal of power: power to reward and punish, house and feed, tax and defend, promote and conserve. Such powers may be both useful and necessary, but where does this concentration of authority in the hands of non-elected officials leave our system of democracy? Indeed, we may put the question in even more basic terms. Can democracy and bureaucracy coexist or are they simply a contradiction in terms?

A system may be judged democratic to the extent that it sets up the means for citizen control of its leaders. The United States is usually referred to as a "representative democracy" meaning that the people do not actually do the lawmaking. Instead they elect certain officials to execute this function and then may hold them accountable through the ballot box. Under such circumstances any inquiry about democracy and bureaucracy must focus on the control of administrative personnel by the elected officials. We are saying, then, that democracy and bureaucracy are compatible indirectly; the people control the elected officials and the elected officials control the bureaucracy. The extent to which this happens in the United States can be examined by analyzing the major institutions that exercise this control over the bureaucracy: The Congress, the President and the Courts.

Earlier in this chapter we discussed the concept of delegated authority and how it allows the Congress to pass power along to the administrative branch. At the time we noted that this practice gave the non-elected official considerably more power than he would have otherwise, but there is another side to this issue. To put the matter very directly, what Congress gives, Congress can also take away. This ability to check the bureaucracy and to withhold, or threaten to withhold, things from it can provide a much-needed counter-balancing power for the Congress. Over the years this counter-balancing power has taken a number of different forms: oversight, the power of the purse and the lawmaking power. Let us briefly consider each of these.

Congressional Oversight

In 1983 the American people learned of a scandalous situation at the Environmental Protection Agency. This office is the federal watchdog over the healthfulness and cleanliness of America's air and of her waterways. One of the ways in which it fulfills this mission of protector is by administering something called "The Superfund." The Superfund is a special item in the national budget whose purpose is to provide money to state and local governments so that they can clean up toxic waste dumps that pose a threat to human health.

In 1983 Congress learned of reports that this Superfund was being manipulated for political purposes. More concretely, it was alleged that the monies were being given to states where clean-ups would help Republican candidates and witheld from those where they might make a Democrat look good. The most striking abuse had to do with the state of California where grants were allegedly witheld in 1982 because it was felt that their announcement might boost Governor Jerry Brown's chances in his run for the U.S. Senate against San Diego Mayor Pete Wilson. If these charges were true, then the bureaucracy had clearly overstepped its authority, and it was up to the Congress to find out if the charges were, indeed, true.

It is the law of the land that Congress must keep itself appraised of exactly how the various departments and agencies are handling the powers given them. Thus the various standing committees are empowered to investigate the agencies over which they have charge. For example the

House Agriculture Committee may wish to examine the Agriculture Department's handling of one of the commodity-price-support programs or the Armed Services Committee may decide to launch an investigation into the procedures used in the awarding of contracts for the MX missile.

The most important oversight bodies are the House and Senate Government Operations Committees which have the authority to review virtually all government activities. Other Congressional committees carry on the oversight function by holding hearings or assigning staff members to undertake independent evaluations. The General Accounting Office (GAO) may also be called upon to provide data on program operation. The GAO provides Congress with a real power base when dealing with the bureaucracy since it reports directly to Congress, not the President.

By and large, however, Congressional oversight tends to be rather weak and sporadic, since the committees and their chairmen have other things to which they give higher priority ranking. Working hard on behalf of the home district or gaining a reputation as an effective legislator are important as tickets to reelection. Will the constituents back home really care if the Congressman has been spending a lot of his time riding herd on the General Services Administration? It is quite unlikely.

The Power of the Purse

In January of each year Congress receives the budget requests of the executive branch. How much money does each agency propose to spend in the next fiscal year? Who will they serve and at what levels of efficiency? What will be the workload? Provisional answers to all these questions are supplied in the agency's budget, but these initial statements mean little until Congress gives its consent. It is often said that we can pass any number of programs, create dozens of new and innovative agencies, but the key to program effectiveness is its funding level. If HUD is given fifty million dollars for urban development action grants it will mean something quite different than if five hundred million dollars are allocated.

Thus, the dollars tell the story, and it is during the appropriations process that Congress is given another opportunity to control the bureaucracy. An appropriation is a congressional grant of money for some specified purpose. This means that each year Congress has a chance to review whatever programs it wants to. If it finds that an agency has been acting in an unresponsive manner all it has to do is lower or raise its budget. The message will be heard "loud and clear." The power of the purse gives our elected officials the chance to re-establish their control over the bureaucracy.

Still, Congress does not always avail itself of this chance, and in actuality only very minor changes are made in the overall budget. Because of the marginal nature of appropriations-changes budgeting has been called an *incremental* process. That is, last year's figures frequently stand as the base and small increments are added onto them. Nonetheless, Congress is at least given the opportunity to step in and control. Sometimes the control may really be a punishment. This was the case with the Federal Trade Commission which had its budget limited in 1979 because of its attempts to restrict advertising on children's television.

More than any other administration in recent years, Ronald Reagan's has moved away from this incremental approach. Instead the emphasis has been on giving large sums to high-priority programs (such as defense) while taking away large sums from programs out of favor (education, income security, etc.).

Lawmaking

Congress' final option is really its most basic one: its power to make laws. If an agency is performing poorly or unresponsively all Congress need do is alter or remove its delegated authority. For example the Food Stamp program has met with congressional displeasure on several occasions, and as a result there have been numerous legislative changes required in the manner in which the U.S. Department of Agriculture administers the program. Granted, the lawmaking process is lengthy and time consuming, but that basic function rests with the Congress, and thus it can always change any program that it wants to.

Another example of how Congress can use its power in this way is provided by an examination of what happened to dozens of federal grant programs during the early 1980's. The federal government has literally hundreds of programs under whose terms it makes grants of money. The money is given to state and local governments to administer and distribute. Examples include federal monies for highways, health, education, agricultural research, etc. Most of this has been very appealing to the recipient governments; but not all of it. State and local governments have been very willing to take the money, but for years have complained about all of the paperwork and all of the red tape.

During President Reagan's first term, Congress finally did something about all of this. It set up a whole series of "block-grant" programs. They were called block grants because they continued the idea of giving free money to state and local governments, while at the same time collapsing the guidelines and purposes down into a much smaller number—into a single block, in fact. Essentially, the Congress was saying to the bureaucracy, "We don't like the way you've been running some of these grant programs, so we are going to re-make the law under which you administer them."

The President's Role in Controlling the Bureaucracy

While the Congress is a real check on the bureaucracy it is also a rather distant one. Officials can be affected and directed by Congress, yes, but it is the President to whom most of them ultimately report. He is the chief-executive officer of the country and as such is given formal authority over the sprawling administrative branch. This chief-executive status plus his budgetary power help to make indirect democracy very real since they provide an elected leader with powerful means of control. In fact, President Reagan has been so vigorous in his control of the bureaucracy that he is often seen as an enemy by his own employees. This has been especially true at offices such as the Environmental Protection Agency and the Department of Health and Human Services.

Chief-Executive Status

The President's role as Chief Executive was examined in an earlier chapter, and thus here we will look at only those aspects which have a direct bearing on his ability to control the bureaucracy: directive power and personnel authority. Much of his directive power, (the ability to set up new procedures and programs, redefine work and sit atop an effective reporting system without becoming isolated) is derived from The Executive Office of the President. This office is composed of units such as The White House Office and the Office of Management and Budget (OMB).

They serve as the President's eyes and ears, commissioning evaluations, recommending alternatives and coordinating activities which all too often can wind up working at cross purposes as discussed above. A good example of this coordinating function is provided by the *central clearance* role of OMB. Under this procedure any laws which administrators wish to place on the Congressional agenda for consideration must first be cleared by OMB. What this means in practice is that all proposed legislation must first be screened by an agency of the White House. Only through such a procedure can the President hope to direct the dozens of agencies under his nominal command. OMB has also been at the center of President Reagan's budget-cutting activities.

The other element of chief-executive status is personnel authority. The president's appointment power covers all department heads and most bureau chiefs and extends to many subordinate positions as well. In all, a new president coming into office has approximately twenty-five hundred appointments to make. Of course this also means that should the governmental apparatus not perform in a manner he thinks appropriate he has approximately twenty-five hundred people whom he can fire in hopes of turning things around.

Some six hundred of these slots involve policymaking—the cabinet, subcabinet and bureau-chief positions. Another twelve hundred are staff positions, which give the President both a source of patronage for his loyal supporters and a ready source of independent information within individual agencies. Having individuals loyal to the chief reporting directly to the White House, rather than being confined to going through the elaborate chain of command, is one of the President's most important tools in keeping from becoming over-dependent on the advice of self-serving bureaucrats. In a large organization it is all too easy for information to be "laundered" as it moves up the hierarchy. However, if the chief has some of his own people down there on the line it is more likely that he will "get the story straight." The remainder of the twenty-five hundred are primarily professional and technical positions.

Before leaving this subject it is important to emphasize that the policymaking positions—the first six hundred mentioned—are absolutely critical to the President's ability to effectively control the bureaucracy. No one person or small group of people could possibly hope to direct and enforce their priorities upon the virtual army of three million federal employees. Remember that even though the President may serve for up to eight years, he and his advisors are just "temporary" job holders. There is an old saying around Washington that "Presidents come and presidents go, but the bureaucracy is always with us." He must thus be able to place loyal individuals in key directive positions, or otherwise he will be left sitting alone and isolated at the top of the pyramid. For this reason appointive power is absolutely essential to control and thus to the functioning of indirect democracy.

The Federal Budget

The federal government is the biggest spender in the nation. No other entity, public or private, even comes close. The billions of dollars in its annual budget make up the largest single component of the gross national product, and it is the president who oversees this expenditure. Through his Office of Management and Budget he is given control over the sums that agencies request from Congress. He has similar control over the actual expenditure. When discussing Congress' power of the purse we said that it is the appropriated dollar amounts that show the representatives' true priorities. This statement is equally true when analyzing the President's budget. Thus Ronald Reagan's spending plan looks very different from the one left behind by Jimmy Carter.

Before an agency's spending requests ever arrive on Capitol Hill they must first be submitted to the OMB. This office trims and coordinates the submissions and then consolidates them together into a single document—the Executive Budget. It is this document which Congress then considers in its appropriations hearings. In practice what this means is that in terms of budgetary oversight it is the President who gets the "first shot" at the bureaucracy. He can raise or lower funding levels, alter functions and stimulate or dampen individual programs.

One of the most fascinating innovations of recent years was Jimmy Carter's attempt to apply a system known as Zero-Base-Budgeting (ZBB) to the federal government. Earlier it was noted that the generation of budget projections usually begins with last year's figures as the base. Incremental changes are then made in that base. The whole idea of ZBB is to start not from a pre-existing base, but from a theoretical base of zero. That is, through an elaborate system of ranking of priorities each agency is forced to justify its existing programs and not merely take them for granted. This means that the "fixed" portion of the budget is considerably reduced and that the President and his advisors are given more discretion and power over agency activities. The net result of ZBB is thus to increase presidential control of the bureaucracy.

The Courts

Because they are the final arbiters under our system of government, the courts—and especially the Supreme Court—are in a unique position to limit the power of administrative agencies. The primary tool at the Court's disposal is *judicial review*, the practice whereby judges can declare the acts of other government officials unconstitutional. The courts also exercise a kind of standby power to control administrative rulemaking.

Suppose that a manufacturing firm disagrees with a factory-safety standard set by the Occupational Safety and Health Administration (OSHA) and thus it does nothing to bring working conditions into compliance. Soon it is cited for a violation and finds itself having to pay a penalty. It appeals the decision within OSHA and loses. Having "exhausted all administrative remedies" first, a key condition, it can next appeal its case to the courts, and ultimately to the Supreme Court if necessary. Grounds may include charges that the requirements were arbitrary and capricious, that due-process rights were violated or that the agency action was *ultra vires,* that is beyond the scope of its authority. One of the Court's key functions is thus to certify that an agency's decisions do not go beyond the bounds of its delegated power. In such cases one question is frequently posed: "What was the intent of the Congress?"

The Courts' main tools for putting a check on the bureaucracy are the declaratory judgement, the injunction and the awarding of damages. The first two are used when agency policies or guidelines are challenged before an action takes place, while the suit for damages takes place after the agency has implemented the program. Specifically a declaratory judgement is a court technique for clarifying the rights of the disputants, either the individual or the agency, prior to the occurrence of any damage. Since its primary purpose is simply clarification it stops short of ordering that anything specific be done. An injunction, on the other hand, is a court order restraining (or in some cases compelling) the performance of a particular act. For example, assume that the

Department of Transportation is seeking to evict me from my home so that it can construct a new highway. I may seek a declaratory judgement on its right to do so, or I may actually try for an injunction ordering it to "cease and desist" from attempting to remove me.

The final tool, the suit for damages, may allow me to be vindicated after the fact. However, it may not be worth much to me if I have already been thrown out and my home demolished. It can develop, however, that the effects of the agency action are not known for a considerable period of time after the act has taken place. Under such circumstances the suit for damages is extremely important. For example in recent years the Defense Department faced hundreds of suits brought by individuals who were exposed to excessive amounts of radiation during nuclear weapons testing in the early 1950s. After a lapse of some thirty years no injunction would be of much help, but the damage suit still might provide some recourse; although one may respond, "Not much, if the people were dying."

Laetrile as a Case Study

A fascinating case study of administrative regulation and judicial review is provided by looking at the controversy surrounding the drug Laetrile. This derivative of the pits of apricots has been used by as many as seventy-five thousand Americans suffering from cancer. They take it on the advice of those touting its curative powers. The hitch in all of this is the fact that the U.S. Food and Drug Administration (FDA) is not among those endorsing it. In fact the agency has done quite the opposite and used its regulatory power to prohibit it from the U.S. market. Large numbers of Americans believe that this is an infringement on their constitutionally-guaranteed freedom of choice. "After all," the argument goes, "if you are dying and even the proven remedies of medical science can do nothing more, you should be allowed to try unproven medications. After all, what have you got to lose?"

The court case which decided the fate of Laetrile originated with a suit filed by Glen Rutherford, an Oklahoma cancer patient. Because the FDA banned the interstate shipment of the drug, Mr. Rutherford argued that the agency had abridged his personal freedom. He won an initial victory in 1977 when an Oklahoma court ruled in his favor. The FDA tried to have the ruling reversed, but in 1978 a federal appeals court in Denver backed Mr. Rutherford again. In their decision the appeals-court judges concluded that the FDA lacked the authority to control drugs sought by the terminally ill. Such individuals were found to constitute a special class of patient. They reasoned this way because the law delegating authority to the FDA specifically states that decisions about a drug's approval must be based on its record of "safety and effectiveness." However, it takes little reflection to realize that a terminally-ill patient is one for whom there are no effective drugs. To quote the judges:

> Therefore we hold as a matter of law that the 'safety' and 'effectiveness' requirements of the statute as now written have no application to terminally ill cancer patients who desire to take the drug.

Upon receipt of the decision the FDA immediately appealed the case to the Supreme Court. It argued, first of all, that the decision would create a large loophole in the law by making it "impossible for the Commissioner to discharge his statutory responsibility to keep unproven drugs out of the marketplace." In other words, they were arguing that the law literally forced them to take action, while this court decision prohibited such action. They also noted certain evidence that the drug may actually be unsafe since it can result in cyanide poisoning. Lastly, agency attorneys argued that the widespread availability of Laetrile and the absence of any government prohibition on its sale would be mistaken by many potential users as an implied endorsement. If the government did not do its job of protecting the unwitting public then many individuals who could be saved might die needlessly. Why? Every year doctors provide early cancer diagnosis to thousands of patients, and many of these lives can be saved—or at least greatly prolonged—if proven remedies, such as surgery and chemotherapy, are applied. However, if an unproven or valueless substitute is also available many will turn to it for help and ignore the dictates of modern medical science. The net result: many will die needlessly.

What would you have done if you were a justice on the U.S. Supreme Court: Would you side with the agency or the individual? Would you rely upon science or upon some vague hope? Should people have the right to try anything—any last resort—or is the government's responsibility to protect society as a whole from grasping at straws more important?

In June of 1979 the Supreme Court did render a decision. It unanimously overturned the lower court ruling, and held that the FDA does have the authority to protect the terminally ill— to protect them from unsafe and unproven drugs. Currently, then, Laetrile *is* banned from interstate commerce, and thousands of lives are directly affected—for better or for worse, depending upon your perspective—by the regulation of this administrative agency.

For Further Reading

Garson, G. D., and Williams, J. O., *Public Administration: Concepts, Readings, Skills.* (Boston, Mass: Allyn and Bacon, Inc., 1982).

Meier, Kenneth, *Politics and the Bureaucracy.* (North Scituate, Mass: Duxbury Press, 1979).

Nigro, Felix and Nigro, Lloyd, *Modern Public Administration.* (New York: Harper and Row, 1980).

Rabin, Jack and Lynch, Thomas, *Handbook on Public Budgeting and Financial Management.* (New York: Marcel Dekker, Inc., 1983).

Wildavsky, Aaron, *The Politics of the Budgetary Process.* (Boston, Mass: Little, Brown and Co., 1984).

Name _____

Section _____

Date _____

Review Questions for Chapter 6: The Administrative Branch

1. List the five types of departments found in the federal government and give an example of each.

Type	Example
_____	_____
_____	_____
_____	_____
_____	_____
_____	_____

2. Governmental agencies are frequently set up in order to serve the needs of some particular group in the economy or society. Such a group is referred to as the agency's _____ .

3. A good example of service-provision departments that have occasionally worked at cross-purposes with each other is provided by the case of The Department of Transportation (DOT) and the _____ .

4. Give two examples of independent regulatory commissions and briefly describe what they do.

   A. First example: _____ ; its function: _____

   _____

   B. Second example: _____ ; its function: _____

   _____

5. What is it that makes independent regulatory commissions independent?

   _____

   _____

6. What is the name of the government agency that regulates the stock market?

   _____

7. According to the concept of _____ , Congress can pass broad statutes empowering administrative agencies to make up their own regulations.

8. Congress has three techniques for counter-balancing and checking the power of the administrative branch. These techniques are:

   _____

   _____

   _____

9. The courts provide a check on the bureaucracy through their power of

   _____ .

10. When an agency acts beyond the scope of its authority, such action may be ruled

    _____ by the courts.

Essay Study Questions

1. Three million men and women work for government. How can a president (who is, after all, just one individual) exercise government control over such a vast, sprawling bureaucracy?

2. Our whole system of government is based on the principle of separation of powers, yet the independent regulatory commissions violate this idea. How/Why?

Chapter 7

Interest Groups

Interest Groups Try to Affect Government Policies

Interest groups are alignments of persons and/or businesses that seek to influence government decision making in ways favorable to themselves. We all have the right—guaranteed by the Constitution—to let our leaders know what we think, but these groups specialize in that kind of activity. They are found in every sector of American life, but their greatest strength lies in industrial corporations, labor unions, finance, the mass media, education and the professions.

The leaders of, and spokespersons for, these groups are constantly dealing with the government. In their dealings they seek favorable decisions on issues affecting them, and they tend to be primarily concerned about two types of policy made in Washington: regulatory and distributive.[1]

Regulatory Policy

Regulatory policies include all those laws aimed at controlling the actions of individuals and groups in the private sector. This includes matters relating to criminal activity, economics and competition (anti-monopoly laws, etc.) access to public goods (such as air, water and the air waves) and public health and safety. Government controls in such areas are necessary to ensure the well-being and orderly functioning of society and the economy. They safeguard the citizenry, but in the process they limit many of the special interest groups.

Interest groups have learned to accept the idea of regulation as a fact of life and thus much of their political activity is focused not on eliminating it, but on influencing the nature of its content. For example, major industrial polluters have sought to delay and weaken clean air and water legislation through groups such as the American Petroleum Institute, the Manufacturing Chemists Association, the Meat Institute, the National Association of Manufacturers and the American Paper Institute.

Another instructive example of interest group politics involves the tobacco industry.[2] For years cigarette manufacturers had to contend with very little government regulation. In fact most of their dealings with Washington focused on agencies whose main concern was the stimulation of the industry: the U.S. Department of Agriculture (USDA) and the Agriculture Committees of the House and Senate. Within a highly permissive atmosphere a very cozy relationship—known as a policy triangle—grew up between three political actors: the industry, the USDA and the Congressional Agriculture Committees. Until 1964 the attention of this unholy alliance was focused almost exclusively on the well-being of the industry, but in that year the U.S. Surgeon General published his famous report on the health hazards of smoking. With that the Federal Trade Commission (FTC) became a fourth force in the field and began seeking regulations to protect the consumer. The eventual result was the mandate that health warnings appear on cigarette packages and advertising. The FTC also succeeded in getting Congress to ban radio and TV advertising for cigarettes. This proconsumer regulation did not take place without a fight, however. For years the FTC stood alone against a powerful tobacco lobby made up of growers, cigarette manufacturers, advertising companies and the mass media. From the "inside," additional sandbagging was done by the USDA and by southern congressmen in whose home districts the industry was based. It might be said that interest group politics is at its heart the politics of building coalitions.

Distributive Policy

The second type of policy that generates a high level of special interest activity concerns what is known as distributive policy. Distributive issues involve the provision of benefits directly to various groups. According to Kenneth Meier[3] there are five main types of distributive policy, and each involves a high level of interest group activity: the distribution of subsidies, the governmental funding of research, the collection and distribution of information, the administration of distributive public goods and the provision of governmental insurance.

Subsidies involve the use of public funds to underwrite private ventures. More will be said of this below. The government also sponsors millions of dollars worth of research every year, research whose most immediate beneficiary is private industry. For example today the Department of Energy is funding a massive research effort on synthetic fuels. Findings will be made available to the petroleum industry for commercial exploitation.

Regarding the collection and dissemination of information, every ten years the Census Bureau gathers comprehensive data on all Americans. Many of the findings of this billion dollar effort are then turned over to manufacturers, advertisers, retailers and others who rely on customer profiles to help market their products. Similarly the U.S. Geological Survey collects and distributes information on valuable mineral deposits. Government insurance programs also provide benefits such as federal crop insurance and federal flood insurance.

Federal largesse also touches the individual citizen through such projects as the national parks, federal highways and airports. While many such projects are ultimately "citizen oriented," in the short run the main beneficiary is again private industry. Consider the building and reclamation projects of the Army Corps of Engineers. Its efforts to construct dams and dredge inland waterways are enthusiastically supported before Congress by numerous qroups that profit directly from such undertakings—the barge companies who use the canals, the dredging firms, the heavy equipment manufacturers like Caterpillar Tractor plus real estate and agribusiness interests whose land is made more valuable by the provision of low-cost irrigation.

While all five of these types of distributive policies affect the welfare of special interests the single most important category is that of subsidies. Many subsidy programs operate through the tax laws. Thus investors are subsidized by a low capital gains tax while businessmen profit through the accounting procedure known as accelerated depreciation. Some of the best examples of subsidies to interest groups, however, are found in the field of agriculture, where the government operates a series of programs designed to raise and stabilize the prices that farmers receive for their goods.

Again, tobacco provides an useful example. In 1979 the government spent approximately forty-eight million dollars on its anti-smoking campaign, operated by the Department of Health and Human Services. During the same year the Agriculture Department spent some three hundred thirty-seven million to subsidize the industry. Occasionally it really does appear that one hand doesn't know what the other is doing, but then that's the way the interest groups like it.

Here is how the system works. Each tobacco farmer is given an allotment by the government specifying how many acres he can plant and how many pounds he can harvest. These growers are then guaranteed the minimum (1980) price of $1.40 per pound. If they cannot sell their harvest on the open market for at least that price then the government will buy it from them at the $1.40 figure. This subsidy has the effect of stabilizing the market and taking all the risk out of growing tobacco. It would perhaps be unfair to term this a system of "welfare for farmers," but the government certainly does use its distributive policies to look after the economic well being of this special interest group.

Interest Groups Use Various Techniques

Interest groups are a critical component of the American political system. All citizens are guaranteed the right to vote and to make their opinions known, but it is only through organization and cooperative group effort that any real impact can be made. When individuals take political action alone the chances of success are rather small. However, when people act in unison and coordinate their efforts government officials are much more likely to listen.

Theoretically this seems to be eminently fair. We live in a democracy. In order to be responsive, those in office must be attentive to the "greatest good for the greatest number;" they must know the needs and wants of large numbers of people. However, interest group politics do not insure that they will hear from the *most* people; only from the loudest, most persistent and best organized. Most people's interests are not represented by organized groups and thus their needs may go unmet.

Nonetheless, for those groups that are organized and do enjoy adequate resources the American system of government can operate in a very responsive manner. For example, in 1980 when the Chrysler Corporation stood on the brink of bankruptcy, it was able to convince the federal government to bail it out with a series of loan guarantees. Other interests are not so successful, of course, and for every interest group effort that succeeds we can point to others that have failed.

One of the elements in any explanation of interest group strength is its selection and use of influence techniques. There are many things that a group can do in an effort to convince government decision makers to do what it wants.

Lobbying

Lobbying is an activity whereby the representatives of an interest group personally approach government officials and supply them with information on why they should vote a certain way on a policy under consideration. Most lobbying is focused on the Congress, and the term originated in the last century when spokespersons for various groups could be found anxiously awaiting Senators and Representatives in the lobbies of the Capitol building. The lobbies were just outside the legislative chambers where the voting would take place, and this was generally the interest groups' last chance to try to win-over the decision makers. Observers who watched their frantic button-holing month-after-month coined the term "lobbying" to describe the political behavior that was taking place in the lobbies.

Campaign Contributions

Election campaigns cost huge sums of money, sums too large for most candidates to put forward on their own. Instead they request and accept contributions from various groups and individuals. Politically active groups are very attentive to the electoral process and are usually ready, willing and able to make substantial contributions to help their "friends."—i.e. officials who have voted "correctly" during the most recent term. There is nothing illegal about such a situation as long as there is no *quid pro quo* involved. In this context, a *quid pro quo*—literally meaning "this for that"—is an arrangement whereby a politician and some interested party agree on a contribution of X dollars *in exchange for* a favorable vote on a particular piece of legislation. "Vote buying" is another name for such an illegal agreement. A bizarre example of this phenomenon occurred in the State of Illinois in 1980 when a female lobbyist for the NOW (National Organization of Women) was convicted of attempting to buy a favorable ERA vote from a state Senator for $1,000.00. She wrote the offer on the back of a NOW business card.

While abuses may occur, there is nothing, *per se,* unlawful about "rewarding your friends." That does not mean, however, that such a system is fair and equitable. Indeed, since some groups can afford to contribute much more than others, it gives a natural advantage to the rich. Most Americans are aware, for example, that members of the medical profession enjoy incomes that are considerably above average. This means, among other things, that their interest group, the American Medical Association (AMA) can invest huge sums in its campaign-contribution efforts. In practical terms all of this becomes visible when we look at a 1982 House of Representatives vote on a bill to outlaw price-fixing by doctors. The medical fraternity did not want this kind of external regulation and thus it contributed more than $2 million to the political campaigns of those candidates sympathetic to their views.

Electioneering

A closely related technique is that of electioneering—working, in ways other than the giving of dollars, for the election of a favored candidate. The main idea here is to influence what the officials do, by affecting who the officials are. Electioneering can take various forms. One is the endorsement, whereby the group's members and friends are urged to support a particular candidate because of his record and/or his promises. Other groups are a bit more indirect, publishing voting records rather than outright endorsements—although the effect is meant to be the same. Electioneering may also involve the provision of speakers, mailing lists and "volunteer" assistance with advertising campaigns.

A good example of electioneering occured in the 1980 presidential campaign when Jimmy Carter received invaluable endorsements and publicity from teachers' groups across the country. While there was no *quid pro quo* involved, Carter had followed through on his 1976 campaign pledge to create a separate Department of Education. This made him a valuable friend to those in the teaching profession and they responded by working hard for his reelection. Similarly in both 1980 and 1984, groups like the Moral Majority and the National Conservative Political Action Committee worked hard for the election of Ronald Reagan.

Testimony

Another technique for affecting governmental decisions involves the provision of testimony at public hearings. Before the Congress passes a law and before the executive branch adopts a new administrative rule, each will frequently hold hearings. The purpose of these is to create a public record and to educate the decision makers on the pros and cons of the proposed action. Because they are well organized the special interests are able to "keep an eye" on what hearings are coming up and appear at those affecting them.

At the hearing either a representative of the group or someone specially recruited by it will make a statement and then answer questions. Frequently the person testifying will not be a group member, but an "outside expert" hired by the group to lend an air of impartiality to his/her comments.

The net result of such hearings is supposed to be the supplying of decision makers with information that they would otherwise lack: information on a proposal's strengths and weaknesses, good points and bad points, probabilities of success and failure. In fact, however, many hearings turn out to be thoroughly one-sided affairs in which only the well organized participate effectively. For example, if an agricultural price-support bill pits farmers against consumers, it is the organized agribusiness interests that will be best represented at the hearings before the House Agriculture Committee. Because the consumers' movement lacks a unified organization it will not really be able to function as a balance to the power of the other side.

Favors

One area where Congress has acted to clean up problems of conflict of interest has involved political favors. Just as elected officials can be rewarded by campaign contributions so too can they be rewarded by numerous favors. Some of the more blatant examples of the use of this technique include the arrangement of lucrative speaking tours, perhaps a trip to Europe for the family, a new consulting job or the finding of a position in the company for a close relative. The acceptance of favors is still a problem, but today there are very definite limits. All such favors must be reported and no member of Congress can exceed a pre-set dollar maximum. Gone are the days when the people's representatives were able to double their salaries by such simple sleights of hand.

Public Relations

A final influence strategy is aimed not at the decision makers themselves but at their constituents. This is an indirect approach that relies on arousing public interest and sentiment on the issue and then translating this into pressure on those in government. The energy companies did this in 1978 and 1979 on the issue of deregulation of natural gas. Instead of focusing all of their attention exclusively on the Congress and its committees, they also spent millions of dollars on advertising in both the print and electronic media. The point of this campaign was to convince the general public that deregulation was in the national interest.

There Is a Bias Built into the Interest Group System

These six techniques are of enormous value to groups seeking to influence the political process. A record of friendliness at contribution time can gain the organization ready access to decision makers. The right of both individuals and groups to bring their cases before the government and to pursue them by all legal means is guaranteed by the U.S. Constitution. That document created a system that was truly open, and for many years political analysts defined the public interest as simply whatever the balance of power (or equilibrium) between contesting groups happened to be. For example when a new logging policy for America's national forests was discussed at public hearings the timber interests outnumbered the campers and conservationists. One way to describe the situation would be to simply claim that since the balance of power clearly rested with the loggers a decision in their favor would automatically represent the public interest. This is sometimes termed the "cash register theory" meaning that the role of Congress is to simply "ring up" a tally of the forces in existence. The public interest translates itself into an exercise in power since, we are told, there is no such thing as a real public interest. Everyone wants something different and everyone has a different idea of what constitutes the public interest. This being so, all we can do is look at the contenders in the political process, establish a winner and declare his/her set of goals to be that elusive thing called the public interest.

Such a theory may well describe what actually happens, but it does little good to term the outcome the "public interest." Ironically, it seems to be the very openness of our system, its highly democratic nature, that brings about an unintended consequence: a bias in the pressure system. If the term "pressure system" is taken to include all those techniques discussed in this chapter, then it is clear that there is an inevitable bias, or tilt, built into it. Because use of the techniques requires strength, organization and money the system is biased in favor of those who are already strong; those who are already in the financial position to make campaign donations, fund public relations campaigns or pay the fees of five hundred dollar per day consultant-witnesses appearing at congressional hearings. The well-heeled and powerful can use these techniques. "So too," the argument runs, "can anyone else. It's a free country." But this begs the question of whether anyone else can really afford to. Rich and poor alike are permitted to spend huge sums of money to convert their goals into favorable political decisions. If the poor fail to do this spending we claim that it is their own fault, but we may also notice that the deck was stacked from the beginning. It is this stacked-deck problem that is known as the bias of the pressure system.

A good example of this problem was the 1975 effort by the British and the French to secure U.S. landing rights for their supersonic passenger plane, the Concorde. Because of feared damage to the atmosphere and the problem of sonic boom, environmental groups were opposed to allowing the plane to land. The plane's backers took full advantage of their considerable financial resources and hired some of the best legal talent money could buy to do their lobbying for them. British Airways engaged the law firm headed by William Ruckelshaus, the first head of the nation's Environmental Protection Agency. France hired former U.S. Senator Charles Goodell—who at the time was also a close advisor to President Gerald Ford. Air France retained the firm of Rogers and Wells—Rogers being former Secretary of State, William Rogers.

Now it may be argued that "it's a free country" and that the environmentalists also had complete freedom to hire whomever they wanted to lobby on their behalf. The simple fact, however, is that they could not afford to; they had to rely on less well-connected spokespersons and on their own staffs. Thus, did the bias of the pressure system send David out to meet Goliath. As we all know, though, this story did not end like its biblical counterpart for the Concorde soon had the landing rights it sought in New York and Washington.

Many college students are familiar with professional sports and the workings of the player selection system. Recruitment is carried out under the terms of a draft system whereby special preference is given to teams that did poorly during the previous season. In the interest of keeping the leagues from being dominated by any single team a rotation system is used giving the less powerful teams a first shot at the best talent. If this equalizing mechanism were not used it is likely that most professional sports events would be no contest at all. The richest teams would simply buy up the best players and there would be a "bias to the sports system." Fortunately we have not let this happen to anything as important as professional football. Why, then, do we tolerate it in politics?

An Attempt Has Been Made at Reform

Lest we sound too negative, it must be noted that some definite progress has been made in this area in recent years. Congress has clamped down on the outside income of its members and has thus severely limited the kinds of favors that special interests can offer to our lawmakers. Secondly, it has placed ceilings on the amounts that these groups can contribute to political campaigns. The 1974 Campaign Finance Reform Law limited them to giving no more than five thousand dollars to any one candidate in any one election. In practice this means ten thousand dollars in any given election year since many candidates have to run in both a primary election and a general election; two elections at five thousand dollars each. Looked at in one way this means that the "day of the fat cat" is over since such excesses as the million dollar contributions of wealthy political backers like Stewart Mott and W. Clement Stone are now a thing of the past. On the other hand it is worth pointing out that ten thousand dollars is still a very substantial sum—enough to turn things around in some races for the House of Representatives. Those who can afford it can still buy a great deal of access.

The third, and most recent, antidote for the bias of the pressure system took effect on July 1, 1979. It concerns not the Congress, but the executive branch of government—another frequent target of the lobbyists. Until that date a great deal of high-level personnel interchange took place between business and government. Individuals often played a game of "musical chairs," working for several months or years in sensitive positions in governmental agencies like the Department of Defense or the Federal Communications Commission. The following year would find them serving as Washington representatives for the very groups they formerly had been in charge of regulating. An official overseeing an antitrust suit for the Justice Department or the Federal Trade Commission thus turns up on the opposite side of the bargaining table during delicate negotiations. In a similar vein, it has not been uncommon for high ranking military officers to retire and then go to work for defense firms with whom they had been negotiating contracts for years. Of course, not everyone could afford to buy such high-powered talent, and thus charges of conflict of interest were frequently heard. Responding to such allegations, Congress curbed the practice by prohibiting such hiring within two years of a "supergrade's" separation from government service.

At first the reader may think that these three reforms touch only the tip of the iceberg, but most political analysts agree that they have gone a long way to deal with the problem. It is true that there is still a bias to the pressure system, but its impact has been greatly alleviated. To go any further would doubtless require limiting certain basic freedoms—a cure worse than the illness.

Political Action Committees

There is a problem about reform: it has the same ability as anything else to fall victim to "Murphy's Law," a law which claims, of course, that if anything can go wrong it will. What has gone wrong with reform? Something very big, and something very rich. Something called the political action committee. A political action committee (hereafter referred to simply as a PAC) is a group of individuals and/or corporations who get together and privately involve themselves in the electoral process.

The 1974 law referred to above sets limits on the total amount that such groups can give directly to candidates. However, a subsequent Supreme Court Case (Buckley v. Valeo) ruled that such groups can spend as much as they want to *independently* on behalf of the candidate(s) of their choice. Thus, for example, in the Democratic Senatorial primary in the state of Texas in 1984 the American Realtors' PAC could donate $5,000 directly to Mr. Kent Hance because his views seemed to agree with theirs. However, it was also completely legal for them to simulta-neously spend more than one-hundred-thousand dollars themselves on a series of media commer-cials on his behalf.

Again, the law has us splitting hairs on this one. You can give only so much ($5,000) directly, but "the sky's the limit" if you want to do something "on the candidate's behalf." Because of this loophole, PACs were able to give some $84 million in 1982 and well over $100 million in 1984. The justification or rationale for all of this is the First Amendment right to freedom of speech. In the Buckley case, the Court ruled that any interference with a PAC's ability to spend its own political money would be a violation of this First Amendment guarantee. In handing down this decree, the Court has equated freedom of speech with freedom to spend. This, of course, does nothing but intensify the already-existing bias built into the pressure system.

Government Structure and Interest Group Access

Earlier in this chapter we examined how interest groups employ certain techniques to put pressure on government leaders. The effectiveness of these techniques is first of all a testimony to group organization and strength. If the groups were ill-prepared, they would fail, regardless of how many techniques they employed. However, group initiative is not the only reason for success. The pressure process is also facilitated by the structure of the U.S. government itself. That is, the way in which the government is organized helps the special interests to gain access, or input, to decision makers. Thus, the structure makes their success more likely. Several factors make this so: federalism, separation of powers, and the modes of Congressional and executive organization.

Federalism

Ours is a federal system, composed of three levels of government: national, state and local. While they have separate identities they do share numerous functions (e.g. all three levels get involved in education policy), and thus substantial overlap exists between them. These multiple levels give multiple access points to groups seeking certain decisions. For example a teachers' organization may be seeking a new policy regarding educational programs for the handicapped. It begins in Washington by lobbying for its goals in Congress, but what if Congress refuses to pass the bill? In most other systems of government, this would be the end of it. Not so, under the American federal system. Instead of accepting defeat the group merely passes the ball to its state affiliates and has them begin working for the policy in fifty state legislatures. Not all will act favorably on the new policy, but some will. Access can also go one step further with local associations taking the case before local school boards.

In a federal system the policy process seldom ends; instead it is much more like a floating crap game where losers at one site merely try again at another. This has been the case with such well-known issues as abortion and prayer in public schools. Groups unhappy with the outcome of one policy process have taken up their causes with another. If ours were a unitary system of government, authority would reside in just one place and once a decision had been received from that place the matter would be closed. Under federalism there is frequently a second or even a third chance. Thus it was that while James Watt was Secretary of the Interior (1981–84) environmental groups like the Sierra Club and the Wilderness Society were forced to turn increasingly to the state governments in their efforts to continue protection and conservation efforts for America's natural resources.

Separation of Powers

Just as federalism provides multiple access points, so too does the arrangement know as separation of powers. The national government is composed of three equal branches (Congress, the Executive and the Courts) each of which can initiate new laws. Groups who believe that they may be at a disadvantage when they bring their cause before one body may choose another instead. This was the strategy followed by the Civil Rights movement. For almost one hundred years after the Civil War blacks could get very little positive action from the Congress. Thus in 1954 they went to the courts instead and in the case of *Brown vs. The Board of Education of Topeka, Kansas* they secured the formal outlawing of segregation in public schools.

Such a formal policy change did not go far enough, however, since the southern states met the court decision with massive resistance. Thus, after trying numerous alternatives for more than a dozen years, in 1968 black leaders convinced the Department of Health, Education and Welfare to adopt a policy of cutting off federal funds for school districts failing to comply with desegregation guidelines. Thus in the pursuit of their goal of equal opportunity for blacks, representatives of these interest groups sought input before, and action from, all three branches of the federal government at different times. The structure of the system provided them with *multiple access points.*

Another good example of how special interests can use the system's separation of powers to good advantage is provided by a series of 1970 events known as "the timber interest shuffle." Early in that year a vote was held on a bill (HR 12025) that would increase the allowable timber harvest in the national forests by some sixty percent each year. The bill had actually been written, not by Congress, but by the lobbyists for several groups that were directly interested: The National Association of Home Builders, The National Forest Products Association and the United Brotherhood of Carpenters and Joiners. They had decided early on to pursue a legislative strategy and then at a trade association meeting in Houston they sat down together and drafted the bill. It was then turned over to a friendly member of the House who introduced it for them.

Because of their confidence in the House of Representatives, the timber interests were considerably surprised when, after a long series of hearings and debates, the bill went down to defeat. This did not signal the end of the drama, however—not in a governmental system based on the separation of powers. After a brief interval, the timber alliance took its proposal to the President who gave it a much warmer reception. He made it law by issuing it as an executive order—something fully within his legal power to do. Thus, although the group was defeated in the Congress all that it had to do was try again with another branch of the government.

Congressional Organization

In order to function effectively any institution has to adopt a set of rules (e.g. by-laws) by which to organize and govern itself. The Congress of the United States is no exception to this general rule. What is worth noting here is that the Senate and House have adopted modes of organization that provide maximum access for the special interests. This has happened because Congress has set up numerous standing committees, each specializing in one particular type of legislation. For example there is a Veterans' Affairs Committee, an Energy Committee, a Merchant Marine Committee, etc. and the representatives who sit on these committees are the key actors in the decisions about whether specific bills pass or fail. This being the case, any group wishing to influence a particular piece of legislation need not worry about lobbying all four hundred and thirty-five members of the House or all one hundred members of the Senate. All they have to do is focus their attention on the few individuals on the committees that will consider their bill. It's as though Congress had done an extensive job of targeting its own membership, and then published a program saying who should be approached for what. This specialization saves the groups a great deal of time and money. Thus when a veterans' group is seeking a change in benefits for ex-GIs it can go directly to the Veterans' Affairs Committee for an initial decision.

Agriculture provides another good example of how Congress has organized itself to promote greater accessibility for interest groups. An examination of the House Agriculture Committee shows how its sub-committee structure facilitates representation. The committee itself has specialized internally by setting up numerous sub-committees, sub-committees established along commodity lines. Thus there is a wheat sub-committee, a tobacco sub-committee, a rice sub-committee, and so forth. Now, congressmen are usually interested in staying in office by doing favors for the constituents back home. In the case of agriculture this means sitting on a sub-committee with jurisdiction over crops grown in your district. The result is that the wheat sub-committee is composed almost entirely of midwestern Republicans while the cotton sub-committee is composed largely of southern Democrats. The situation is similar with the other sub-committees. This makes the specialization and similarity of interests complete so that when the wheat farmers come to Washington to plead their case they are talking primarily to just one small group of lawmakers. The members of this group just happen to be their representatives elected from the wheat belt, who are already pledged to do all they can to help their constituents, the wheat farmers.

One further aspect of group access to Congress needs to be mentioned before we leave this topic, and that concerns a question about the basic fairness of our system of representation. Seats in the House of Representatives are allocated among the fifty states on the basis of population. This means that more than forty slots go to a large state like California, while Nevada has only two. This is as it should be for our system is designed to represent people, not acres of land. In the Senate, however, each state has two seats regardless of the size of its population. Thus both Alaska and New York are treated equally even though they do not have equal populations. This means that certain interest groups are afforded representation far in excess of what their numerical strength can justify. For example, timber constitutes a significant industry in states like Oregon, Washington, Idaho, Colorado, Wyoming, Maine, West Virginia, Vermont, New Hampshire and Utah. These ten states are sparsely populated and together have a total of only thirty-four seats out of four hundred thirty-five in the House of Representatives. In the Senate, however, they have a whopping twenty percent of the total membership. That means a twenty percent factor already favorably disposed to many of the demands that may be made on the federal government by the timber industry. Their interest groups can thus enter certain legislative battles with a built-in advantage, an advantage assured by the way in which Congress is organized.

Executive Organization

Just as Congress has specialized via its committee structure, so too has the executive branch been divided up into departments. This is obvious to us all, but the relevant point here is that many department lines have been drawn so as to make administrative officials as accessible as possible to the appropriate interest groups. For example, we do not have a consolidated Department of Economic Affairs within which labor and management would have to compete for attention. Instead we have one department for each of these powerful groups: The Department of Commerce and the Department of Labor. In the interest of efficiency several presidents have tried to merge these two departments, but none has succeeded. Political muscle often overrules rationality on the banks of the Potomac. Similarly the farmers have their own department—the U.S. Department of Agriculture—to represent them, and since the teachers were such strong Carter supporters in 1976 they were given their own separate department.

One mechanism used to heighten the impact of this type of closeness is the agency advisory committee. Hundreds of these exist in Washington and they work like this. Frequently a department or bureau seeks some systematic and formal means for sounding out its clientele group on matters affecting it and thus establishes a committee whose members are drawn from the ranks of the group. For example the Department of Energy has numerous advisory committees made up of personnel from the major oil companies while the Department of Transportation has similar committees manned by the highway builders.

These committees meet periodically and serve as institutionalized channels of information exchange between the administrative agencies and their clientele groups. Through them the groups can initiate communication about needed policy changes and the administrators can find out many of the likely effects of proposed policies and regulations.

Summary

In this chapter we have considered the functioning of interest group politics in the United States. We saw first of all that groups are most active regarding two main types of public policy: distributive and regulatory. In the pursuit of their goals in these areas interest groups use six main techniques: campaign contributions, lobbying, electioneering, testimony, favors and public relations. We noted during this discussion that there is a distinct bias to how these techniques can be employed—a bias in favor of those who are already rich and powerful. Finally, we examined the relationship between the structure of United States government and the ability of the various groups to be heard.

Notes

1. Theodore Lowi, "Four Systems of Policy, Politics and Choice," *Public Administration Review* 32 July/August, 1972, pp. 298–310.
2. A. Lee Fritschler, *Smoking and Politics* (Englewood Cliffs, N.J.: Prentice-Hall, 1975).
3. Kenneth Meier, *Politics and The Bureaucracy* (N. Scituate, Mass.: Duxbury Press, 1979).

For Further Reading

Cigler, A. J. and Loomis, B. A., *Interest Group Politics*. (Washington, D.C.: Congressional Quarterly Press, 1983).

Drew, Elizabeth, *Politics and Money*. (New York: Macmillan Publishing Co., 1983).

Dye, Thomas, *Who's Running America? The Reagan Years*. (Englewood Cliffs, N.J.: Prentice-Hall, Inc., 1983).

Sherrill, Robert, *Why They Call It Politics*. (New York: Harcourt Brace Jovanovich, Publishers, 1984).

Sorauf, Frank, *What Price PACs?* (New York: The Twentieth Century Fund, 1984).

Name _____

Section _____

Date _____

Review Questions for Chapter 7: Interest Groups

1. "_____ policy" is the term used for laws that control the actions of individuals and groups in the private sector.

2. Distinct from this is "_____ policy" which involves the provision of benefits directly to groups.

3. "_____" is the name given to the "cozy relationship" that often exists between an interest group, the Congressional committee that drafts laws affecting it and the administrative department that is supposed to regulate or serve the group.

4. What are the five main types of distributive policy?

   _____

   _____

   _____

   _____

   _____

5. List the six techniques used by interest groups to influence government decision makers.

   _____

   _____

   _____

   _____

   _____

   _____

6. Explain what is meant by the term "bias of the pressure system."

   _____

   _____

   _____

7. Within the context of Political Science, the term "quid pro quo" usually means

   _____

   _____

   _____

8. The idea that Congress should simply tally or "ring up" the balance of forces among contending interest groups is known as the _____ theory.

9. The four elements of U.S. governmental structure that affect interest-group access are:

   _____

   _____

   _____

   _____

10. In which house of the U.S. Congress are timber-producing states over-represented?

    The _____

    Why/How _____

    _____

    _____

Essay Study Questions

1. Compare and contrast the concepts of distributive and regulatory policy.
2. How can our political system remain free and democratic and, at the same time, do something to limit the bias of the pressure system?

Chapter 8

Political Parties

Let me warn you in the most solemn manner against the baneful effects of the spirit of party generally. This spirit . . . exists under different shapes in all government, more or less stifled, controlled, or repressed; but in those of the popular form it is seen in its greatest rankness and is truly their worst enemy.

President George Washington

The political parties created democracy and . . . modern democracy is unthinkable save in terms of the parties.

Political Scientist E. E. Schattschneider

The parties do more to confuse the issue than to provide a clear choice on them.

Political Scientist J. Dennis

Rather than promoting competition over national goals and programs, the parties reinforce social consensus and limit the area of legitimate political conflict.

Political Scientist W. D. Burnham

For most Americans, politics boils down simply to choosing between the Democrats and the Republicans. It is around the banners of these two major political organizations that elections have turned for more than a century. Some analysts now detect a gradual weakening in their structures, but the two major parties still dominate the American political process. If politics is characterized by conflict, there must be institutions that channel that conflict into a peaceful resolution of differences. In democracies, political parties are supposed to function as the vehicles through which people attempt to gain control of government through elections. By identifying issues, establishing choices among programs, and proposing candidates for office, parties "structure the conflict" and facilitate decision making. Because they must appeal to a majority, parties moderate the conflict by avoiding extreme positions and discouraging proponents of radical positions.

There is no mention of political parties in the Constitution. Why and how did they evolve as important political institutions? Is there any particular reason for a two-party system in the United States? What are the major differences between the Democratic and Republican parties? Political parties serve as the organizational bases for legislative activity and electoral competition. How well do the Democratic and Republican parties perform these functions? The parties offer a channel of communication between the government and the people. Is this channel used? Parties must be judged by how well they perform their basic functions. How effectively do parties choose candidates and contest elections? Do parties provide meaningful alternatives or are they focusing on images of candidates, not issues? Are we witnessing what some analysts term a "decomposition of the American party system?"[1] Finally, what is the future of the American party system?

Definition and Functions of Parties

Political parties may be defined as organizations whose basic purpose is to control the choice of governmental personnel and policies. The functions of political parties are quite different in competitive, fragmented, and noncompetitive governmental systems, but they are also similar in some important respects. In all three systems parties are educational institutions that seek to inform people of the rightness of their political views; they act as connecting links or conveyor belts between the governed and the ruling leaders; and they are symbols of political representation. Even in countries where political parties are not powerful in the sense of affecting the policies of the government, they act as agents of legitimacy.

There are very significant distinctions among different types of party systems. In competitive states, political parties are essential participants in the political process. They act as aggregating agencies converting individual and group demands into national programs and policies. Thus they moderate these narrow demands and in so doing render their countries governable. Equally significant is the fact that because parties train and select candidates for leading government positions, they are major agencies for producing the political leadership in their respective countries. In short, political parties are essentially agents of political competition. They regulate the process and establish the rules by which competition may successfully be conducted.

Political parties are generally ineffective institutions in fragmented states. They are unable to aggregate individual and group demands and to present national programs and leaders with broad national support. Because such fragmented countries have deep, apparently irreconcilable divisions in their societies, political parties are weak and generally remain ineffectual vis-a-vis such other institutions as the bureaucracy or the military.

Political parties can be extremely powerful in noncompetitive states, but they are not agents of political competition. In competitive states, government has to moderate among rival demands, and political parties are very important in this moderating (aggregating) process. In noncompetitive states, parties do not aggregate and instruct as much because they simply present the views of an elite leadership to a population organized to follow. Actually, the single unitary party in a noncompetitive political system becomes more important than the very institutions of the state (e.g., the official executive or the legislature), because there are no other parties to compete with and because the unitary party is the primary organizing structure in society. In such noncompetitive states as Cuba and the Soviet Union the party can exercise monolithic control over the entire political life of the state.

The American political system, as established by the Founders of the Republic, probably could not function without the political parties; they are essential elements of our system of democratic government. They make possible giving the American people a choice of candidates and programs, and they also provide alternatives to the existing governing leadership when they want a change.

Ideally, any political party should represent the wishes of constituents, including their desires for change and reform. However, in one-party states, the party itself may be the leading obstacle to change. In Cuba and in the Soviet Union (or in the few remaining one-party states of the American South) it is harder for voters who want change to influence the party to accept change than it is for the party, once convinced, to change other parts of the political system. In multiparty states such as we find in many of the countries of Western Europe, every major interest group finds itself represented by one party.

Background and Development

James Madison, one of the most perceptive founders of the republic, foresaw that we would have a multifaction system, with different legislative factions representing different interests, but he and the other Founders did not anticipate that the factions would constitute themselves as political parties so soon. The Founders were originally strongly opposed to what Washington referred to as "the baneful effects of the spirit of party." They hoped to see the new nation move ahead as one united citizenry rather than divide into opposing factions or parties. To provide for the selection of the president and vice-president, the Founders devised the electoral college system which fulfilled the function of both nominating and electing these officials. Nominations for other offices were by self-announcement or by caucuses of local leaders.

The Founders were Federalists because they supported the federal system set forth in the Constitution. They were also pragmatic politicians who knew that conflict among factions is inevitable in a free society. It is important to know the argument of *The Federalist #10:* unchan-nelled conflict will result in chaos, therefore conflict must be limited and regulated. Washington enjoyed a tremendous prestige and was elected unanimously by the electors. He sought to direct the government in a nonpartisan fashion; and Adams, Hamilton, and Jefferson, men of very diverse ideas and temperaments, worked together. The ideal was a bipartisan administration, free of faction. But despite Washington's efforts, it was impossible to avoid political turmoil and dissen-tion. Men of good faith and high intelligence were not of one opinion, and when their ideas were not accepted, they fought for them. There had to be some way to resolve such conflicts. Although Washington attempted to be nonpartisan, eventually he came to accept the policies advocated by the leader of the emerging Federalist Party, Secretary of the Treasury Alexander Hamilton. Actually, the group referred to as the Federalist Party did not really form what could be called a political party before 1800. Only the aggressive organization of the developing political oppo-sition by Jefferson and Madison and its increasing success in mobilizing popular support for its cause forced the Federalists to defend their positions of power and eventually close ranks as a party. Hamilton and the other Federalists favored a government based on strong executive lead-ership, emphasized the need for order and stability, centralized power, and policies beneficial to the commercial and business community. Jefferson and his supporters, on the other hand, stressed a limited and decentralized government, individual freedoms, a strong legislature, and policies that would benefit farmers, workers, and small shopkeepers. Thus the ideological roots of the American party system developed out of the conflict between Hamilton and Jefferson and their followers in the early years of the Republic. Jefferson differed so strongly with Hamilton and the other Federalists in the government that shortly after Washington's second inauguration he re-signed as Secretary of State to organize and lead the opposition party. Thus Jefferson is considered the founder of the modern Democratic Party, first known as the Anti-Federalist and Jeffersonian-Republican Party. The first electoral contest between the two parties occurred in 1796 when John Adams, the Federalist candidate, defeated Jefferson for the presidency.

The political repression that accompanied the ideological controversy concerning the French revolutionary wars eventually reached its climax in the Alien and Sedition Acts of 1798 which equated dissent with treason. The Adams administration favored the British and accused the Jeffersonians of plotting treason because the latter favored the French. Obviously, Jeffersonians and Federalists differed in their social philosophies as well as in their economic interests and their constitutional views. The foreign policy implications of the French Revolution further intensified the conflict between the government and the rising political opposition. Americans adopted different views about the events in France, the Federalists denouncing and the Republican Anti-Federalists applauding them. Indeed, many of the Jeffersonian Republicans imitated the French radicals, the Jacobins, by cutting their hair short, wearing pantaloons, and addressing one another as "Citizen" Brown or "Citizeness" Smith. Thus, for a time, it was possible to tell a man's party by his manners and appearance, for the Federalists kept the old-fashioned long hair, knee breeches, and traditional etiquette of the gentleman. Republicans accused the Federalists of being aristocratic and even "monarchical." Federalists referred to the Republicans, in horrified tones, as "radicals" and as "Jacobinical rabble"—terms which then had much the same implication as "communism" many years later was to have. Like the symbolic expressions of certain political beliefs in the 1960's (long hair, short hair, sideburns, modes of attire, simple, incorrect, and even vulgar language, etc.) the symbolism of the Federalists and Republicans reflected their ideologies.

Jubilant after their success in the elections of 1798, the Federalists were determined to smash the political opposition. Some of them schemed to go on winning elections by passing laws, such as the Alien and Sedition Acts, to weaken and completely silence the opposition. They had as an excuse the necessity or supposed necessity of protecting the nation from dangerous foreign influence in the midst of an undeclared war. By persecuting their critics, the Federalists produced a number of Republican martyrs, gave rise to protests against their disregard of the Constitution, and provoked a reaction that brought about their defeat in the election of 1800. Out of power, the Federalists continued to draw support mainly from the upper classes, from established men of substance. One could characterize the Federalist Party in the following way: they were nativists in a land swelling with immigrants; they were anti-popular in a time of expanding suffrage; they were uncompromising in the face of constant change; they were faction-ridden; and, finally, they were very reluctant to be a party at all. By 1820, the Federalist Party faded away, but through the work of Chief Justice John Marshall and the power of judicial review the Federalists have left their permanent imprint on the American political system.

The Jeffersonian Republicans organized an effective party machine, and the vigor and unity resulting from their organizational efforts completely shattered the Federalists. Jefferson and his followers reasoned that a government based upon the consent of the governed needed a dynamic link between the people and their political institutions. They went riding about the country, talking to important local and state officials, organizing a national party machine. Madison helped Jefferson by working in Congress, organizing a strong party caucus that helped bridge the gap between President and Congress. When Madison became President the power of the caucus expanded: it chose nominees for President whose names would appear on the ballots of the electors. During the Age of Jackson the national party conventions replaced the caucuses in the presidential nominating process, reflecting the vast expansion of suffrage. That procedure has been used ever since.

Eras of One Party Dominance

Most political scientists today tend to accept the view that American history has been characterized by relatively long periods during which one of the major parties has dominated the scene. Each era reflected a major phase of economic and social development and the dominant party tended to establish the "agenda" for the nation. Although the period between Jefferson's election in 1800 and the Civil War is considered the first "Democratic Era," from the standpoint of American politics the most important contribution of these decades was the firm entrenchment of the two-party system. There was competition between Federalists and Jeffersonian Republicans, Whigs and Democrats, and by the 1850's, between Democrats and Republicans. A single party has been able to win most presidential elections for long periods, but in every election since 1824, two parties have competed vigorously and seriously and usually on fairly even terms. With the split of the Democratic Party into northern and southern wings, it became possible to elect the Republican Party candidate Lincoln in 1860 (he received less than 40% of the popular vote). Lincoln's presidency and the Civil War ushered in the "Republican Era" that tended to dominate national politics until the Depression and the election of Franklin Roosevelt on the Democratic ticket in 1932. Like the election of 1860, Roosevelt's victory represents one of the landmark elections in the nation's history. The second "Democratic Era" has lasted down to the present. The Republican Administrations of Eisenhower, Nixon, and Ford had to contend with a Democratic Congress most of the time.

There are several reasons for the periods of one party dominance in the American two-party system. The most obvious reason would seem to be that the dominant party was able to win more votes than the other because it successfully organized a national coalition representing the major socioeconomic interests of that era. The party in power has numerous advantages that it can exploit to maintain itself in power. It is in a position to recommend programs and it can award honors, favors, preferments; it can provide jobs, grant contracts, select locations for governmental facilities; it can reduce substantially the problem of raising campaign funds; it can promote the interests of candidates aspiring to high office, and can induce ambitious persons in the opposition to change party affiliation. Because Americans tend to vote for incumbents, the party with the largest number of officeholders may expect to benefit at the polls in subsequent elections. Proving the old adage that nothing succeeds like success, the party that has been in office continually attracts more and more loyal supporters until it becomes firmly entrenched as the majority party. Most significantly, the major changes in political reorientation that resulted in the ousting of one party and the dominance of another have taken place at times of great national crises. After 1800, the Federalist Party was discredited by the repression associated with the Alien and Sedition Acts and the attempts at secession by New England Federalists at the Hartford Convention; after the Civil War, the Democrats were stigmatized as the party of rebellion and secession; and for decades the Republicans were blamed for the Depression. In each of these instances the party in power exploited the accusations to its advantage.

Nature and Characteristics

Despite their ideological roots in the 18th and 19th centuries, the two major parties are not organized to support specific ideologies or the specific interests of social classes. The Democratic and Republican parties are pragmatic, non-ideological coalitions of interest groups, with no clear-cut doctrines holding them together. In short, the American two-party system is almost unique, consisting of multigroup organizations. In any other country that has a two-party system, it is natural to ask what bases underlie the party division. In Britain it is fairly clear that the Conservative and Labour parties are divided along ideological and social-class lines, but in the U.S. the reasons why some people support one party and others do not are harder to spell out. Because of the heterogeneous nature of American society, consisting of many social, economic, ethnic, racial, and religious groups spread through 50 states, any party that obtains a majority of the vote must of necessity be composed of different groups. In their efforts to achieve majority coalitions, both parties have to appeal to every major segment of the population—business, labor, farmers, ethnic, racial, and religious groups, wage earners, professionals, and to every section of the country. Although it is hard to define exactly which groups support which party, there are some general tendencies. We normally think of the Republican party as the party of the well-to-do, of Anglo-Saxon Protestants, of business and professional people, of non-Southern agrarian areas and of the suburbs. The Democratic party usually represents the poor, second or third generation Americans, religious, ethnic, and racial minorities, urban residents and Southerners. One must remember, however, that many groups of voters do not follow this pattern. Jewish voters, many of whom are business and professional people, are an ethnic-religious minority and generally vote Democratic. The Democrats have traditionally controlled the big cities through their strong political machines, which distributed so many favors to loyal voters that the Republicans could not compete. In the current stage of transition in American politics, changes in the voting behavior of certain groups have become noticeable, and it is possible that further changes may occur in forthcoming elections. In the 1972 presidential elections considerable numbers of Jewish people deserted the Democrats and voted Republican. Large numbers of workers we think of as "hard hats" also voted Republican in the same election. Now that the issue of urban crime has become so highly charged, the Republicans may begin to make in-roads in the cities because of their law-and-order image. There is considerable evidence indicating that the strong anti-busing stands of the Nixon and Ford Administrations have helped the Republicans obtain large blocks of voters in such former Democratic strongholds as the South and in a number of the nation's biggest cities particularly plagued by forced, court-ordered busing aimed at integrating schools. White ethnic groups, traditionally Democratic, also have shown signs of possible change in party support because of what many consider threats to their ethnic heritage. Jimmy Carter's ill-chosen term "ethnic purity" was used in the primary campaign in 1976 to indicate his and the Democratic Party's concern with the numerous groups of white ethnics who felt threatened by the influx of blacks and who might vote Republican in the forthcoming presidential election. In addition to the transitional state of flux or "partisan fluidity" the evidence available indicates that the percentage of independents among the electorate has increased substantially during the past decade.

Probably the most significant factor that has contributed to the development of the two-party system in the U.S. is the method used to elect the President and members of Congress. The American "winner takes all" system contrasts sharply with systems of proportional representation in other countries. All members of the Congress are elected under the single-member, simple plurality system: the one candidate in each geographic area with the largest number of votes is elected. The system obviously works to the disadvantage of all except the two major parties. The separate election of the President also helps to create and to maintain the two-party system. Customarily, one nominee receives the entire electoral vote of a state, and the candidate who receives the highest number of electoral votes becomes President. Political leaders and party organizations in the various states know that in order to participate in this, the ultimate victory, they must join one of the two major parties. Historical, legal, psychological, and other factors have also been influential in the establishment and maintenance of the two-party system. The early American leaders were undoubtedly influenced by the practices of the British two-party system. Once the system was firmly entrenched, legal provisions and practices, especially in Congress, worked against third parties. The inherent dualism of many American political issues is another factor. Such issues as the early question of the "strict" versus the "loose" interpretation of the Constitution, the issue of property rights versus the rights of the people, the division of the nation along sectional lines, and others have tended to divide the American electorate naturally into two parties, whereas the political questions confronting the French and Italian voters have been responsible for their multi-party system. Finally, once the system is established, it forces individuals and groups to compromise their demands and unite with others in order to share political power. Splinter parties, such as the Progressive Party that temporarily split from the Republican Party in 1912, and the States' Rights or Dixiecrat movement of 1948, eventually rejoined the parties of their origin. The American Independent Party led by George Wallace became the first third party in 1972 to gain a place on the ballots of all states. But his chances ended when he was shot and seriously wounded while campaigning in the Maryland primary. By 1976, he was no longer a viable contender when he tried to get the Democratic nomination.

Ideologies, Issues, and Personalities

In contrast to ideological party systems in Europe and elsewhere, the American two-party system results in moderate programs and policies. The party platform is determined both by the desire to attract new voters and by the need to retain the support of groups within the party. As a result, party platforms of both major parties tend to be compromises negotiated by party leaders between the often conflicting policies advocated by different groups. Thus the "Tweedledee and Tweedledum" image of American parties, subscribing to the same fundamental ideology, based on democratic values: individual liberty, limited government, majority rule, due process of law, the sanctity of private property, and a free enterprise economy. Furthermore, the Republicans have accepted and supported such public-oriented, mass-welfare domestic programs of the Democrats as social security, fair labor standards, unemployment compensation, government regulation of public utilities, a federally aided welfare system, and many others. The basic outlines of American foreign and military policy since World War II have also been supported by both parties. No wonder that some political analysts charge that our major parties merely reinforce societal consensus and limit the area of legitimate political conflict rather than promote competition over national goals and programs.[2] But of course no one can claim that the major parties have identical ideologies. Because their social bases are not exactly identical and because the aspirations of the two broad groups differ, the thrust of the two parties' ideologies differs. However, the magnitude of this difference is not very great. Since there are only two major parties and a basically non-ideological electorate, it is imperative that party ideologies be moderate and ambiguous. Because American parties are organizations whose basic motive is to capture political office, strong ideology and radical innovation are unlikely. The stress on clear "conservative" or "liberal" ideology has usually cost the parties votes. For example, the defeats of Goldwater and McGovern can be attributed to some error in perception on their part: they overestimated the number of voters who prefer clear alternatives to the dominant value consensus of the American people.

In general, personalities and specific issues are more important in the American party system than ideology. In some European and other countries we see the opposite tendency: politicians often have to leave their parties if they deviate from the party line, even in democratic countries like Britain. Franklin Roosevelt probably owed his election less to his endorsement of Keynesian economic schemes to end the Depression than to the fact that voters saw him as a father figure who inspired confidence. Eisenhower and Kennedy won votes because they were attractive personalities. Issues can also be important. Goldwater was probably hurt as much by his stand on the Vietnam War as by his extremely conservative ideological stance in 1964. McGovern's extremely liberal ideology and his association with radical left wingers in 1972 made him totally unacceptable to the vast majority of the American people. Success in American elections requires the right balance of issue-orientation and ideological commitment together with a winning personality. Candidates will emphasize one or another aspect of their appeal depending on what sort of voters they are addressing, stressing personality with simple-minded voters and issues and ideology among the more educated and sophisticated.

Organization of Parties

The two major American parties, unlike European mass-membership parties, are not "organizations" in the sense normally understood by that term. For the average American, to be a Democrat or a Republican involves no greater commitment to the organization than voting, occasionally, for the nominees of that party. The official organization charts of the parties, indicating neatly the various echelons of party structure, are deceptive. Because of the federal form of government, our parties are decentralized. They are coalitions of a variety of socioeconomic groups and alliances of state and local party organizations. The national organizations have little power over the state and local ones; power flows up rather than down. As the state and local organizations are largely autonomous units, the national leaders seldom have sanctions that may be employed to discipline them. As for the official organization, at the top is the national presidential nominating convention, which meets every four years and sets policy for the party. Below it is the national committee headed by the national party chairman. One of the best studies of the national committees is by C. P. Cotter and B. C. Hennessy and has the revealing title *Politics Without Power,* a judgment perhaps a bit harsh, but fairly close to the truth. Below the national committee there are state committees on top of hundreds of county and city committees on top of thousands of ward, town, and precinct committees. Real power rests at the wide base of the pyramid, and not at the top. Thus our parties are national without being hierarchical. E. E. Schattschneider, one of the most astute political analysts of our parties, has correctly stated that "Decentralization is by all odds the most important single characteristic of the American major party."[3]

The party is made up of people ranging from committed activists to nominal party members. The leadership of a party, like that of any group, almost always comprises the full-time officials (at times called the "bosses"), a core of activists, and a larger number of fairly active members. The inner circle of the elite leadership consists of office-holding (or office-seeking) men and women: The President, Vice-President, governors, the national party chairperson, highly influential senators and representatives, elected state party chairpersons, and some other party officials. The inner circle of our party leadership is neither as homogeneous nor as numerically small as the famous model provided by Roberto Michels requires. His "iron law of oligarchy" states that "every party . . . becomes divided into a minority of directors and a majority of directed."[4] Michels' dictum is only partially applicable to American parties because while there is, indeed, an active minority in control of the party machinery, we do not have a passive majority in the sense of European-style mass party membership. Our party in the electorate, the masses, does not consist of card carrying party members.

Functions

As noted before, the primary function of political parties in competitive states is to select and present candidates for public office to the electorate. Political parties in democracies also provide peaceful and orderly means for succession to office, a major concern for any political system. In Cuba, the Soviet Union, the People's Republic of China, and other noncompetitive political systems there is no regular and orderly procedure to remove governmental leaders from office. Often force and violence are used for that purpose. Through the nominating and elective process American parties provide links between the governing leadership and the people and are supposed to assure majority rule and the will of the people, i.e., of those who participate in the process by casting their votes. Parties are engaged in resolving conflicts by serving as aggregators and artic-ulators of group interests; they try to unify the electorate, conciliate groups, sections and ideologies, formulate and present problems and costs of each alternative function. In addition, parties simplify the alternatives, inform and educate the electorate, help stimulate interest in public affairs, provide some help and services to people, serve as channels for upward mobility (notice the spectacular success of Irish-Americans in the Democratic leadership!), give people a sense of participation, and generally try to project consensus on major issues. In accordance with the so-called consensus theory, parties must act as if classes did not exist in spite of identifiable class voting patterns. To win a national election, parties have to appeal to all segments and sections of American society. The opposition party also serves a useful function although we have not institutionalized the concept of "loyal opposition" the way the British have it. As noted in a previous chapter, they value the role of a responsible and alert opposition so highly that its leader is paid a government salary. In the U.S., we consider the role of the opposition party as one of scrutinizing and pointing out defects in governmental policies and presenting alternative proposals. However, this role often appears intended merely to harass the party in power.

The Electoral Process

Today, the electorate consists of every man and woman who is over 18 years old, a citizen, and meets residential requirements. Registration is generally a prerequisite for voting. The relative importance of elections helps to determine how many voters will participate. Fewer people vote in primary elections than in other elections, even though real political decisions are often made in these contests, especially in areas like the South where the minority party has little chance of winning. Local elections rarely draw as many voters as national contests, unless there is some particularly emotional issue, like forced busing or building a freeway through a residential neigh-borhood. In such cases a local election may draw a bigger turnout than even a presidential election.

Theoretically, one might expect better turnout at local elections, where the issues are more immediate, than in national elections, but, perhaps because of the excitement over national elections created by the media and others, national elections usually interest more voters. Elections for executive-branch offices, presidency, governorship, nearly always draw more voters than elections for legislative posts at every level of government.

American parties are very much election year phenomena. They are much more cohesive in presidential election campaigns than they ever are in state legislatures or in Congress. The presidency is the highest prize in the political system, and both parties concentrate their major efforts on the presidential race. One important consideration in choosing a presidential nominee is that he be able to rally the whole party around him and give it the cohesion it needs to win in November. A strong presidential candidate can help his party by pulling other nominees into office "on his coattails."

Choosing and presenting to the public their respective presidential and vice-presidential candidates is the most important single function that the parties perform. It is significant for two different reasons. First, nomination represents a far greater part of the process of political choice than does the actual election. In the election, voters can choose between two candidates. It is the nominating process that reduces the alternatives to two by eliminating all other contenders. At times, the choice of candidates virtually predetermines the outcome of the election, as with Goldwater in 1964 and McGovern in 1972, neither of whom stood much of a chance in the national election. But even when the election is a genuine contest, it is still limited to persons—those who have dealt most successfully with their parties' candidate selection procedures.

The other significance of the nominating process is that it determines who will have control of the party itself. Control of the nomination is control of the party. If the nominee wins the election, he is indisputably the party leader. And even if he loses he may still retain influence within the party so long as he loses in a way that indicates that he might win the next time. The parties choose their presidential candidates in national conventions held in the summer of the election year. Whether the conventions are actual decision-making bodies or merely occasions for crowning a well established winner depends on the results of the primaries. Irrespective of the answer, the most important parts of the nominating process occur before the convention, in the long and tortuous series of primary elections designed for selecting the delegates. One of the most conspicuous trends in American politics has been the growth of presidential primaries. Less than half of the delegates to the 1968 conventions were chosen in primaries. By 1972, almost two-thirds of the delegates were from primary states, and in 1976 and 1980 over three-quarters of the delegates were chosen in primary elections. The caucus-convention method for selecting convention delegates used to be quite popular, but it has lost ground rapidly as states have switched to the primary system. The number of delegates at the convention varies from year to year as well as from one party to another. It ranges anywhere from around 1,400 to more than 3,000. Both parties follow a policy of apportioning delegates to states on a basis of both population and past support for the party. Critics of the primary system claim that it is a "costly endurance contest . . . lacking any kind of uniformity . . . not a reasonable yardstick of a candidate's support. The results are sometimes meaningless, sometimes indecipherable . . . campaign sameness turns off many voters even before the country reaches the November day of decision."[5] It is claimed that our present system is responsible for getting Carters and Reagans—men who are not viewed by their peers and much of the public as unusually gifted in governmental leadership. What distinguishes men like Carter and Reagan is that they are capable freelance campaigners, self-proclaimed outsiders, most remarkable for their dogged ambition and relentless energy, and prepared to spend years of their lives seeking the presidential prize.[6]

Being the "supreme governing bodies" of their respective parties, the conventions nominate candidates, make rules for the party, and write the platform. Although not binding in the sense of the European-type ideological parties, party platforms have become increasingly important. They indicate the influence of the party nominee and his supporters on crucial issues and point out the policy guidelines his administration would follow. At the July 1980 Republican Convention in Detroit there were serious fights over such controversial issues as abortion and the equal rights amendment. But the Republican platform that finally emerged was tailored to the views of Ronald Reagan. The GOP went on record to support a constitutional amendment prohibiting abortions and refused to endorse the equal rights amendment by stating that the states had "the constitutional right to accept or reject the amendment without federal interference or pressure."

Given the overwhelming support Reagan received at the convention, he was able to present a Republican platform which included tax cuts and tax incentives, reduced federal spending, policies to fight inflation, support for equal rights and equal opportunities for women, exemption of women from the military draft, an aggressive energy policy, decentralization of the federal government, increased spending for national defense and support for a foreign policy through strength, efforts to end unemployment, opposition to "socialized medicine," end to welfare fraud, support for medicare and medicaid, opposition to forced busing, increased efforts to fight crime, and many other issues.[7]

These pledges were designed to draw attention to issues which are usually overshadowed by the emphasis of the media on personalities. As a former movie actor who knew how to use the news media, Reagan seemed to capitalize on the general dissatisfaction with the Carter Administration and the split within the Democratic party due to Senator Kennedy's opposition to Carter. In the summer of 1980, the GOP seemed to have reappeared in a most favorable position in national politics. Public opinion polls confirmed Reagan as the favorite over President Carter and showed Republicans on a near-par with Democrats in the Congressional races. Polls also showed that Republicans were regarded by the voters as the party best able to control inflation, government spending and taxes, to maintain world peace and military security and to assure adequate energy supplies. The survey results showed that "the Democrats (were) as low as the Republicans were in 1974—and (were) going down."[8]

Issues, Challenges, and the Future of the American Party System

In the 1960's and 1970's an increasing number of Americans have developed feelings of alienation and cynicism toward political parties and public officials. The decline in the proportion of the electorate who have voted can be traced largely to apathy and alienation (only 45.9 percent of those eligible cast their ballots in 1978). In 1958, over 88 percent of the people believed they could "trust the government" to do what was right all or most of the time. That figure declined dramatically to 55 percent by 1972. In a 1974 study in Wisconsin two-thirds of the voters agreed that "it would be better if in all elections we put no party labels on the ballot," and five out of six voters thought that the parties had done "no good" for people like themselves.[9]

The Vietnam War, widespread corruption in the administration of the welfare system, loss of faith in the judicial system, the Watergate, "Koreagate," "Billy-gate" and other scandals have tarnished the image of both parties. The glaring failures of the Carter Administration to deal with inflation, recession, unemployment, energy, arms control, and other foreign policy issues (especially those related to the Middle East) exposed President Carter as an ineffective and even incompetent leader.

By 1980, increasing numbers of Americans were frustrated by an incompetent government, disillusioned with politicians, and apathetic toward political parties. The national convention became a "$40-million circus," part ritual, part TV show extravaganza, designed to entertain.[10] The primary election system has preempted the major role once played by the conventions, the nominating of candidates for the presidency, and television has replaced the political bosses as the major influence on the nominating process. Each year, the share of audience watching the conventions declines. So does the number of Americans identifying with the two major parties. Perhaps the greatest danger to our party system could be the inability of the two major parties to respond to the issues and challenges of the 1980's. Long before the 1980 presidential election, increasing numbers of Americans had begun mobilizing around simple issues outside the traditional party structures. People who were flocking to single-issue movements saw them as the best way to achieve change or get relief in the face of unresponsive politicians or bureaucrats.[11] Taxes, abortion, nuclear power, rent control, school busing, the equal rights amendment and capital punishment, to name a few, all generated their own movements. If this fragmentation continues, it could lead to political paralysis and possibly even to destruction of the two-party system. In California, Nevada, and some other states it is possible for single-issue politics to succeed on specific issues that agitate the minds of people (e.g. the Jarvis-initiated initiatives on property taxes, busing, etc.). On the national level, however, only the cumbersome and difficult procedure of constitutional amendment can bring about basic changes. If traditional politics does not respond to the need for change that people demand, the impatient and skeptical citizens become cynical about the political process and the candidates of the two major parties. For these people single-issue politics is the most promising arena for change. If the trend toward single-issue politics continues, some analysts see a multi-party system ultimately replacing the two-party system as issue groups form their own political parties. Unless the two major parties become more responsive to the demands of the issue groups, the ends of the spectrum are going to get sliced up into these different divisions and the middle is going to shrink.

When Ronald Reagan accepted the nomination of the Republican Party at Detroit in July 1980, he expressed the goal of building a "New Consensus," a new majority based on the dissatisfaction of practically all segments of the American people with the Carter Administration. Skillfully capitalizing on Carter's almost unprecedented lack of popularity, Reagan proclaimed the major issue of the 1980 presidential campaign: "the direct political, personal and moral responsibility of Democratic Party leadership—in the White House and in the Congress—for a disintegrating economy, a weakened defense and an energy policy based on the sharing of scarcity."[12] Senator Edward Kennedy, challenging President Carter for the Democratic nomination, accused Reagan of "speaking the language of the Democrats" in order to attract the broad masses of the American people.[13]

The increasing number of independent voters, ticket splitting, and single-issue politics are causing alarm in both parties. The changing patterns of voting behavior, noted before, also provide evidence for possible realignments. In short, the American people are showing displeasure at the ways the two parties have responded to the problems facing the nation. Historically the American party system has more than once shown flexibility. The inflexible party is a doomed party. Only the future will tell whether Ronald Reagan, in addition to capturing the presidency, can also build a new broad-based Republican majority. If he succeeds, he will have contributed to changing the American party system from coalitions dominated by interest groups to broad-based parties depending more on appeals to the individual citizen than on the concept of coalition. Many Americans seem to be loosening their emotional ties to the groups with which they formerly identified including the political parties themselves. This does not mean the end of the American party system. Rather it can be viewed as the dawning of a new political day, with Democratic and Republican party officials finding it necessary to change their methods in light of the voters' new-found independence from parties.

Notes

1. The term seems to have been coined by W. D. Burnham. See his *Critical Elections and the Mainsprings of American Politics* (New York: Norton, 1970).
2. See Robert E. Lane, "The Politics of Consensus in An Age of Affluence," *American Political Science Review,* March, 1965, p. 880, and the essays in William N. Chambers and Walter D. Durnham, eds., *The American Party System: Stages of Political Development* (New York: Oxford University Press, 1967).
3. E. E. Schattschneider, *Party Government* (New York: Farrar and Rinehart, 1942) p. 129.
4. Roberto Michels, *Political Parties: A Sociological Study of the Oligarchical Tendencies of Modern Democracy* (New York: Dover, 1959) p. 32.
5. Howard Flieger, "Endurance Contest," *U.S. News and World Report,* June 21, 1976, p. 80.
6. See David S. Broder, "And That's How the System Works," *San Francisco Chronicle,* June 4, 1980, p. 44.
7. "The Platform Reagan Will Run On," *U.S. News and World Report,* July 28, 1980, pp. 72–73.
8. "GOP in Its Best Position in Years, New Poll Shows," *Los Angeles Times,* July 6, 1980, p. 5.
9. Jack Dennis, "Trends in Public Support for the American Political Party System." Paper presented at the 1974 Annual Meeting of the American Political Science Association (mimeographed); Arthur H. Miller, "Political Issues and Trust in Government," *American Political Science Review,* September, 1974, pp. 951–972; William Watts and L. A. Free, *State of the Nation 1974* (Washington, D.C.: Potomac), pp. 70–74.
10. "Part Ritual, Part TV Show," *Time,* July 28, 1980, pp. 22–23.
11. "Single-Issue Politics Jolt the 'System'," *Los Angeles Times,* February 14, 1980, pp. 1, 14.
12. *Los Angeles Times,* July 18, 1980, p. 16.
13. Senator Edward Kennedy on NBC's "Meet the Press" program, July 27, 1980.

For Further Reading

Broder, David S. *The Party's Over: The Failure of Politics in America.* New York, Harper and Row, 1972.
Crotty, William J. and Gary C. Jacobson. *American Parties in Decline.* Boston, Little, Brown, 1980.
Ranney, Austin. *Curing the Mischiefs of Faction: Party Reform in America.* Berkeley, California, University of California Press, 1975.
Rossiter, Clinton. *Parties and Politics in America.* Ithaca, N.Y., Cornell University Press, 1960.
Sorauf, Frank J. *Party Politics in America,* 4th ed. Boston, Little, Brown, 1980.

Name _____

Section _____

Date _____

Review Questions for Chapter 8: Political Parties

1. What is the difference between competitive, non-competitive, and fragmented political systems?

_____

_____

_____

_____

2. What were the ideological differences between the Federalists and the Jeffersonians, and what groups of society supported each?

_____

_____

_____

_____

3. What is the most significant factor that has contributed to the development of the two-party system in the United States?

_____

_____

_____

_____

4. What is the "Tweedledee Tweedledum" image of American parties and to what extent is that image right or wrong?

_____

_____

_____

_____

5. What were the main reasons for the overwhelming defeats of Goldwater in 1964 and Mc-Govern in 1972 as presidential candidates?

_____

_____

_____

_____

_____

6. Why did the political scientist E. E. Schattschneider consider decentralization the most important single characteristic of the major American parties?

_____

_____

_____

_____

_____

7. List the major functions of the major political parties in the United States—How different are those functions from parties in such non-competitive political systems as the Soviet Union or Cuba?

_____

_____

_____

_____

_____

8. What procedures do the parties follow to select their presidential and vice presidential candidates?

_____

_____

_____

_____

_____

9. How important are the parties' platforms and to what extent are they binding on the presidential candidates?

_____

_____

_____

_____

_____

10. What were the reasons for the apathy, cynicism, and alienation of many Americans in the 1960's and 1970's? How were those feelings reflected in the elections?

_____

_____

_____

_____

_____

11. Why did some reporters refer to national conventions as "$40-million circuses?"

_____

_____

_____

_____

12. What do we mean by "single issue" politics? Give two examples of such single issues.

_____

_____

_____

_____

_____

Chapter 9

Campaigns and Elections

We differ from other states regarding the man who holds aloof from public life not as quiet, but as useless; we decide or debate, carefully and in person, all matters of policy holding not that words and deeds go ill together, but that acts are foredoomed to failure when undertaken undiscussed.

Pericles

The voice of the people is the voice of God.

Machiavelli

The right to vote is the most basic right without which all others are meaningless. It gives people—people as individuals—control over their destinies.

President Lyndon Johnson

The voters have little effect on public policy. The prime function of elections is a ritual of symbolic reassurance that serves to quiet doubts about the democratic character of the system and the resentments about particular political acts.

Political Scientist Murray Edelman

The American electoral system is one of the most fascinating of all political institutions. Campaigns and elections are key elements in the American political system and they provide a colorful and entertaining array of political practices. The primary means by which the Constitution guarantees that the government will be responsive to the people is the electoral process, which gives citizens a chance to change their political leaders and to pass judgment on the performance of elected officials. Many elections are held in the United States at every level from township commissioner to President. The common thread that runs through all such contests is that the people have the final say in choosing their leaders. Voting is really an expression of opinion by means of a definite action.

Winning a share of political power has been a long and even violent struggle for most people. Thus it is understandable that the importance of voting has been emphasized and exaggerated. But the hopes placed on gaining the ballot have not been fully realized. Like the swing of a pendulum, the consequent disillusionment with the ballot has been as exaggerated as the most extreme hopes. Elections are under attack among both the general public and scholars. New myths may be superseding old ones; unsubstantiated despair may be replacing unsubstantiated optimism. The American electoral system does not operate perfectly; in some ways it does not operate well at all. But the system is constantly changing in response to the issues and challenges of the time. The American political scene of the 1980's is very different from that of the previous two decades in which the nation was tormented by Vietnam and its aftermath, race conflict, and assassination. Yet America was also prosperous, democratically involved, and apparently able—if it had the will—to solve its problems. In the 1980's the immediate problems of the earlier time have been either resolved or repressed, but there is less confidence in the future. The economy is stagnant and hostage to foreign energy producers. The big issues of the 1980's are inflation, unemployment, energy, national defense, to name some of the most crucial ones. Public allegiance to leaders and political institutions has steadily declined. Political parties, earlier presented as the critical link between the electorate and the government, have been enfeebled.

The discussion of campaigns and elections centers on the questions whether the American electoral process has retained its vitality in confronting the issues and replacing one group of politicians with another, and whether elections are effective means to protect the vital interests of the citizens. Plato's myth was designed to result in popular consent to the actual rule of an elite group. If elections are the modern equivalent of Plato's myth, how much truth is in the charge that in the United States Plato's myth and ruling oligarchy have become realities and that elections are mere images of reality? There is also the question concerning the relationship between the voters' policy desires expressed through the choice of officials and the policy actions of those officials. After "the people have spoken," a winning politician could represent the wishes of the majority or be independent and deaf to the inchoate speech of the voters. He can rely on the support of special interest groups whose support is essential for the financing of campaigns and elections.

The United States is an election-happy country. Over a four-year period more than 500,000 public offices are filled by election, more per capita than in any other country in the world. Unlike most other democracies, the United States is characterized by long and expensive campaigns and, unlike most other democracies, party organizations in the United States tend to be scrawny creatures unequipped for such arduous efforts. What has arisen to play the leading role in campaigns is the candidate-centered organization, an organization brought into existence to advance a particular candidate in a particular race. David Hartman concluded his report on the furious platform fight concerning unemployment and other economic issues between Carter and Kennedy delegates at the Democratic National Convention at New York in 1980 by saying: "Once the nomination is over, the platform will take a back seat to the candidates." In short, personalities, and not issues tend to be in the center of most campaigns and elections.

Campaigning for public office in the United States, from town council to the presidency, has grown enormously in cost and complexity through the years. George Washington expended little effort and literally no money to become the nation's first President in 1789. Today, national campaigns have evolved into multimillion dollar extravaganzas complete with professional campaign managers, pollsters, computerized voting lists, television advertising, advance men, and a great deal of hoopla. In many respects, statewide, congressional, and local campaigns have developed into miniature copies of races for the presidency, different only in scale. Early-day campaigning required little more than filing for office and a few blasts of political oratory. The candidate with a well-known name and good reputation among landowners was rarely even opposed at the polls. Those leisurely elections have given way to the "packaging" of modern-day candidates who are carefully selected with emphasis on television presence, good looks, and a high-powered image maker to lead the way.

Drawing by Richard Milholland from the Los Angeles Times. Copyright © 1980.

Who Runs for Office and Why?

Why do people choose to run for public office? Once they decide to run, how do they attempt to secure their party's nomination and win the election? Running for office is an uncommon form of political participation. Only a small proportion, certainly less than 5 percent, of the adult population have ever run for public office. The reasons why individuals become candidates for public office are many and varied. The range of motives that people may have for running for office reflects the numerous types of offices that people can run for and the variety of political contexts in which people live and operate. Individuals who run for office usually have a high level of political awareness and past involvement. Even if we look at individuals who are running for office for the first time, we find that they generally have been interested in politics for a long time and have been active in various ways. Thus, candidates are not recruited evenly from the entire population, but disproportionately from the stratum of highly involved citizens. Occasionally, a person may become aroused by some political decisions or actions, perhaps because they affect him or her directly, and respond by filing for an elective public office. Becoming a candidate also depends on personal circumstances. For many candidates, one important factor is the support of family and friends. Such encouragement and support have been most noticeable in the political careers of the Kennedys ever since their Irish immigrant grandfather set foot on American soil. It is a well known fact that Ronald Reagan and Jimmy Carter have been motivated greatly, and perhaps even decisively, by their wives to aspire to the highest office of the land. An equally important factor is the personal freedom to run. Most individuals lack the time and money to enter an election and serve in office. In most states, for example, the office of state legislator is a poorly-paid, part-time position. Very few people have occupations that permit the continuation of their professional pursuits while serving in the state legislature. Persons in business for themselves, lawyers, insurance salesmen, and some others may be able to combine public office with a private career. In fact, some may find that holding public office furthers their private business or career. But for most people, occupational constraints preclude their holding public offices. Numerous case studies have illustrated the relevance of these personal factors. The ability of Jimmy Carter to campaign full-time for over one year before the first presidential primary (while his brother Billy minded the family peanut business) undoubtedly influenced his decision to run. The financial independence of Ronald Reagan and the Kennedys, to name a few, has certainly influenced them to enter presidential elections. The occupation most associated with American politics is that of lawyer. Characteristic is Woodrow Wilson's statement: "The profession I chose was politics; the profession I entered was the law. I entered one because I thought it would lead to the other."[1] In general, candidates are not representative of the population in social or demographic terms. They are higher in social status, usually having college and even post-graduate degrees and professional or managerial occupational backgrounds. In short, political office holders in the United States represent a political elite consisting mainly of white males. Candidates and office holders tend to have these social characteristics in part because these traits are associated with political involvement and personal opportunity and in part because people with these characteristics find it easier to obtain support for their candidacy.

Nominations, Primaries, Conventions

The Democratic and Republican parties dominate the process of nominating candidates for office. In presidential elections, candidates compete for a party's nomination in a long, hard primary campaign. Are the primaries an effective way of choosing candidates? Do voters have a chance to find out about the abilities and positions of the candidates during the primaries? What determines a candidate's primary campaign strategy? Do the primaries and national conventions produce candidates of high caliber?

Most states use the primary system to nominate candidates for the U.S. Senate and House of Representatives, the governorship, and most important state and local offices. Presidential candidates compete for their party's nomination through state primary elections or state party conventions. By 1980, about three-fourths of the delegates to the national conventions were elected in primaries. The goal of the primary campaign is to gather the pledges of enough delegates to the national convention to win the party's nomination. The American system of nominating presidential candidates is complex, physically taxing, and financially burdensome. To a large extent it removes the process of choosing a candidate from the control of party organizations and opens it to anyone who wants to run in the primaries and conventions. It is only in recent years that the presidential nomination process has been altered by the spread of primaries to new states—between 1968 and 1980 the number of primary states more than doubled to 35—and by the adoption of new rules affecting delegate selection in the Democratic party.

The period of rapidly changing rules in the Democratic Party began in 1968, a year marked by public recognition by the American government that the Vietnam war was unwinnable, by the pressured decision of President Johnson not to seek the Democratic renomination, and by the assassinations of Senator Robert F. Kennedy and Martin Luther King. It was not an easy year for the Democratic Party to nominate a presidential candidate. The Democratic convention in Chicago attracted thousands of antiwar protesters intent upon making life miserable for Johnson's party. Protestors nominated a pig for President, then threatened to eat their candidate. On one of the most tumultuous nights in the tumultuous history of the Democratic Party, policemen and thousands of antiwar and anticonvention demonstrators became embroiled in a televised riot. The convention was portrayed by television as one in which Chicago Mayor Richard Daley, the last of the big political bosses, ruled with a heavy hand and an obscene finger.[2] The convention, it was widely felt, had given the party a poor image. After the defeat of its presidential candidate Hubert Humphrey, Democratic leaders agreed that change was needed in the way the party nominated its candidates. A Commission on Party Structure and Delegate Selection, headed by Senator George McGovern, recommended a number of changes to ensure "fair representation of minority views." Just as some Democrats interpreted the 1968 defeat as a reason for reform, some interpreted the 1972 defeat as evidence that the reforms (particularly the demographic group quotas) should not be enforced with undue zeal.

The 1980 Democratic and Republican conventions seemed to confirm the fact that the "Part Ritual, Part TV Show,"[3] organized by the two parties every four years at the cost of well over 100 million dollars, no longer served the purpose of selecting the presidential candidates of the two parties. The 35 state primaries in which some 32 million citizens had voted left little doubt about the nominations of Ronald Reagan and Jimmy Carter as the standard bearers of their parties. Both men won most of their respective primaries and delegates to the conventions simply registered their predetermined votes. The majority of the 3,331 Democratic convention delegates in New York refused to change the party rules that the results of primaries were binding on delegates. With that vote on the first day of the convention, Senator Kennedy's challenge to the renomination of President Carter collapsed. Ronald Reagan, an old hand at theatricals with overwhelming primary victories behind him, emerged as the superstar of the four-day extravaganza officially labeled the Republican National Convention.[4] As observers noted, the term nominating convention was really a misnomer; confirmation, or perhaps coronation, would be a better description for the spectacular shows staged by the two parties. To try to lure as many viewers as possible for 18 hours of TV time, the conventions were overflowing with such show business celebrities as Wayne Newton, Pat Boone, Glen Campbell, Willie Nelson, Tanya Tucker, Vikki Carr, Dorothy Hamill, Ginger Rogers, and Donny and Marie Osmond, among others, who rivaled the politicians on the rostrum, a far cry from oldtime conventions where delegates lustily bargained, brawled, and demonstrated to choose a delegate. Senator Kennedy's supporters made a brave effort to resist the Carter steamroller at the Democratic convention. All they could accomplish was to change some statements in the platform and to add another non-binding plank concerning the creation of a 12 billion dollar job program.[5] As every student of politics knows, platform promises are just one type of "side payment" to a losing faction. Another one is the choice of a vice presidential running mate, selected by the nominee, to appeal to a faction that did not win the presidential nomination. Reagan's selection of George Bush was a good example of this type of strategy.

Importance of Television

For years, primaries had been essentially "beauty contests" that tested a candidate's appeal to the voters but did not usually bind the convention delegates. In 1952, for example, Estes Kefauver swept through the 15 primaries, only to be denied the nomination by party bosses who gave it to Adlai Stevenson instead. With the results of the primaries binding on the delegates, "direct democracy" triumphed. As the 1980 national conventions have demonstrated, their function is no longer to select the nominees but simply to celebrate the result. And celebrate they did. The convention floors were packed not only with hordes of television network reporters but also flocks of local TV crews from all over the country, videotaping their delegations so that folks back home could see their delegates.[6] The importance of television can hardly be overstated. Television *is* American politics in the way that television *is* American sports. And television determines what we hear by what speeches it chooses to cover. Seeing makes for believing. All the surveys indicate that people find television more credible than newspapers or magazines. To the average viewer, it is hard to determine where show biz ends and politics begins. Gazing down on the delegates of the 1980 Democratic Convention from his CBS News twin anchor booth, Bill Moyers expressed a somber mood when he remarked: "There are moments when I think this whole affair is being staged by Hollywood, but Hollywood's on strike and this is for real. Or is it?"[7] Well, is it? How real is it to the millions watching, some of the millions accustomed to reality through "Mork and Mindy" or "Lou Grant?" Are the conventions with all their hoopla and pageantry just the "wordiest show on earth?"[8] In their consequences they are certainly not.

Few political analysts and professionals are satisfied with the way the two parties select their presidential nominees. Many feel that instead of producing better qualified, more widely accepted candidates for President, the system has put too high a premium on a candidate's ability to build an organization that can manipulate the early primaries, caucuses, and ultimately the national convention. The way the system works now, the primaries, rising costs, exaggerated focus on the candidates at the expense of the issues require skills which, in the words of political scientist Jeane Kirkpatrick, "bear virtually no relationship to the skills needed to govern the country. We have created a process which is functioning almost to eliminate qualified people."[9]

The 1980 presidential nominating process ended with a prize political paradox. On the face of it, the system worked perfectly. The two men who were the favorites of their parties' rank and file, according to the polls in January 1980, emerged as the victors. Carter and Reagan were not anomalies: they were the logical, predictable products of the presidential selection system Americans used in 1980. Undoubtedly, the media have become the great anointers, deciding in large measure which candidates are to be taken seriously and which will sink into obscurity. It is a self-appointed role that many Americans resent.[10]

Candidates in 19th-century elections rarely left their homes or places of business to campaign—actually a forced choice, since roads often were impassable anyway. In the absence of television or radio, politicians relied on newspaper advertising that often was slow to catch on. Campaigning was virtually restricted to a word-of-mouth approach in which the candidate sought out people wherever they could be found in large groups—civic meeting, public debates, church picnics, county fairs or the occasional staged rally. Even presidential races remained casual affairs for many years. As late as 1896, Republican William McKinley won a "front porch" campaign from his home in Ohio. Compare that nonchalant approach with today's demands on candidates in major races who find themselves the center-ring attraction in a "flying circus," living out of suitcases for months as they jet from one stop to another. Ronald Reagan, for example, started running four years before Election day, 1980, and was on the road almost continuously.

Importance of Specialists and Experts

Before candidates even launch a campaign these days, they frequently attend special schools and may even take professional speech lessons to correct regional accents, as was the case with Jimmy Carter when he first decided to run for President. Managing a political campaign used to be a relatively simple chore. The operation was limited to a few close friends, and the electorate was smaller and more interested in politics. Today, while methods of communication have grown immensely sophisticated, the number of eligible voters has mushroomed to an estimated 160 million, and people are often apathetic about even bothering to go to the polls.

A modern political campaign requires an elaborate structure with a number of specialists and experts. Many of these workers wind up on staffs of elected officials, so the connection can be a fruitful one. Some campaign workers, however, are not personal followers of a candidate but are professional political consultants who provide guidance for a fee. Such a consultant is often the first person hired. Another crucial individual on the campaign team is a financial chairman or treasurer to raise money to pay expenses, which can run into the millions of dollars. A presidential campaign requires personnel and offices in virtually every state. Statewide races usually have county organizations, and local contests frequently are divided into precincts and wards. Managers are named at each level to coordinate activity. Most candidates for public office must put together an effective campaign organization, often for both a primary and a general election. Running a campaign involves both acquiring sufficient resources and using the resources in an effective manner.

To win, the candidate must raise money. He must learn about the electorate. The candidate must reach the voters and convince them that he is the best candidate for the position. The basic election organizational effort is aimed at the grass roots. Winning elections is a deceptively simple business: get out the full potential of the candidate's favorable vote, and convert the fence straddlers.

Financing Campaigns

The veteran California politician Jesse M. Unruh referred to money as "the mother's milk of politics."[11] Although it may be a slight exaggeration, there can be no doubt that the raising and spending of campaign funds has always been at the heart of the electoral process—perhaps today more than ever. Campaign expenditures go for a variety of things. The purchase of television and radio time can use up a substantial portion of campaign resources. Besides broadcast expenditures, advertising through newspapers and mass mailings takes a significant share of campaign funds. Money also goes for a variety of campaign services. Professional pollsters, advertising agencies, campaign managers, and fund-raising consultants are regularly employed by candidates for higher-level offices. Finally, money must be available for establishing campaign headquarters, providing for sufficient travel, and purchasing campaign materials.

Campaigns have become increasingly expensive. Increases are especially visible at the presidential level. It has been estimated that Abraham Lincoln's presidential campaign of 1860 cost about $100,000, the equivalent of $5 million today, counting inflation and population growth. In 1960, Richard Nixon and John Kennedy each spent about $10 million. In 1972, Nixon spent six times that amount to get elected, and George McGovern spent $30 million in his losing campaign, more than any previous presidential candidate had spent. Public financing is now available for presidential candidates. In 1976 and 1980, the two major candidates each were entitled to $21.8 and $29.4 million respectively for their general election campaign.[12] The establishment of public financing for presidential primaries and elections came about by the Federal Election Campaign Act of 1974. While presidential candidates have the option not to participate in the system, they still are bound by another provision of the law limiting individual contributions of $1,000 to each candidate in a single race and a total of $25,000 a year. Political action committees can donate up to $5,000 to a candidate. Even with public financing, money does make a difference. It was estimated that in 1980 the "independent" committees, allowed under the Supreme Court ruling on the public financing law, raised about $5 million on Reagan's behalf, and that the Republican national, state, and local committees spent more than $20 million. Help from organized labor for Carter was no match for the business and corporate political action committees' record funds to GOP committees and candidates, directly and indirectly helping Reagan.[13]

Looking at presidential election expenditures can give a misleading picture of campaign financing in general. Of the elected offices in this country 95 percent probably require less than $10,000 to wage a competitive campaign, and many take no more than $1,000.[14] For these offices the candidate can usually rely on his own funds, contributions from friends and associates, and money obtained from informal fund raising efforts. The offices that usually require substantial campaign funds are, besides the presidency, the other elected national offices and the more visible statewide offices. Gubernatorial election expenses naturally vary with the state. A large and competitive state can require a million-dollar campaign. Ronald Reagan spent $5 million getting elected governor of California in 1966, and Nelson Rockefeller spent $8 million in his 1970 reelection as governor of New York.[15] U.S. senatorial candidates in large states often spend over a million dollars. A candidate in a safe rural congressional district might spend only a few thousand dollars, but a competitive urban House seat will require $100,000 or more in campaign funds. Even lesser offices can be expensive in some cases. Running for the California State Senate from a competitive district was estimated to cost $20,000, and becoming County Executive in populous Suffolk County in Long Island could require $100,000.[16] Spending a great deal of money does not guarantee victory. But in trying to predict the outcome of a particular campaign, professional politicians usually begin by asking "Who has the bucks?" That was clearly a critical question in 1968, when Humphrey spent $12 million compared with Nixon's $25 million. Humphrey's expenditures were not only less, but they came later, and they required far more hours of the candidate's time to obtain than did Nixon's. Had there been public financing in 1968, Humphrey would probably have been elected. Public financing for presidential elections (efforts to include congressional campaigns have not succeeded) and tighter monitoring of contributions and spending, however, have not altered the fact that, next to a good candidate, nothing is more vital to a campaign than money to pay the bills.

The 1980 general election campaign was dominated by money as never before. Experts calculated that more than $800 million would be spent in local, state, and national races by Election Day on November 4, a record amount far exceeding the $540 million expended in 1976. At this pace, authorities predict, 1984 could well bring the nation's first billion-dollar election. The long grind of the presidential campaign alone absorbed more than $250 million in taxpayer subsidies and private donations. It was expected that months after the election some losing candidates would still be paying off debts from primary elections. For instance, bills totaling some $12 million for Republican John Connolly and an estimated $17 million for Democrat Edward Kennedy.[17] The main force behind the skyrocketing cost of winning public office: the 45 percent increase in living costs that took place between 1976 and 1980. It is more than inflation, however, that makes money both a prime worry and principal goal of politicians. Pressures on candidates are rising to assemble manpower and equipment capable of competing in increasingly sophisticated campaigns that have developed from parades and stump speeches to slick TV commercials and computers capable of targeting specific blocs of voters. At the same time, multiplying laws, court decisions and bureaucratic regulations are weaving a complex web of rules that governs virtually every aspect of how political funds are raised and spent. The result is that handling political money, once regarded as a routine if slightly distasteful chore for campaign volunteers, has been transformed into big business that requires the attention of not only the candidate but of a horde of lawyers, accountants, and hired consultants.

The hectic scrambling for campaign money has produced a new breed of experts who provide a candidate with total services, including the molding of a campaign image. There is some concern that a new caste of powerful political elitists is in the making. At the national level, virtually all candidates are turning to direct mail to raise funds. This highly specialized method is relatively new and expensive, but its use is considered essential to reaching enough contributors.

As indicated before, political action committees are playing a growing role in fund raising. The number and power of PAC's have mushroomed since court rulings in the mid-1970's interpreted election-reform laws to allow corporations to collect voluntary donations from employees and use the money for political purposes. In September 1980, the Federal Election Commission listed in its active file 1,106 PAC's formed by corporations, 542 established by trade associations, and 266 set up by labor unions.[18] Federal election laws limit PAC contributions to $5,000 per candidate per election. The committees may support local and state candidates, but they are forbidden to contribute to nominees for President if the candidates accept public funding. However, federal law permits individuals and organizations to spend money backing presidential candidates if they do it independently of the candidate's regular campaign committee. In 1980, there were at least four independent groups raising money to back Reagan after beating a legal challenge by Common Cause.

Money, or more specifically lack of it was a major problem for independent presidential candidate John Anderson in 1980. He raised 6 million dollars but did not qualify for the public funds granted Carter and Reagan, each of whom accepted 29.4 million dollars in public funds in addition to 4.8 million and 7.2 million respectively in matching funds in the primaries. Fortunately for Anderson, the Federal Election Commission eventually ruled that Anderson could claim a belated share of the federal subsidy if he received at least 5 percent of the popular vote in the election in November.

Corporations and Campaign Contributions

Four centuries ago, British jurist Sir Edward Coke wrote that corporations "cannot commit treason, nor be outlawed, nor excommunicated, for they have no souls." These days, however, American courts are taking a different view. No judge has decided whether U.S. corporations have souls, but the current Supreme Court has decided they at least have mouths, windboxes, and the legal right to speak. In a series of rulings over the last five years, the Court headed by Chief Justice Warren E. Burger has been granting official recognition and new constitutional protections to the role of corporations and money in the American political system. This slowly evolving series of decisions has brought about a quiet revolution that has radically changed the nature of public debate in this country and has become a major issue of our times.

The effect of the decisions has been to undercut efforts by the federal and state governments to keep corporations and large sums of money from exercising too much influence in election campaigns. The high court is basing its rulings on the First Amendment guarantee of freedom of speech. In one line of decisions, dating back to 1976, the justices have held that money, that is expenditures in political campaigns, is a form of speech. In a second line of rulings that began in 1978, the court has held that the First Amendment protects the speech of corporations exactly as it does the speech of individuals. The consequences of these Supreme Court rulings can be felt every month and in every election campaign. When a group of Republicans announced in June 1980, that they hoped to raise and spend $20 million to $30 million on behalf of Ronald Reagan's presidential campaign, they had the Supreme Court rulings in mind. Under the principles set down by the high court, as long as that group operated independently of the formal campaign structure its spending was a form of constitutionally protected speech. The court's rulings thus provide a means of skirting a congressionally mandated prohibition on spending by presidential candidates who agree to accept $29.4 million in federal funds.

At the state and local levels, the high court has opened the door for corporations to take part in election campaigns or votes on nuclear power, energy measures, taxes, and other matters affecting their welfare. In one of the whole series of Supreme Court rulings, handed down June 20, 1980, the justices held that states cannot prevent utility companies from using their monthly bills to tell customers their views about nuclear power and other issues, or to advertise their products. If these decisions are important, they are also highly controversial, although in an unusual fashion that defies traditional ideologies. To supporters, the idea of granting corporations the protection of the First Amendment amounts to a net gain for freedom of expression. In this view, all the Supreme Court is doing is allowing businesses a chance to take part in public debate on issues that affect them. To do otherwise, it is argued, would be to allow a form of government censorship over a corporation's ideas. Critics contend that the First Amendment guarantee of free speech was meant to cover individuals, not corporations. They cite the words of former Chief Justice John Marshall who wrote in 1819 that a corporation is "an artificial being, intangible, existing only in contemplation of law." Unlike people, these critics argue, corporations must be created or chartered under state laws, and therefore can be regulated by state laws. They say the First Amendment may give individual corporate executives or shareholders the right to speak or to take part in elections, but that few other people have the financial means to do so.

The debate has produced some odd bedfellows, breaking down the usual divisions between liberals and conservatives. Within the court, for example, Justices William J. Brennan Jr. and Thurgood Marshall, the court's two most liberal and, ordinarily, its two strongest defenders of freedom of expression, opposed extending First Amendment protection to corporations. So did Justice William H. Rehnquist, the court's most conservative member, who seldom aligns himself with Brennan and Marshall on any issue of importance, but who believes strongly that a corporation is merely an economic entity and is not entitled to political liberties. Rehnquist's most frequent ally on the court, Chief Justice Burger, has been on the other side, supporting the court's extension of First Amendment protection to corporate entities. But the key figure in developing the court's new doctrine has been Justice Lewis F. Powell Jr., the former Richmond lawyer who spent much of his career representing corporate clients before he joined the Supreme Court bench. It was Powell who wrote the key 1978 decision, *First National Bank v. Bellotti,* which first established the principle that corporations are entitled to freedom of speech. And it was Powell who wrote the court's two decisions regarding utility companies in June 1980.

The Burger court's ruling effectively cut off government attempts to curb the role of corporations and the influence of wealth on American political campaigns. These governmental efforts were themselves a response to two separate developments in American public life of the twentieth century. First, an increasing amount of money is in the hands of corporations. The effects of personal income and inheritance taxes have made it more difficult than it was in the nineteenth century to amass personal fortunes and pass them on to heirs. Meanwhile, small, family-run businesses are selling out to large corporations, which can profit from the economies of scale made possible by mass merchandising. Second, speech, that is public or political speech, costs increasing amounts of money. The best way to reach an audience is through television, radio, and mass-circulation newspapers and magazines. As everybody knows, advertising through these news media is not cheap.

By the early 1970's, both Congress and a number of state legislatures had begun to act to limit the effects of corporate wealth on election campaigns. In the wake of the Watergate scandal and its revelations of huge, often hidden corporate campaign contributions, Congress in 1974 enacted a new campaign reform law limiting the amount of money that could be spent on elections. On the state level, Massachusetts passed a law in 1972 barring any corporation from taking part in any ballot measure that did not directly affect its business activities. These laws themselves reflected two fundamentally different legislative approaches: you might try to limit the expenditures of money in elections, or you might simply regulate the extent to which corporations could participate in elections. The recent court rulings have, in effect, restricted both of these approaches. In the 1976 case of *Buckley v. Valeo,* the Supreme Court decided that campaign expenditures are a form of speech protected by the First Amendment. As a result, the justices struck down the sections of the 1974 campaign reform law limiting the amount of money an individual or group can spend during an election. In the 1978 case, *First National Bank v. Bellotti,* the court granted corporations the right to freedom of speech. As a result, the court struck down the Massachusetts law prohibiting corporations from taking part in most state ballot measures.

Justice Powell's opinions for the court in the "corporate free speech" cases invoke the tenets of classical liberalism, the ideas advanced in the eighteenth and nineteenth centuries by such writers as John Stuart Mill and Thomas Jefferson to advance the cause of freedom of expression. Under this theory, the truth will eventually emerge from competing points of view so long as debate is not restricted in any way. "The best test of truth is the power of the thought to get itself accepted in the competition of the market," wrote Justice Oliver Wendell Holmes in a 1919 opinion cited recently by Powell.

A number of critics are now beginning to question whether the introduction of corporations and large amounts of money into the political process may turn the competition that Justice Holmes wrote about into a hopelessly unfair contest. In a case involving bill inserts, for example, a number of public interest groups pointed out that a utility company is a state-created monopoly. By using its bills to propagate political views, these groups argued, a utility company gains an essentially cost-free method of communicating with a mass audience, in a fashion that opponents of nuclear power might not be able to match. In short, critics of the series of court rulings are contending both that corporations have fewer rights than individuals and that the nation should aim for a sort of equality of speech. Some constitutional scholars claim that one could never really have exact equality of opportunity to speak. It is asserted that the dominant class is always going to monopolize the major means of communication and that one simply cannot equalize things. Common Cause and other public interest groups claim that under the current system money can be used to drown out free speech. The ones who spend money can dominate the airwaves, and those with insufficient funds don't get heard. That is why Common Cause and other reform minded groups continue fighting for the imposition of limits on campaign spending.

Use of Federal Money in Elections

The powers of the presidency have often been used in hitching state and local officials to the incumbent President's campaign bandwagon with a classic carrot-and-stick routine. In 1980, for example, there was dangling before politicians 29 billion dollars' worth of discretionary funds at the Carter administration's disposal. In order to receive some of the available funds for their communities, officials had to get in harness with President Carter. Republicans and Democrats not supporting the reelection of Carter were shooed away. Federal dollars were flooding into states just before each held its caucus or primary. Right before Pennsylvania's primary in April, the Commerce Department granted 2.2 million dollars to establish an American shoe center in Philadelphia. Four days before New York's March primary, Carter granted 500 million dollars in new urban aid to the state. New Hampshire was awarded 45.2 million dollars in grants in the month before its February primary. In the six weeks before the fall 1979 straw vote in Florida, Carter flooded the state with more than 1 billion dollars in federal funds. A local Democratic congressman marveled: "One more grant and the state will sink under the weight of these projects."[17] A senior White House aid was dispatched to Ohio a few days before the June 3 primary to remind local and state officials of all the federal money they had received from the Carter administration.

Early in the 1980 presidential race, aides to Senator Edward Kennedy accused the Carter administration of using federal aid to threaten or bribe officials into backing the President. Kennedy supporters filed suit charging vote buying, but the Supreme Court refused to hear the case. The record indicates that it was not so much that aid totals were being manipulated. It was just the timing of approvals. Maine, for instance, received 373 million dollars in the year before its primary, no marked increase over 1978. But in the month before its caususes, 75 million dollars' worth of grants were unveiled for Maine—up from 23 million in the previous month. On the day the mayor of East St. Louis, Illinois, endorsed President Carter, he was visited by a White House aid who announced a new 7.8 million dollar courthouse for the city. By comparison, after mayor Jane Byrne of Chicago had endorsed Kennedy, newly-appointed Secretary of Transportation Neil Goldschmidt declared flatly: "I am paying attention to where this money is being spent and who is getting it, and Jane Byrne is not at the top of my list." Goldschmidt's remarks inevitably set off political fireworks. He backed down and promised that Chicago would not be punished. But Carter aides were not bashful to point out that they only wanted to make sure that federal aid did not flow through those who opposed the President. The results in the presidential primaries confirmed that such tactics did work. Carter had the support of 23 of the 31 Democratic governors and all but three of his party's big-city mayors. All this maneuvering by the President usually invites severe criticism from the opposition party. "It's amazing," commented Representative Guy Vander Jagt, House Republican campaign chairman, "that the administration is so good at using the office for domestic politics but can't do a better job using that skill for solving our nation's problems."[19]

In the movie *The Candidate* Robert Redford portrays Bill McKay, a young, attractive lawyer who is approached by a political consultant to run for the United States Senate. At first the lawyer is reluctant to challenge the incumbent senator, but gradually he is talked into running. When he finally agrees to run, he says "I want to go where I want, say what I want, do what I want." Shaking his head, the consultant writes his reply on the back of a matchbook. It says simply, "you lose." Probably most Americans would identify with the honesty and openness of the kind of campaign Bill McKay wants to run. But in reality most campaigns for major public office are far more structured, far more organized, and far more controlled. Individuals who become members of Congress, or governors, let alone Presidents, simply do not go where they want, say what they want, or do what they want. Candidates need a staff and an organization. To succeed a campaign must have structure. In addition to raising and spending money, the candidate must learn about the electorate; he must reach the voters and convince them that he is the best person for the position. At earlier periods of American history, candidates for major office did not need their own organization. The Democratic and Republican parties could usually provide the staff and personnel necessary to stage a campaign. But over the years state party organizations have become weaker and weaker. Usually the party's state committee can give the candidates some help, raise some money, and generally be supportive. But in most situations candidates need to have their own organizations. With as many as one-third of all voters belonging to no party, these organizations must find ways of attracting the independent voters.

During the past three decades, candidates for political office have been able to learn more about voters and what they want. In addition, candidates have been able to reach more voters with less mediation by others, and have been able, or have been forced to campaign for longer periods, with more money and more professional staff. Associated with these trends have been new research methods including opinion polling, new media of communication including television and computerized direct mail, and the weakening of political parties. There have been such changes in nominating politics as the growth of presidential primaries, public financing, and the availability of new campaign professionals.

Plans and Strategies to Win

At the outset of a campaign the candidate and campaign managers usually agree on a plan. The higher the office the more elaborate and detailed is the plan. Most plans sequence campaign events by time. For a local campaign the plan, or activity calendar, might cover only the six months before the first vote. For a statewide campaign a plan is usually agreed upon a year before the primary election. Gubernatorial candidates and, more frequently, presidential candidates, begin their efforts as soon as the previous election is over, almost four years ahead of time. Hamilton Jordan, as aide to the then Governor Jimmy Carter, wrote a memorandum on November 4, 1972, the day before Richard Nixon's landslide reelection. The memo outlined what Carter needed to do to win the Democratic presidential nomination in 1976. Among other things, Jordan emphasized the need for press relations by recommending that " . . . it is necessary that we begin immediately to generate favorable stories and comments in the national press. Stories in the *New York Times* and *Washington Post* do not just happen, but have to be carefully planned and planted . . . you need to appear on television talk shows, write articles for national publications . . . develop and/or maintain a close personal relationship with the principal national columnists and reporters. . . . Fortunately, a disproportionate number of these opinionmakers are southerners by birth and tradition."[20]

Jimmy Carter's plan to win the 1980 election included the near sweep of the South, his home base. Stressing regional loyalty and the need to boost a fellow Southerner, "after more than 100 years, we need a President with no accent," the President hoped to gain 145 electoral votes from the Southern states. Second, Carter planned to carry normally Democratic strongholds in the Northeast, counting on voters to follow habitual patterns and on distrust of Ronald Reagan as an alternative, adding to a total of 244 electoral votes. Third, the Carter plan included challenging Reagan in the West, but with low expectations in a region that went practically solid for Gerald Ford in 1976, and that remained largely hostile to Carter. Counting only Hawaii's four electoral votes, Carter's total was calculated to be 248 electoral votes. Fourth, Carter planned to go over the top in the Midwest by carrying Minnesota, Vice President Mondale's home state, and adding traditionally Democratic Michigan thus achieving a total of 279 electoral votes, 9 more than needed to win. Fifth, the Carter plan provided a cushion by going all out for victories in two Midwest and two Far West states by appealing to wavering Democratic loyalists, labor, and minorities. Ohio, Wisconsin, Oregon, and Washington could add another 51 electoral votes for Carter.[21]

Reagan's strategy consisted of capturing as many Democratic and independent votes as possible, and to build a successful coalition for the 1980 presidential campaign and possibly for the future. The plan also called for a "coast to coast, border to border" campaign, hammering away at Carter's management of the economy and conduct of foreign affairs. According to the plan, Reagan campaigned not only in areas of GOP strength but also in states where Republicans often fared badly: the industrial Midwest, the Northeast, and the rural South. Reagan's plan counted heavily on the support of white Baptists and other politically and socially conservative religious groups, many of whom had grown disillusioned with Carter. In order to win, Reagan had to go beyond his party's conservative wing and draw more votes from blue-collar workers, women, and minority groups that usually vote Democratic.[22]

Independent presidential candidate John Anderson's strategists insisted in 1980 that not only could he win the presidency, but that he could do it by following a trail blazed by Abraham Lincoln in 1860. Anderson's strategy was based on states carried by Lincoln, another Illinois Republican, in a four-man race for the White House in 1860.[23]

Issues and Elections

The role of public policy issues in elections is of special interest to political analysts. In democratic theory, elections are widely viewed as providing a means for citizens to influence their government by selecting among contenders for office. The assumption is that the electorate will shape governmental policy by choosing candidates on the basis of what the candidates stand for. When this does not appear to be the case, there is reason to be critical. In the 1976 presidential campaign there were many complaints that Ford and Carter did not sufficiently address the issues. And in the last month of the 1980 campaign President Carter found it hard to keep his pledge to stick to the high road in what turned into an endless exchange of bitter invective with challenger Ronald Reagan. Two days after Carter announced on October 8 that he would stop making harsh personal attacks on his opponent, the President told a TV interviewer in St. Petersburg, Florida: "I think it would be a bad thing for our country if Governor Reagan were elected President. He would not be a good President, a good man to trust with the affairs of this nation in the future."[24] Carter had promised to change tactics on the advice of top aides, who kept getting reports that the President was hurting himself more than Reagan. "The meanness of Carter's campaign has rubbed folks the wrong way," said Claiborne Darden, an Atlanta-based pollster who found Reagan suddenly pulling ahead in the South, the base of Carter's political strength.

The harsh tone of the 1980 campaign escalated in the last few weeks before the election. Reagan used the word "unforgiveable" to describe Carter's claim that the choice between them was one of peace or war. When Carter refused to apologize, Reagan said: "That's in character." One of Carter's most controversial remarks came in October when he told fellow Democrats" You'll determine whether or not America will be unified or, if I lose this election, whether Americans might be separated, black from white, Jew from Christian, North from South, rural from urban, whether this nation will be guided from a sense of long-range commitment to peace, whether our adversaries will be tempted to end the peace, sound judgment and broad consultation." Reagan responded that Carter was a "badly misinformed and prejudiced man" who was "reaching a point of hysteria that's hard to understand." Former President Ford said Carter was "getting arrogant and mean . . . and on the borderline of demeaning the Presidency."[25] Reagan hurled his own barbs at Carter when he accused the President of opening his campaign in the birthplace of the Ku Klux Klan, "Jimmying" price statistics for political purposes and playing "Russian Roulette" with private pension funds.

A number of political analysts were convinced by the end of October that the 1980 campaign was one of the most negative in decades. The basic strategy of the two candidates appeared to be to attack each other instead of debating the issues, while independent candidate John Anderson claimed neither was worth a ballot. When *New York Times* columnist James Reston called Carter's campaign "vicious and personal," he also added that "even if he wins, it will be difficult for him to regain the support he needs to govern." An editorial of the *Washington Post* joined the President's critics and concluded: "Jimmy Carter is campaigning like a politician gone haywire. . . . Where is 'the President?' " And the Boston *Globe* stated flatly: "The President seems to be bent on discarding his last ace, his reputation as a decent and compassionate man."[26] Carter's outbursts undoubtedly reflected his frustration at running behind a challenger whom he could not fight on his terms. In 1976, it was Carter who was the challenger, attacking the incumbent President Ford. Given Carter's performance in the 1980 campaign, political observers wondered if he knew how to run as an incumbent, especially one with a record that was difficult to defend. A dominant issue in any presidential election campaign is the record of the incumbent administration. This is especially true if the incumbent President is running for reelection. The public has formed an opinion of the effectiveness of the government during the past four years. The candidate of the party in power always gets the credit or takes the blame for whatever has taken place during that period, people vote for or against what has gone before. There is no way to judge what a change of administration will bring, but despite its lack of knowledge when it comes to specific details of certain issues, the public is quite capable of voicing its disapproval of the government's past performance.

Incumbents and Challengers

Any President running for reelection has to defend his record. Any candidate opposing him tries to emphasize the negative aspects, failures, and mistakes of the incumbent. In the 1976 campaign President Ford had to defend the record of his administration while disassociating it from the inglorious end of the Nixon administration. He had to defend the strategy of detente with the Soviet Union, assure that the Soviet arms buildup did not endanger the United States, and still promise to deter Soviet aggression. On the domestic scene, Ford had to blame the continuing high rate of unemployment on previous administrations and Congress while taking credit for the economic recovery that began in 1975. This kind of effort to balance good and bad is the major campaign goal of any incumbent President running for reelection. President Carter's reelection campaign in 1980 was seriously handicapped by his very poor record. When he was elected President the inflation rate was less than 5 percent and he pledged to bring the figure down to 4 percent or less by the end of his term. Actually inflation edged steadily upward, jumping to an annual rate of 18 percent early in 1980, and remaining between 13 and 14 percent by November. Unemployment was nearly 8 percent during the 1976 campaign. Carter promised to cut the rate in half during the next four years. But while he made some progress, the recession deepened by 1980, and unemployment became one of the major issues of the campaign. Carter blamed the rise in the price of imported oil and poor economic conditions beyond his control. Campaigning at a time of a 66-billion-dollar deficit in 1976, Carter promised and failed to balance the federal budget. In foreign policy, Carter pledged to maintain detente with the Soviet Union, deny American support to nations that violate their citizens' human rights, promote peace in the Middle East, officially recognize China, and transfer control of the Panama Canal to Panama. Actually American-Soviet relations chilled even before Russia invaded Afghanistan and the U.S. took counter measures. Many countries received American support despite their repressive policies. And despite the agreement between Israel and Egypt on a "framework" for settling their differences, some of the most crucial details of the peace agreement remained unresolved. Diplomatic relations with China were established and the Senate approved the Panama Canal treaties. But despite strong administration support for the SALT II treaty with the Soviets the Senate failed to ratify it. This kind of effort to balance good and bad is the major campaign goal of any incumbent President running for reelection.

The challenger, by contrast, can offer only the promise of a better performance. Unlike the election of 1976, when there was little discussion or difference between Ford and Carter on the issues, in 1980 substantive disagreement on almost every problem meant voters could decide on issues and policies rather than style or personality. In his successful campaign Reagan promised a series of dramatic steps to reverse many of the policies of President Carter. He assured the American people that unlike Carter, who in 1976 also promised to lower taxes, cut spending, and reduce the federal bureaucracy, his promises were "with an important difference: he intended to keep his promises."[27]

Challenger Reagan blamed President Carter for bringing the United States to a low point in power, prestige, and prosperity. At home, Reagan was determined to unleash the forces of a free market economy to combat high unemployment and inflation. He promised to push for tax cuts totalling 30 percent over three years, a balanced federal budget, and the repeal of many government regulations on business. Abroad, Reagan promised to reestablish America's traditional military superiority and revive the muscular diplomacy of the 1950's. Abandoning the SALT II nuclear-arms pact, Reagan planned to reopen weapons talks with the Soviet Union while beefing up American defenses.

Issues are usually defined as differences between candidates on substantive policy matters. In 1980, for example, Reagan was for a massive tax cut, prayer in public schools, and a constitutional ban on abortions; Carter was against them. Carter, on the other hand, supported a limited tax cut, SALT II, the Equal Rights Amendment, the Departments of Education and Energy, the 55-mile-per-hour speed limit, and a gradually implemented plan of national health insurance; Reagan was against them. As for winning the election, probably the decisive element of the 1980 election was the fact that American voters increasingly make their presidential choices on questions of competence and character, in addition to specific issues, as the results of the election so clearly indicated. Reagan's charge that "Carter has failed on the economy, defense, and diplomacy" found acceptance among a substantial majority of the American people. Sensing defeat in the last few weeks of the campaign, Carter also revealed himself as a very mean and vindictive man as compared to the congenial and self-assured Ronald Reagan. Characteristic of the thinking concerning Carter's competency as President were the comments of Southern pollster Clay Darden: "I had hundreds of people tell me he was totally inept. One fellow told me he considered Carter to be five feet ten inches and the water six feet deep. That overrides any regional pride."[28]

The campaign planning, the targeting of voting groups as potential supporters, the door-knocking, television appearances and debates, all of this is directed to influencing the behavior of potential voters on election day. Whether it is a primary or a general election, the goals of a campaign remain the same: reinforce and activate your supporters and, where possible, convert your opponents. Candidates are concerned, strictly speaking, with winning elections, not winning votes. Votes must be combined or aggregated according to some system for a candidate to be declared a winner. Voting occurs within prescribed geographical areas. States and localities have a variety of choices as to how constituencies will be defined, what their geographical scope will be, and the number of candidates who will compete within them. City Council members might be elected on partisan or non-partisan ballots. Council members and state legislators might be elected in single-member districts in which they must reside, (a city ward or district system) or all candidates in a jurisdiction could compete against one another, with the top vote-getters across the entire area declared the winners (an at-large system). A plurality is usually sufficient to win the general election. This is true of congressional and statewide offices.

In a presidential election each state has electoral votes equal to the number of its U.S. senators (two) and U.S. representatives (based on population). A presidential candidate could win a plurality or even a majority of the popular votes in the general election, yet lose the office because he failed to win a majority of the electoral votes of the states. This actually happened in the nineteenth century. Current concern grows out of the close elections of 1960, 1968, and 1976, in which small changes in popular votes could have altered the Electoral College outcome. In 1960, Kennedy won only 118,000 more popular votes than Nixon. Kennedy carried Illinois by less than 9,000 out of 4.75 million votes cast, but because of the winner-take-all plurality principle that operates in the awarding of electoral votes, Kennedy received all of its electoral votes. In 1968, Humphrey trailed Nixon by only 510,000 popular votes, but lost by a 301–191 margin in the Electoral College. If no candidate wins a majority of electoral votes, and assuming that no electors defied tradition and cast their votes for someone other than the winner in their states, the selection of the President would be left to the U.S. House of Representatives. In the House Congressmen would vote by states with each state having one vote for President. In 1976, Ford trailed Carter by 1,681,000 votes out of 80 million votes cast, but it was only 11,116 votes in Ohio and 35,245 votes in Wisconsin that kept him from retaining the presidency. Winning those two states would have given Ford an Electoral College majority. In the 1960, 1968, and 1976 elections the plurality winner in popular votes also won a majority of electoral votes, but the margins have been so close as to encourage proposals to abolish the Electoral College and have only the popular vote decide the election of the President.

FRANK AND ERNEST by Bob Thaves

RIGHT NOW, I'M JUST THANKFUL THAT ONLY ONE OF THEM CAN BE ELECTED.

THAVES 9-25

Reprinted by permission. © 1980 Newspaper Enterprise Association, Inc.

Analysis of the 1980 Reagan Victory

In sharp contrast to 1960, 1968, and 1976, the presidential election of 1980 gave Ronald Reagan a mandate to get the country back on track. In the process, Americans turned their nation on a new conservative course and, possibly, laid the groundwork for a far-reaching political realignment of the country. The decision was overwhelming. Reagan won 44 states. He received 51 percent of the popular vote and 489 electoral votes to 41 percent and 49 electoral votes for President Carter. Independent candidate John Anderson received 7 percent and no electoral votes. Reagan's Republican Party took control of the Senate, gained 33 seats in the House, and added four governorships. Reagan's victory invited comparison with Nixon's 1972 landslide. Nixon defeated McGovern by more than 20 percentage points in the popular vote and held him to one state, Massachusetts, and the District of Columbia. Carter lost to Reagan by 10 points in a three-man race, and won six states and Washington, D.C. Nixon failed to do much to help the Republican candidates for Congress, but Reagan's coattails helped the GOP capture a dozen Democratic Senate seats and gain control of that body for the first time since 1954. At the same time the Republicans slashed the once top-heavy Democratic majority in the House by 33 seats.

From all evidence, the American people were fed up with the nation's economic situation and with its loss of influence abroad. They blamed President Carter for high inflation, high interest rates, and continuing unemployment. The unending captivity of the 52 American hostages in Iran hurt. "The Iranian thing reminded people of all their frustrations," said Robert Strauss, Carter's campaign chief. Reagan emerged from the election with the makings of a new political alignment that was going to be shaped and tested during his years in the White House.

When American voters went to the polls on November 6, 1980 they made an irrevocable choice with which they would have to live for at least four years. Despite the confusion caused by the shifting positions of the presidential candidates and the hyperbole and innuendo of a disappointing campaign, Carter and Reagan offered, in many ways, clearcut and contrasting choices. Whatever other complaints American voters may have had in 1980, they could not complain that they were confronted with Tweedledum and Tweedledee. The outcome of the electoral struggle between the conservative California Republican and the centrist Georgia Democrat could become one of the true watershed elections of this century, the end of one era and a decisive turn into another. Reagan's victory could affect the role of the Federal Government in domestic affairs, create a clear split in political philosophy between the two major parties, profoundly affect the nation's economy and energy directions, and deeply influence the role America plays on the global stage, thus raising the prospect of increased international tension.

There were striking similarities between the campaigns of 1976 and 1980. In 1976, Carter opposed Big Government, just as Reagan did in 1980. Carter would up settling for some civil service reforms and deregulation of the airline and trucking industries. But these were modest improvements in making the government work rather than any dismantling of the existing power structure. When Reagan promised to "getting the government off the backs of the people," he expressed a deep conviction that "the permanent structure" of Washington bureaucracy stifles free enterprise and individual initiative. When Reagan vowed to reduce the regulatory role of government, eliminate such recent bureaucratic creations as the departments of Education and Energy, and wipe out countless petty federal forms that businessmen must fill out, he could be counted on to fight hard to do just that. Despite talk of a new "pragmatism" in Reagan's thinking, he has not really abandoned any of the fundamental beliefs he has held for many years. For purely political purposes, he has made some token shifts, such as favoring federal aid for both New York City and the Chrysler Corporation. But both were questions that had already been firmly resolved. In short, Reagan really is not a moderate on any major domestic issue, although, as his record as Governor shows, circumstances can force him to change his policies.

Carter and Reagan differed sharply in their views of the role of the Federal Government in solving the nation's social problems. Because of fiscal restraints, Carter had not pushed hard for new programs, but he had no philosophical quarrel with the long-held tenet of the Democratic Party that it is the government's responsibility to help uplift the lowly, keep a watch on the powerful, and legislate equal opportunity. In sharp contrast, Reagan had always been deeply suspicious of Washington's trying to cure the ills of American society. He had been much more inclined to let the job be done on a state or local basis, and wherever possible, by private enterprise rather than by government. There was another fascinating contrast between Carter and Reagan in their views of the proper role of the federal government. Reagan saw no contradiction with his basic philosophy when he waged federal action to support the so-called traditional values. For example, he endorsed constitutional amendments to limit abortion and to permit prayers in the classrooms. Carter, on the other hand, felt that the government should stay out of such matters.

As far as national defense was concerned, Reagan had long demanded an increase in spending to strengthen both strategic and conventional military forces. On specific weapons, Reagan criticized Carter's decision to delay production of the neutron bomb and cancel the B–1 bomber. Carter contended that the cruise missile had made the B–1 obsolete, but he suggested, with a great deal of campaign fanfare, that a bomber employing "stealth" radar-baffling technology might be built instead. Both men supported the new MX missile, although they differed about how the land-based weapon should be deployed. Attacking Carter's foreign policy as conveying a sense of meekness and vacillation, Reagan promised to project more American power abroad. His stands on specific issues were to unfold after inauguration. What was certain was a firmer stance backed by beefed-up armed forces.

The election of 1980 was a referendum on Carter's record as President. By electing Reagan and by replacing old-line liberal lawmakers with more conservative Republicans, voters signaled a sharp turn to the right. It was the most dramatic shift in philosophy of government since a Democratic tide swept Franklin D. Roosevelt into office in 1932. The presidential election of 1980 was no more a "negative landslide" than the 1932 election, when disheartened Republicans rejected their party's incumbent President, Herbert Hooover, and joined the Democrats to elect FDR, whom they scarcely knew. The voters in 1932 had had enough of the sterile, established political philosophy of that time, and they signaled their desire for a basic change. In 1980, the American electorate again signaled a sharp turn, this time rightward.

The accomplishment of the Reagan campaign in 1980 was not that it convinced the majority that conservatism is right. Rather it was that it convinced the majority, in circumstances less than those of an immediate crisis, that conservatism was credible enough to deserve a try. In short, the Reagan majority was made up of one part devout believers and another sympathetic skeptics. The great realignment of our era has not yet taken place. One could only state that it has begun to take place. It can be completed only if the program of conservatism shows promise for success. Based on his solid electoral victory, Ronald Reagan could, within the broad range of conservative principles, chart his own course. After all, he was the victorious candidate of New York no less than California, of Connecticut no less than Mississippi. In applying conservative principles he was unlikely to sacrifice the opportunity for a political majority on the altar of a moral majority. Reagan was to be busy for the next years giving conservatism a fair chance.

Concluding the analysis of the 1980 election one could say that the Reagan landslide, unlike the Nixon victory of 1972, was more than a personal triumph. It was a Republican Party triumph or, if one prefers, a Democratic Party defeat. In the Senate, the Democrats lost more seats to the opposition party in 1980 than they have ever lost in the party's 180-year history. In the House of Representatives, the swing was less dramatic, though still impressive. The GOP picked up 33 seats, its largest gain since 1946. But a look at the electoral map revealed a great deal about the fragility of the Democratic majority. Many of its members still came from the South and clung to their party label from tradition, not ideology. In fact, there was already a conservative majority in the House, and it seemed possible that some Southern Democrats might soon come to caucus with Republicans. To say that the Democrats lost the 1980 election because of Jimmy Carter's personal failures would be like saying that it is the last inch of rain that causes all the damage of a flood. In fact, something else was happening in 1980: a slow but steady rise of the level of opposition to liberalism that swept beyond the banks of presidential politics into the Senate and the House. Reagan's choice of George Bush as his running mate and the many speeches directed at all segments of the American people clearly indicated that he had his eyes not only on the White House, but also on the restoration of a Republican majority. The scope and size of Reagan's victory revived hopes for a "new Republican majority" that had been kindled by Richard Nixon's landslide victory over George McGovern in 1972. The big question for Reagan was whether he could solidify his broad voter support in the following years. For good or ill, he has succeeded in transforming the Republican Party into a party of the agenda in American politics, the party that sets and defines the issues that come before the public for consideration.

Historically, a presidential election in the United States is almost always a referendum on the incumbent. If things seem to be going well domestically and internationally, then the incumbent usually wins favorable ratings and he, or his party, stands a good chance of being reelected. That seemed to be the situation when Ronald Reagan ran for reelection in 1984. In sharp contrast to President Jimmy Carter's so-called "national malaise" speech in 1979, in which he spoke about a "crisis of confidence . . . that strikes at the very heart and soul and spirit of our national will," President Reagan's campaign speeches in 1984 expressed the pride and confidence of Americans in themselves and in their country. Carter's intention of delivering that impassioned, fretful analysis of the country's bad mood in the summer of 1979 was to inspire his countrymen and to plead for a "rebirth of the American spirit." But many Americans felt Carter was blaming them for his failures of leadership. His reputation as a weak and ineffective leader never really recovered after the national malaise speech.

It seems clear now that Carter touched on something real and powerful. Americans in 1979 did feel defensive and dispirited about their nation: cynical about its faded grandeur, alarmed by what felt like the beginnings of economic chaos and despairing of prospects for improvement. The notion of even a quiet national contentment and pride seemed quaint, implausible, slightly foolish. Not so in 1984.

To millions of Americans watching the evening news the images of the traditional Labor Day launching of the 1984 presidential campaign showed the upbeat scene of President Reagan standing tall in bright California sunshine before almost 50,000 enthusiastic citizens. Balloons floated, flags waived, America's upbeat mood was reflected in the optimism of the wildly cheering crowds. "You ain't seen nothing yet," declared the President. "Four more years!," the crowd roared. "You talked me into it!," chortled Reagan, pink cheeks glowing, head bobbing happily. The scene was in sharp contrast to the TV camera's downbeat shot of Democratic presidential candidate Walter Mondale and his running mate Geraldine Ferraro trudging down New York City streets that were almost eerily empty. Smiles fixed, they waved energetically at no one in particular. CBS described the Labor Day parade crowd as "puny." Poor timing was blamed: the 9 A.M. start on a holiday was too early for most New Yorkers. Mondale and Ferraro went on to Merrill, Wisconsin, where Congressman David Obey warmed up the crowd by exclaiming: "When the sun comes out in Merrill, the Democrats are going to win!" Intermittent rain began to fall. Mondale gamely pushed on to Long Beach, California; the sound system failed three times, and each time Mondale had to stop, pretend to be emotionally worked up as he started again. Not many were moved. So stark were the contrasts between the two campaigns that they almost seemed contrived, a TV producer's artifice. They were not. Rarely in American history has one presidential candidate set out on the trail seeming so buoyant and secure, his challenger appearing so dull and snake-bit.

The new upbeat mood of Americans reflecting the fact that the country was at peace, with fading inflation and rising employment and the economy aglow. Americans were feeling more sanguine and comfortable about their country, more than they had felt in two decades. A rebirth of the American spirit as Jimmy Carter had hoped five summers before. It sure felt like it. Even the walkouts called against General Motors on September 22 were reluctant and selective. Optimism became a central element in the Reagan reelection campaign. Ronald Reagan tried to capture the flag by stressing the nation's economic recovery and his huge military buildup. Most Reagan campaign events were masterpieces in Yankee Doodle pondering. The Democrats too made a point of waving Old Glory at their convention in San Francisco. And Mondale insisted "There is not one party that is patriotic and one that is not."

The ebullient surge did not happen overnight, but in fits and starts from the mid 1970's onward. After Vietnam and Watergate, the United States seemed to have lost much of its confidence and moral energy. As measured by the polling firm YANKELOVICH, Skelly and White for *Time* magazine, the nation's mood reached a low point in 1975. During the Bicentennial celebrations all sorts of Americans were surprised to find themselves feeling proud of their country. Between June and September 1976, the survey showed a 10% jump in the "state of the nation index," the fastest rise recorded by Yankelovich before or since. Jimmy Carter's improbable, romantic victory sent spirits still higher, to a level not reached again until 1984. But after his first year, the mood started to sour, declining further after the American embassy staff was imprisoned in Tehran.

A few days after the hostages were freed, a *New York Times* editorial marveled that they had "returned to a different country than the one they knew only 14 months ago." The editorial further stated: "Now the pride and patriotism that many people tried to unfurl during the Bicentennial have erupted without embarrassment. It's not as though there were not more divisions in the country. . . . But on every side, there has suddenly appeared a need to express national unity, to demonstrate an unashamed patriotism." From the onset Reagan benefited from the yearning: the hostages left Iran on his Inauguration Day. In 1981, after a pair of Navy F-14s blasted two Libyan jets over the Gulf of Sidra, the jolt of home-team pride was strong, and the taking of tiny Grenada in 1983 prompted more V-G-Day celebrating than seemed strictly appropriate. Jesse Jackson's presidential candidacy, despite the antogonisms it sometimes stirred, was a salutary symbol of black progress. And the Democrats' historic nomination of Geraldine Ferraro for Vice President added to the political self-esteem. The high spirits surrounding the Los Angeles Olympic Games struck some observers as jingoistic and ungracious. But with American athletes winning nearly everything in sight, the country was able to see itself as it liked: wholesome, powerful, a touch rowdy. Americans could celebrate as they had not done in a long time. Of course, once ignited, a sense of optimism (like pessimism) can be self-fulfilling: the United States has cheered up partly because enough Americans willed such a change. It was the power of positive thinking writ large.

Beneath the political hoopla and the posturing of the candidates lurked many serious and even critical issues, from arms control to tax reform. The newest issue was also one of the nation's oldest: the role religion should play in political and public affairs. In a potentially explosive flare-up, ignited by Reagan and Mondale themselves, such ponderous matters as the federal deficit and relations with the Soviet Union took a back seat to topics more commonly debated by theologians than politicians. While the impact on the election's outcome was uncertain, the religion argument reflected a growing attempt by church groups to exert more influence. Both candidates made major pronouncements concerning the religion issue in September. Mondale attacked Reagan for embracing zealots on the "extreme fringe" who wanted to impose their beliefs on the nation. "Most Americans would be surprised to learn that God is a Republican," he told a Jewish gathering. "No President should attempt to transform policy decision into theological disputes." A few minutes later, Reagan assured the same group that the United States "is and must remain a nation of openness to people of all beliefs." It was a clear attempt to temper remarks at an August prayer breakfast during the Republican National Convention in Dallas, where the President said "religion and politics are necessarily related" and accused opponents of optional school prayer of being "intolerant of religion." Democratic vice presidential candidate Ferraro, an Italian Catholic, was compelled to defend her pro-choice position on abortion after Roman Catholic bishops warned that public actions of Catholic politicians should reflect their private beliefs. Earlier, Ferraro herself was the critic, saying she did not believe Reagan was a good Christian because his policies were "terribly unfair."

From the Reverend Jerry Falwell's benediction at the GOP convention to the sight of Democrats swaying to a gospel singer's strains at their own, religious images filled the political landscape in 1984. Even the much heralded meeting between the President and Soviet foreign minister

Gromyko at the end of September, designed to indicate Reagan's willingness to engage in personal discussions to reduce the serious tensions between the superpowers, was soon overshadowed by the significance of the religion issue. The controversy concerning religion and public policy reflected the complexity of the constitutional separation of church and state in the 1980's. The development went far beyond mere symbolism. Candidates for office as well as the proponents and opponents of the so-called Christian Right movement were aware of the fact that voters in November would elect a President whose Supreme Court appointments and legislative agenda could decide the fate of such emotional issues as abortion, school prayer, and tuition tax credits.

Many observers of the 1984 presidential campaign believed that the issue of religion could make a big difference in the election. Fundamentalist Christian Right groups had claimed credit for helping Reagan win in 1980, particularly in the South, and were now wholeheartedly supporting the President in his campaign for a second term. Recognizing the influence of religious groups, the White House assigned four staff members, up from one during the Carter years, to strengthen ties with religious leaders. As in 1980, the religious conservatives of the Christian Right were also working hard to help elect candidates favoring their position and help defeat those opposing them. Among chief targets of the Fundamentalist Christian Right in 1984 were Democratic Senators Carl Levin of Michigan, Max Baucus of Montana, and David Pryor of Arkansas. In contrast, the fundamentalists worked hard for the reelection of GOP Senator Jesse Helms of North Carolina and Roger Jensen of Iowa. Not unexpectedly, a storm of Democratic criticism arose when in a controversial move Nevada Senator Paul Laxalt, chairman of the Reagan-Bush campaign committee, sent a letter to 80,000 ministers asking them to register members of their congregations and create "a voice that will surely help secure the reelection of President Reagan."

The conservative Christian Right was not the only religious group pursuing political goals in line with its beliefs. On the issue of banning abortions by a constitutional amendment the Roman Catholic bishops supported the Protestant fundamentalists. However, the bishops parted company with the Christian Right by opposing such Reagan administration policies as military aid to El Salvador and MX-missile development. Following their controversial pastoral letter in 1983, condemning the nuclear-arms race, the bishops decided to release the draft of a letter on the U.S. economy in November, after the election. Just as the Christian Right was rallying behind Reagan, the president of the 6.8 million National Baptist Convention was backing Mondale, and in July leaders of the African Methodist Episcopal Church called upon its 3 million members to defeat Reagan. Throughout his unsuccessful campaign for the Democratic nomination Jesse Jackson, a Baptist minister, skillfully used black churches and religious rhetoric. As every student of American history knows, political activism among churches and religious organizations is not unusual in the United States. Churches and individual members of the clergy have regularly spoken out on public issues, ranging from slavery and Prohibition to civil rights and the Vietnam War. In writing the Constitution, the nation's founders did not ban religion from public debate but merely prohibited the establishment of a state religion. What Jefferson called the "wall of separation between church and state" has been understood by most Americans to be broader than the simple, constitutional hands-off requirement. By informal consensus, the separation has been regarded as more of a two-way affair, with undue incursions of organized religion into politics also limited.

As Reagan and Mondale prepared for their first debate on national television the risks were substantial for the two candidates and for the country. Reagan may have misread a national hunger for moral and spiritual uplift as a desire for a specific religious regimen. Mondale could be hurt if he was perceived as insensitive to religious yearnings. In either case, new religious tensions could be stirred. Like many Americans, Reagan has a religious sense that lacks much formal institutional grounding, but nonetheless seems earnest and powerful. Mondale, the pious and principled son of a Methodist minister, has a temperamental aversion to wearing his faith on his sleeve; but he apparently feels his faith deeply and knows what he believes. What was at issue, or should have been, was neither the sincerity nor the righteousness of the two men's beliefs. Rather the point was their basic difference in outlook, reflected within the electorate over the proper role of religion in the political realm. Most people would tend to believe that one cannot ultimately separate religion from politics. The question is how they are to be related in such a way that civility and respect for religious minorities are guaranteed and nurtured. American society has a large capacity for this kind of discourse. Fearful lest they inflame devisive sectarian passions, aides to Reagan and Mondale announced that the candidates were hoping to turn their campaigns back from the brink of religious division. But, as both men pointed out, Americans just now seemed to be searching for deep urgency for stable values and deeper meanings to their lives. That stirring seemed to be emotional enough to keep matters of faith at the forefront of the 1984 campaign.

A few weeks before the election it was mainly the contrasting personalities of Reagan and Mondale which impressed people. Reagan seemed to be on the go, Mondale limping along in search of the spark he so desperately needed in order to save his come-from-behind campaign. Though Reagan's lead in the polls, usually between 15 and 30 points, did not in itself seem insurmountable, there was a growing feeling among political insiders that unless Mondale found a way of personally catching fire with voters, he was heading for political disaster. The Democrats realized that although the choice of Geraldine Ferraro as a running mate did not seem to have helped Mondale in the polls, it may have stemmed further erosion. Many reporters watching Ferraro in the campaign felt that the excitement she generated at almost every stop might translate into an unexpectedly large number of votes for the Democratic ticket in November. Reagan's advisers were eagerly eying what they called "the Big Kill," an overwhelming electoral mandate to carry through the Reagan Revolution. They believed that 1984 could be for the Republicans what 1936 had been for the Democrats: the beginning of at least a decade of party dominance. They felt so confident that they planned to play it safe, to ride the wave of economic prosperity and renewed patriotism. Reagan's speeches were full of phrases like "the surging spirit of boundless opportunity." His television ads were "soft," evocations of the American spirit, not discussions of substantive issues. Reagan did his best to appear "presidential," to float above political acrimony. He didn't even mention his opponent by name. Asked why not by reporters, Reagan loftily replied, "Why should I?" Though the President did not hesitate to turn on his opponent if pressed, Mondale bashing was left to Reagan's surrogates, principally Vice President George Bush. Mondale's aides seemed to have given up hope of making their man telegenic. Journalists described him a "buttoned-up Norwegian" with a reedy voice who liked to say about himself "What you see is what you get." Mondale tried to do his best following House Speaker Tip O'Neill's advice not to allow himself "to be punched around by Reagan," and to "stop acting like a gentleman and come out fighting, to come out slugging." The Democratic candidate indeed tried to show the fire that earned him the name "Fighting Fritz" during the primaries. He took off his jacket, pulled down his tie, and pounded on the lectern. Yet even when giving impashioned speeches in his shirtsleeves, he still appeared, particularly on television, to be stiff, mechanical, and uninspiring. Despite his strong social conscience and heartfelt political convictions, Mondale often seemed incapable of conveying an aura of zeal or inspiring passion. Often when Mondale and Ferraro appeared together Ferraro usually spoke first. When Mondale began speaking the crowd often started to thin out. Hard as he tried, Mondale simply could not engage an audience. But his problem ran deeper than a poor speaking voice and stiff manner. It was not surprising that most people would rather hear Reagan's good tidings than Mondale's jeremiads. Mondale's empathy with the poor was noble but was not really a major problem given the popular mood. Most important of all, Reagan was able to convey a simple, powerful vision of America. Mondale didn't seem to. He was essentially a retail politician, familiar with the back room and able to appeal to special interest groups by intimately understanding their issues and voicing their concerns. After two long and exhausting years campaigning for the presidency, Mondale did not seem to shape an overarching theme or articulate an inspiring vision that could spark zeal among those who agreed with him on specific issues. A few weeks before the election, he didn't seem to be kindling any fires.

By usual standards of presidential performance, Reagan might have been judged a failure. He regularly lost track of his facts, or got them wrong, and he followed his ideology no matter where it led him. Several of his subordinates showed serious lapses in judgment. Many others were mediocre. His budget was preposterously out of balance, and generally his programs tended to hurt the poor. For those reasons, a large minority of Americans were neither charmed nor disarmed by the easy Reagan smile, the low-key Reagan warmth, and the relentless Reagan sincerity. But with most citizens, he seemed to have established an uncanny rapport, beyond political agreement or disagreement, as if he were a favorite twinkly uncle who happened to make it to the Oval Office. Not since Dwight Eisenhower had the American public felt such fondness for its leader, and not since Franklin Roosevelt had any President seemed quite so relaxed about the job. Reagan's political adversaries conceded his special knack for coming across as both engagingly human and larger than life. To explain the American public's generosity toward Reagan, analysts resorted to a kind of mystical non-analysis: some unprecedented "Teflon factor," it was said, permitted him to escape public blame; no failure would stick. Actually the zigzags in support for Reagan indicated that voters were ambivalent, fond of him personally but uneasy about many of his policies.

The Reagan campaign depended to an unusual degree on the candidate's personal magic. But the President did go to the voters with a message and a record in office. He ran on the same broad principles he had run in 1980. Reagan remained devoted to cutting back social programs (although he declined to be specific), to increasing the Pentagon budget further, to hanging tough with the Soviet Union, and to preaching the New Right line on social issues. Moreover, the President was still trying to pitch himself as a crusading outsider, even after a term in the White House because he believed Congress and the bureaucracy were the government. Although his ideological bent was virtually unchanged since 1980, Reagan had accommodated himself to the political exigencies of governing. He adhered to the terms of the unratified SALT II nuclear arms treaty that he had condemned as a candidate four years before. Giving in to public pressure, he met with Soviet Foreign Minister Gromyko a few week before the election to indicate his willingness to sit down and talk with the Soviets. In all, the Democrats found it hard to portray Reagan as a right wing radical. Indeed, the GOP platform its language on taxes and classroom prayer sessions toughened up by the party's dominant right wing at the Dallas convention in August, put Reagan in the remarkable position of running a bit to the left of his party's position. In the last few weeks of the campaign the big question, to be answered at the polls in November, remained: which of the two candidates could attract the crucial swing voters? Both could fairly well count on their core constituencies: for Mondale, minorities, the poor, organized labor; for Reagan, religious fundamentalists, the well-to-do, and conservatives of every stripe. The real battle was for the huge masses of the middle, in particular two key groups: the blue-collar middle class and the smaller but influential core of young professionals sometimes called Yuppies.

In sharp contrast to Labor Day a few weeks before, Mondale and Ferraro celebrated Columbus Day in New York in an atmosphere of triumph and enthusiasm. In the first nationally televised debate between Reagan and Mondale the day before, the Democratic challenger had not only stood his ground facing the President but seemed to have scored points. Although most commentators agreed that neither Reagan nor Mondale emerged as the clear winner in the debate, Democrats were clearly enthusiastic about their candidate's performance. Mondale had presented himself to the nation as an alert, knowledgeable, polite and respectful but determined opponent of the incumbent's policies. There seemed to be nothing "boring" about Fritz Mondale anymore. Still, the question remained, how many of those favoring the President could be persuaded to vote for the Democratic challenger at a time when most, though by no means all, Americans seemed to be satisfied with the status quo. That question, of course could only be answered on Election Day.

Elections are essential to maintain the stability of the democratic process and to permit some change within the system. The American electoral process has fulfilled its basic function of giving the citizens a periodic opportunity to review the performance of their leaders. Elections, however, are only indicators how the electorate feels about the past performance of their representatives. If the voters are roughly in accord with what the government is doing, things will not change. At crucial times in history, though, critical elections have acted as safety valves for the voters' anger. Such elections have allowed the voters to express their dissatisfaction by replacing leaders and the party in power and keeping it out of power for considerable periods of time.

Given the representative nature of the American system, citizens can influence, but not control, the government. Elections merely determine who the people want to have represent and govern them. It is the representatives who effect the real change in policy. The evidence concerning the electoral process does not confirm the most idealistic expectations of popular sovereignty. Neither are elections meaningless. Most basically, the ballot has been an effective means for the protection of citizen interest. Elections in the United States ultimately provide only one, but the most vital, mandate. Echoing the words but not the despair of Linda Loman, in *Death of a Salesman,* the voters give politicians their marching orders: "Attention must be paid." Thus from the standpoint of encouraging governmental responsiveness to the people, the American electoral process appears to be effective.

On November 6, 1984, President Reagan was reelected by a historic landslide because voters of almost every description agreed with his boast that "America's back and standing tall." According to Election Day polls, voters of almost every age, income, occupation, and ethnic group credited the President with fixing an ailing economy and restoring the nation's battered international prestige. As a result, the contest between the seventy-three year old Republican incumbent and Democratic challenger Walter Mondale turned out to be one of the most one-sided in the twentieth century.

In final returns, Reagan won 59 percent of the popular vote and carried every state except Minnesota, the home of his opponent. Mondale also won the District of Columbia, giving him a total of 13 electoral votes. Reagan's total of 525 electoral votes exceeded the 523 won by President Roosevelt over Alf M. Landon in 1936. By carrying 49 states, Reagan tied another record, set by President Richard Nixon in the 1972 election when he defeated George McGovern who carried only Massachusetts.

Despite the magnitude of his victory, Mr. Reagan failed to lift his party to major gains in Congress, and Democratic leaders moved quickly to define the election as a tribute to the President's personal popularity rather than a mandate for unrestricted extension of his economic, social, and military policies. The Republicans lost two seats in the Senate, where they retained a majority of 53 to 47, and they fell short of attaining a working majority in the House of Representatives. The President's party gained 15 new seats in the House, 11 fewer than it lost to the Democrats in 1982. Consequently the new lineup was 252 Democratic and 183 Republican Representatives. Because the Congressional returns were so much less favorable to the Republicans than the Presidential voting, Mr. Reagan promised that he would "take his case to the people" in pursuing a conservative economic agenda. At another news conference, White House chief of staff James A. Baker indicated that the second term, would bring a renewed effort to cut Federal spending but promised that two areas, defense and social security, would be sacrosanct. One area of clear bipartisan agreement emerged: that President Reagan would not face an easy time with a House of Representatives that the Democrats still controlled by 71 seats. Speaker of the House "Tip" O'Neill flatly denied that "there was any mandate out there whatsoever," and Republicans acknowledged that the continued Democratic dominance promised to make it very difficult to push some of the things the President wanted through Congress. However, few Republicans endorsed the Democrats' assertions that their party's relatively strong showing in Congress meant that the voters were trying to limit Mr. Reagan's ability to institutionalize the conservative philosophy he brought to Washington four years before.

Since surveys of voters leaving polling places detected the Reagan landslide long before the voting was over, the House and Senate races provided most of the suspense on Election Day. In a contest that drew wide national attention, Senator Jesse Helms of North Carolina, a Republican with a following among conservative religious leaders, defeated Governor James B. Hunt, Jr. after the most expensive Senate campaign ever. Together, the two men spent $22 million in a contest polarized along religious and racial lines. Fundamentalist white Protestants voted for Helms by a 3-to-1 margin, while more than 85 percent of the black voters went for Hunt. In another important Senate contest, Charles H. Percy of Illinois, chairman of the Foreign Relations Committee, lost to representative Paul Simon, a liberal Democrat who survived despite Percy's effort to grasp the President's coattails. In sum, the Congressional returns for the Republicans seemed anemic compared with gains they made behind Mr. Reagan in 1980. Then, they gained 12 Senate seats to take control of that chamber and also picked up 33 House seats. As for governorships, the Republicans were aided by President Reagan's historic sweep and captured 8 of 13 governors' seats that were up for grabs in 1984. Thus despite stunning defeats of two sitting Republican governors and the election of a female Democrat in Vermont, the Republicans put a small dent in the ranks of Democrats occupying most governors' mansions. Since six of the contested seats were held by Republicans, the GOP victories represented a gain of only two, with Democrats holding 35 governors' offices to the Republicans' 15.

In 1984, President Reagan succeeded in expanding beyond the 51 percent he attained in 1980, and he also reached deeper into some traditionally Democratic constituencies. Black and Jewish voters were exceptions to this pattern, according to exit polls by the *New York Times* and CBS News: 90 percent of the black voters voted for Mr. Mondale, and Reagan got only 9 percent, against the 11 percent he got in 1980. Mr. Mondale won 66 percent of the Jewish voters, according to *The New York Times*/CBS News Poll, and Mr. Reagan 32 percent. In 1980, Mr. Reagan got 39 percent of the Jewish vote in defeating President Carter, who got 45 percent. Nationally, President Reagan got two-thirds of the white voters, and in some Southern states the racial polarization was striking. For example, more than 80 percent of the white voters in Alabama and Mississippi voted for Reagan. The poll also showed that leaders of organized labor who endorsed Mondale already in 1983, fell dramatically short of delivering the labor vote for the Democrat. A quarter of the nation's voters live in union households, and President Reagan got 45 percent of those voters to Mondale's 53 percent. Although the poll found Reagan ran more strongly among men than among women, only in one state did the difference prove decisive. Mondale carried Minnesota on the strength of his stronger showing among women. Three Democratic Senate candidates, Paul Simon in Illinois, John F. Kerry of Massachusetts, and Senator Carl Levin of Michigan, won on the basis of their additional support among women. Women also provided the margin of victory for Madeleine Kunin's election as the Governor of Vermont. On the negative side, Geraldine Ferraro failed to carry her home state of New York.

President Reagan's landslide election victory was more than an endorsement of certain policies or a defeat of a ragged Democratic army. Many experts felt it was an enormous personal triumph establishing Reagan as the most powerful political phenomenon in decades. For more than a year, as the opinion polls showed Reagan strong against sharp criticism from the group of Democratic candidates running for President, political experts began realizing that the President had become more than a politician. He had become, in their view, a phenomenon existing outside his policies, many of which were not being embraced nearly as warmly by Americans. Reagan's aides and critics disagreed about many things but there was surprising agreement on many of the facts that contributed to his popularity. More than his predecessors, Reagan had been able to articulate a sweeping sense of the direction in which he wanted to take the country. Aides of Mondale admitted that their candidate never succeeded in giving similar coherence to his own collection of policies. Among the other factors adding to Reagan's popularity was the simplicity and consistency of his message, his practice of speaking in the broadest of terms about values rather than issues, his identification with America's myths and the apparent sincerity of his beliefs. In the view of most observers, Reagan's major asset was the perception of his qualities as a leader.

Added to the phenomenon of his consistency was Reagan's willingness to repeat what he said over and over again. It was hard to imagine that Reagan could have been as successful as he was without his abilities as a television performer, without the smoothness of his voice and the seeming genuineness of his smile. Finally, Reagan was a master at evoking a nostaligic view of America which was rooted in small-town values of hard work, neighborhoods, and patriotism, that he had long embraced. To those who said that it was a Hollywood vision of America, Reagan supporters said that America was a part of his own past, and something in which he genuinely believed. There was enough evidence in 1984 that people felt they agreed with Reagan even if they really didn't. The question was why should they have felt that way? Apparently because people felt Reagan's policies were working. Americans have a pragmatic approach to the issues: whatever works must be right. If big government policies had worked during the New Deal, then they had probably been right, at least for that time. If Reagan's anti-government policies were working in the 1980s then they were probably right, at least for the time being. The American public's basic conviction could be summed up in the phrase "One doesn't quarrel with success."

Notes

1. Quoted in Joseph A. Schlesinger, *Ambition and Politics* (Skokie, Illinois: Rand McNally, 1966), p. 17.
2. See J. P. Robinson, "Public Reaction to Political Protest: Chicago, 1968," *Public Opinion Quarterly,* 34 (Spring 1970), pp. 1–9.
3. *Time,* July 28, 1980, pp. 22–23.
4. "Reagan Takes Command," *Time,* July 21, 1980, pp. 6–7.
5. *Los Angeles Times,* August 13, 1980, p. 1.
6. *Time,* July 28, 1980.
7. "Moyer's Eyeful Tower," *Los Angles Times,* August 14, 1980 Part VI, p. 1.
8. Neil Hickley, "It's a $40-Million Circus," *TV Guide,* July 12, 1980, pp. 4–8.
9. Quoted in "What's Wrong with the Way Americans Pick a President," *U.S. News and World Report,* March 31, 1980, p. 35.
10. "Now Television's the Kingmaker," *TV Guide,* May 10, 1980, pp. 4–8.
11. Quoted in George Thayer, *Who Shakes the Money Tree?*(New York: Simon and Schuster, 1973), p. 208.
12. See Herbert E. Alexander, *Financing Politics* (Washington: Congressional Quarterly, 1976), pp. 20, 27, and *CQ Guide to Current American Government, Fall 1980* (Washington: Congressional Quarterly, 1980), pp. 37 and 44.
13. "Campaign 1980: Now the Race is Really On," *Los Angeles Times,* August 31, 1980, Part V, p. 1.
14. Thayer, *op. cit.,* p. 165.
15. Ibid., p. 166.
16. Ibid.
17. "White House Grants: Carter's $29 Billion Campaign Fund?," *U.S. News and World Report,* June 9, 1980, p. 27.
18. Ibid.
19. Ibid.
20. Martin Schram, *Running for President* (New York: Pocket Books, 1976), pp. 67–69.
21. "Carter's Second Chance," *U.S. News and World Report,* August 25, 1980, pp. 16–19.
22. "Reagan Takes Command," ibid., July 21, 1980, pp. 6–10.
23. "A Plan for Winning the Presidency," ibid., May 19, 1980, pp. 31–34.
24. Quoted in "A Biting, Gouging Race for President," ibid., October 20, 1980, p. 11.
25. "A Vow to Zip His Lip," *Time,* October 20, 1980, p. 16.
26. Ibid.
27. "Head To Head On the Issues," *U.S. News and World Report,* October 6, 1980, p. 59.
28. *Los Angeles Times,* November 6, 1980, p. 1.

For Further Reading

Abranison, Paul R. et al, *Change and Continuity in the 1980 Elections,* revised edition, Washington, D.C., Congressional Quarterly, 1982.

Alexander, Herbert E. *Financing Politics: Money, Elections and Political Reforms* 2nd ed. Washington, D.C.: Congressional Quarterly Press, 1980.

Barber, James. *The Pulse of Politics: Electing Presidents in the Media Age.* New York: W. W. Norton, 1980.

Baxter, Sandra and Marjorie Lansing. *Women and Politics: The Invisible Majority.* Ann Arbor, Michigan: University of Michigan Press, 1980.

Peirce, Neil and Lawrence Longley.*The People's President: The Electoral College in American History and the Direct-Vote Alternative.* New Haven, Conn.: Yale University Press, 1981.

Polsby, Nelson and Aaron B. Wildawsky. *Presidential Elections: Strategies of American Electoral Politics* 6th ed. New York: Charles Scribner's Sons, 1984.

Name _____

Section _____

Date _____

Review Questions for Chapter 9: Campaigns and Elections

1. Nominations _____

_____

_____

_____

_____

2. Primaries _____

_____

_____

_____

_____

3. Conventions _____

_____

_____

_____

_____

4. Political "Experts" _____

_____

_____

_____

_____

5. "Mother's Milk of Politics" _____

_____

_____

_____

_____

6. Federal Election Commission _____

_____

_____

_____

_____

7. Corporation _____

_____

_____

_____

_____

8. First National Bank v. Bellotti (1978) _____

_____

_____

_____

_____

9. Buckley v. Valeo (1976) _____

_____

_____

_____

_____

10. John Anderson _____

_____

_____

_____

_____

11. "New Republican Majority" _____

_____

_____

_____

_____

Essay Study Questions

1. Discuss the reasons why people choose to run for political office.
2. How does television influence political campaigns?
3. How are political campaigns financed? Can you support any reforms?
4. Discuss the different plans and strategies utilized in waging political campaigns.

Chapter 10

Voting Behavior

Most Americans do not hold truly meaningful political attitudes because most individuals' opinions or belief systems consist primarily of "nonattitudes," lacking consistency and stability. Politics does not compete in interest with sports, local gossip, and television dramas. Given this low concern of salience of politics, few Americans vote on the basis of issues.

Political Scientist Philip E. Converse

American voters are not fools. They are neither strait-jacketed by social determinants nor moved by subconscious urges triggered by devilishly skillful propagandists. Voters are moved by concern about central and relevant questions of public policy, of governmental performance, and of executive personality.

Political Scientist V. O. Key

Why do people vote for the presidential candidate of one party and the Congressional candidates of another? Why do so many Americans fail to vote? What is the implication of low levels of participation in presidential elections? Analyses of voting behavior tell us much about the political perceptions of citizens. They also help explain the actions of political leaders.

The central focus of research on American political behavior is vote choice, especially presidential vote choice. No other single form of mass political activity has the popular interest or analytic significance that surrounds the selection of a President every four years. Most Americans follow presidential campaigns with greater attention than they give other elections. The results of this balloting are reported and analyzed far more extensively than any other.

Ever since V. O. Key challenged the findings published by a group of Michigan researchers in *The American Voter* and other studies concerning the uninformed, often irrational, and disinterested voters of the 1950's, political analysts have claimed that the American electorate has changed substantially. Events like the Cold War, the civil rights and student movements, the Vietnam War, Watergate, the energy crisis, and the recession of the 1970's, have had a profound effect on the electorate.[1] It can be argued that the Eisenhower years were a peculiarly benign time, one in which few political events which stirred the electorate occurred. Because of the relatively quiet political atmosphere of the 1950's, some analysts have concluded that it is no wonder that *The American Voter* found such a disinterested and docile citizenry.

Changes in Electoral Behavior

The turmoil of the 1960's and 1970's brought about a number of changes in the behavior of the electorate. Probably the most often cited change in American electoral behavior has been the decline of partisanship and the role of parties. The evidence indicates significant increases in the

By Bob Englehart. Copyright © 1977 Copley News Service. Reprinted by permission.

number of persons who classify themselves as Independents rather than Republicans or Democrats. In addition, many other voters who claim to be partisan actually vote as we might expect independents to vote. For example, they frequently vote a split-ticket. This split-ticket voting has resulted in an increase of split outcomes which occur when a state or congressional district votes for the candidate of one party for one office and a candidate of the other party for another office. One of the many examples for such voting behavior occurred in the 1980 elections in Nevada. The voters of that state voted overwhelmingly for Reagan as President. At the same time, however, they reelected Democratic Representative Jim Santini and voted for a predominantly Democratic state legislature. Substantial, split-ticket, non-party voting must have occurred to cause this split outcome. Another aspect of the decline in partisanship involves an increase in the role of issues and candidate images in voting behavior. A number of researchers argue that because voters increasingly vote on the basis of these two factors, they have less need to depend on their partisanship. Gerald Pomper has articulated most clearly the position of political scientists who perceive a rising role for issues in electoral behavior. Based on the evidence, Pomper concludes that in contrast to the past, party loyalty and policy views are significantly related. Furthermore, he and other analysts claim that the effect of issues on the vote has increased considerably, while the effect of partisanship has decreased. These important changes, in addition to a developing ideological coherence in voters' attitudes, are claimed to be altering the way most citizens think about political parties, candidates, and issues.[2] *The American Voter* summarized the forces present in any voting decision as issues, images, and partisanship.[3] The last factor was considered the primary determinant in most Americans' voting decisions. Since the publication of *The American Voter* and the 1950's, most political scientists agree there have been increases in the roles played by issues and images in voter decision making. As for the many pessimistic predictions about the demise of the American party system, D. B. Hill and N. R. Luttbeg sum up the conclusions of most political scientists who believe that "some clouds are beginning to form; but the storm has not fully arrived."[4] Only the future will tell whether the roles of increasing independency and issue voting have been exaggerated. The return of the Republican Party to power in 1980, following its decline after Richard Nixon's resignation in 1973, would seem to confirm the guarded optimism concerning the vitality of the two major parties. One can assume that partisanship will continue to be a dynamic force in American politics.

Analysts of voting behavior saw Americans move from an attitude of benign affection for government during the 1950's and early 1960's to a state of apparent distrust, lack of confidence, and alienation in the 1970's. *The American Voter,* dating from the period of trust in government, gave scant attention in its conceptualization to distrust, protests, or any form of violent political behavior. In contrast, survey data from the 1960's and 1970's showed a dramatic decline in public confidence in elections and parties, to the point where negative attitudes tended to prevail. In their study *American Parties in Decline,* political scientists W. J. Crotty and Gary C. Jacobson concluded that "The American electorate of the late twentieth century is a "turned-off" electorate."[5] In short, voting behavior in the 1970's was characterized by low levels of voter participation, a decline in party loyalty, split-ticket voting, an increasing emphasis on issue voting, and unpredictable swings in outcomes and vote margins from one election to the next.

In a national survey, conducted by the Center for Political Studies in 1976, respondents were asked which national political institution—President, Congress, Supreme Court, or political parties—they least trusted to do the right thing. The overwhelming majority, 70 percent, singled out parties as the institution they least trusted. In the same survey, 64 percent of the respondents agreed that political parties were interested only in people's votes, not in their opinions.[6] The available data from other opinion polls in the 1970's tended to confirm what these results suggested: the American people had limited faith in the electoral process, and suspicion, distrust, and cynicism characterized the reaction of many to elections, candidates, and political parties. The growth of negative attitudes toward the electoral process was part of a broader decline in the confidence that Americans had in their political institutions. The 1960's and 1970's were a period of growing political alienation, which was manifested in public reactions along several dimensions. In general, people expressed far less confidence in their government, less trust in their political leaders, and less faith in the political process. These negative attitudes began to spread in the mid-1960's and continued to grow through the 1970's.[7]

Reasons for the Loss of Confidence
In the Government and Big Interests

Most nationwide surveys of public opinion in the 1970's showed that positive evaluations of government and of the political process declined noticeably since about 1964. That the crisis of confidence began in 1964 is very important. Many times journalists and other political observers claimed that public disaffection was a result of the Watergate scandal and its related events. But the evidence indicates that people had begun to doubt their leaders long before Richard Nixon was elected President in 1968.[8] There is no doubt that the events associated with Watergate stimulated and accelerated the trend toward a cynical public. But it would be a mistake to put all of the blame for it on Watergate. It was especially the Vietnam War that deeply divided the American people, turned their attention to the deceitful handling of that conflict by the government, and produced intense dissatisfaction from both the left and the right with government policy. The urban riots and domestic unrest of the late 1960's, exemplified by the violent demonstrations surrounding the 1968 Democratic National Convention, also contributed to a growing lack of confidence in the system. Coming when it did, Watergate did more than just discredit the Nixon administration and embarrass the Republican Party; it reinforced and fostered the already growing feeling that political leaders were not to be trusted. Although there have not been such divisive issues or events in the late 1970's, the inability of the Carter administration to deal with the problems of inflation, unemployment, energy, and foreign policy has focused the attention of the public on the ineffectiveness of the incumbent political leadership. The impressive victory of Reagan over Carter demonstrated the belief of the electorate that a change in leadership could bring about improvements.

In its quadrennial studies of political attitudes, the University of Michigan Survey Research Center published the results of two highly revealing surveys in 1964 and 1974. The decline in political trust is best captured in the respondents' answers to the first question of how much of the time they think they can trust the government in Washington to do what is right. In 1964, 76 percent of those surveyed felt that you can trust the government in Washington at least most of the time to do what is right. By 1974, this figure had declined to 36 percent. So, in one decade the American public made a substantial reassessment of its orientations toward the trustworthiness of Washington.[9]

Government is not the only institution singled out for public criticism. The second item in the University of Michigan Survey Research Center's questionnaire on "Measures of Alienation, Trust and Efficacy, 1964–1978" suggests that Americans grew increasingly distrustful of big interests during the decade between 1964 and 1974. Only 29 percent felt that government was run by a few big interest groups in 1964. By 1974, more than twice that number, 65 percent, believed that government was run by a few big interest groups looking out for themselves. Additional evidence indicates that distrust has been generalized to other levels of government and institutions as well.

Political efficacy is the term used by political analysts to refer to a person's belief that he or she can influence government. The evidence seems to indicate that there has been an increase in the belief that we cannot have much to say about what the government does. Americans in the mid-seventies were less likely to feel politically efficacious than was the populace in the mid-sixties. The trend in alienation and powerlessness was clearly demonstrated by the data produced by the University of Michigan survey. The items used by the Michigan questionnaire form the basis of a scale of alienation, powerlessness, and cynicism used by the Louis Harris polling firm since 1966. The data show that between 1966 and 1977 there was an increase of 32 percent in the average percentage of respondents reporting feelings of alienation and powerlessness as measured by the scale. This average change was influenced most by massive changes in the attitudes on two of the items. The second greatest change came on the item which measured the belief that "The rich get richer and the poor get poorer." In 1966, only 45 percent of the Harris sample held this belief. By 1977, 76 percent agreed with this statement, for a change of 31 percent between 1966 and 1977. An even greater change was noted on the item which asked respondents to agree or disagree that "People running the country don't really care what happens to you." Only 26 percent of the Harris sample agreed with this statement in 1966, but by 1977 a clear majority of 60 percent felt that this was true.[10] The last question relates to one aspect of political efficacy which political analysts call systems efficacy. An individual who agrees that the people running the country don't really care what happens to you is saying that the individual has little power. One can conclude that both the University of Michigan Survey Research Center items and the Louis Harris data suggested that political alienation in the 1970's increased on almost every dimension.

Voters' High Regard for the System and Low Estimate of Politicians

Political analysts disagree about the nature of contemporary mass disaffection. One of the two opposing points of view contends that recent declines in traditional support indicators, such as those discussed previously, portend great danger for the American system of government. David Easton has expressed the view of political scientists who believe the United States is now suffering a "crisis of regime."[11] Opposed to this view is one which holds that Americans are not so much alienated from what Easton calls the regime as they are from incumbent officeholders. Most of the polls conducted in connection with the 1980 general elections tended to support the latter view. A survey prepared by *Los Angeles Times* public opinion analyst George Skelton for the *Times* and the John F. Kennedy School of Government at Harvard University was a serious and most up-to-date effort to measure the attitude of Americans toward the primaries, the politicians, the

FRANK AND ERNEST

Reprinted by permission. © 1980 Newspaper Enterprise Association, Inc.

parties, the press, and the political system generally. Those surveyed were asked whether they were satisfied or dissatisfied with these elements of the American political process: political parties, debates between candidates, public financing of campaigns, national nominating conventions, opinion polls, and primaries. The results of the survey confirmed the view that most Americans "like the political system, but not the politicians" in power who were blamed for the nation's problems.[12]

The *Los Angeles Times* poll interviewed 1,047 adults, including 766 registered voters, and came up with the following specific results: most Americans like primaries, the polls, the debates, the national conventions, and even the use of their tax money to help finance campaigns. They thought the voters in primary elections should have more influence over who become the nominees, and felt that contributors, political leaders, and special interest groups had too much power. Voters admitted to learning little during the primaries about a candidates' leadership qualities, administrative abilities, solutions to problems, and trustworthiness. "Taking everything into consideration," 8 in 10 said the nation had a "good" way of "choosing the people who are going to run for President." When measured against America's system of business and industry, the presidential nominating process rated virtually as high, 71 percent considering business and industry "basically sound" and 70 percent considering the nominating process in the same category. The political system was considered "basically sound" by 62 percent, far surpassing in esteem the nation's "system of administering justice," which was viewed "basically sound" by only 49 percent. The political system was particularly favored by people with at least some college education and those whose families earn more than $25,000 annually.

The voters' high regard for the political system contrasted sharply with their low estimation of politicians. Those surveyed were asked "which one or two of the following kinds of people do you respect the most: policemen, public officeholders, newsmen, judges, businessmen, ministers or union leaders?" Ministers and policemen were by far the most respected. The least respected were union leaders and officeholders. The "personal qualities" people said were missing the most in politicians who run for office were "honesty" and "leadership." Roughly three-fourths of those surveyed said they were able to learn only "a little" during the campaigns about whether the candidates could be trusted, whether "they are able to run the country effectively" and "how they will solve the important problems of the country." But a majority nevertheless felt that primary voters should have more influence over who is nominated. Those interviewed said these elements, in order, should have less influence: campaign contributors, party leaders and officeholders, organized groups with strong beliefs, people not registered in the party, and the press.

Of those surveyed, 74 percent said they "regularly follow news about politics and government by reading newspapers." This was particularly true of college-educated and higher income people. An even larger number, 85 percent, said they "regularly watch television news." This was especially true of Democrats. The most interesting running news story for those surveyed was the fate of the American hostages held in Iran, with 92 percent saying they were following it "closely." After that came energy and gas shortages, 86 percent; which prices were going up and down, 78 percent; relations between Israel and the Arab countries, 52 percent; the 1980 presidential campaign, 51 percent (another 41 percent were following it "casually"); what happened to Senator Kennedy at Chappaquiddick, 29 percent; and the stock market, 15 percent. Slightly more than half those surveyed desired more news about the presidential campaign; only one in ten wanted less. But almost half also said they wanted less news about Chappaquiddick, with only roughly one-fourth wanting more. People particularly asked for more news about energy prices. The *Los Angeles Times* survey considered the margin of error for this size sample about 4 percent in either direction.

The Average Voter is Conservative
but Anti-Washington

All in all, the conclusion is inescapable that the average American voter in the 1980's is basically conservative in his views concerning the political process. He is not the uninformed and disinterested citizen as described in *The American Voter*. The results of the 1980 general election also confirm the fact that voter dissatisfaction is stronger with the performance of politicians whose lack of leadership and inefficiency are blamed for the problems of the nation. That the majority of voters are conservative concerning the political process should not conceal the fact that there is a strong anti-Washington sentiment among Americans. In 1976, Jimmy Carter profited from his strong anti-Washington anti-bureaucracy stand in his bid for the presidency. And in 1980, Reagan's promise to "get the government off the backs of the people" gained him the votes of those who were sick and tired of the inefficiency, corruption, and general waste of the taxpayers' money. The anti-Washington sentiment has often been misinterpreted as anti-political system. Some voting behavior studies fail to draw the distinction between the two different sources of dissatisfaction.

One of the most conspicuous examples of the anti-Washington reaction of American voters was the voting pattern of the South in the 1980 presidential election. According to a survey by the Southern Regional Council, a bipartisan, nonprofit research organization, white Southerners voted overwhelmingly for Ronald Reagan and rejected their fellow-Southerner Jimmy Carter. Black voters, on the other hand, gave President Carter even stronger support than he got from them in 1976. But the split of the vote, along almost strictly racial lines in Carter's native region, was interpreted by the Council's executive director, Steve Smitts, as essentially a "negative," or "anti-Washington," response by voters in 43 surveyed precincts of 11 states of the Old Confederacy. The Republicans' near-sweep of the South gave Reagan every state in the region except Carter's native Georgia. It was not "Reagan's coattails," Smitts said, that left only two Southern states, Louisiana and Arkansas, without a Republican United States Senator. Rather, he said, it was the "anti-Washington vote, the feeling here that the government is giving the country away . . . that the entire status of the country was deteriorating while its social programs gave preference to blacks."[13]

In its cover story "The Mood of the Voter" *Time* magazine described the American electorate in September 1980 as "disenchanted, but not apathetic." The American voter cared about issues, although he was much more concerned about character. He longed for a strong person to trust, but was fearful of strength lacking sound judgment. Leery of weakness, but edgy about brashness, all too mindful of the disappointments of the past, he sought hope in the future. Leaning toward one man, but often out of desperation and a sense of disdain for the others. Uncommitted, unpredictable. Having described the American voter in these terms,[14] *Time* accepted the conclusions of most of the public opinion polls which declared the American electorate evenly divided between Carter and Reagan with 39 percent for each of the two candidates and 15 percent for

Anderson. The Yankelovich, Skelly and White polls, based on a national sample of 1,644 registered voters interviewed between August 26 and 28 for *Time,* indicated a surprisingly low 7 percent of voters who claimed to be undecided about whom they favored. But the survey also disclosed how shaky those preferences were at the time when the poll was taken. Fully 55 percent said they were not "personally interested or excited about" any of the candidates. Only 11 percent reported genuine enthusiasm for Reagan, and a mere 9 percent felt that way about Carter and 6 percent about Anderson. In fact, much of the support given their preferred candidates was based on voters' opposition to the others; the choices were essentially anti-votes. Thus 43 percent of the voters who preferred Reagan said they did so because they were "really voting against Carter." Similarly, 34 percent of Carter's supporters said their choice was based on opposition to Reagan, while a hefty 61 percent of Anderson's followers admitted that they were motivated by being "against Carter and Reagan."

Political Polls

Were the polls wrong in the 1980 presidential election, claiming that the American electorate was almost evenly divided between Carter and Reagan before November 4? Many Americans, including political analysts, must have thought so. They heard on Sunday and Monday before the election that Carter and Reagan were running about even. Then, on election night, they saw Reagan win by 10 percent and carry practically every state in every part of the country. Even professional analysts and journalists were shocked by the size of Reagan's victory. Obviously, the polls had not prepared observers for what happened on November 4, 1980. Had they been wrong? Are political polls worthless?

One could argue that while most pollsters were wrong as far as the outcome of the 1980 presidential election was concerned, polls are still useful for the study of American voting behavior. The first thing to realize is that a poll is not a prediction, but a picture—to some extent an imprecise picture—of opinion at the time the poll was taken. Nonetheless, the apparent discrepancies between the published polls and the results do need to be explained. One can point out three important reasons for the difference. The first one relates to the differential in turnout between Democrats and Republicans, which the polls did not take into account. Nationally, turnout was down: only 52 percent of those eligible to vote actually bothered to do so. But the biggest decline in turnout was among Democrats. Throughout 1980, samplings of voter opinion showed greater interest in the election and enthusiasm for the candidates among Republicans than Democrats. So it is reasonable to suppose that the electorate in 1980 was 1 or 2 percent more Republican than in a year like 1974, when the Democrats were enthusiastic and the Republicans down-hearted. Of course, turnout did not affect the result of the presidential election. But it increased Reagan's margin, and it hurt Democrats in Senate and House races. The second reason for the discrepancy between the published polls and the actual results was the significant change in voters' attitudes in the week before the election. In fact, there were two shifts. On Thursday, two nights after the debate between Reagan and Carter, telephone polls for both candidates showed a 5 percent increase in support for Reagan. The former California governor's low-key, unthreatening performance in the debate resolved many voters' doubts about him and left them determined to vote against Carter. That Thursday-Friday surge for Reagan was confirmed in the networks' Election Day polls of voters. Unfortunately for Carter, and for the reputation of the pollsters, there was another surge on Sunday and Monday. The Gallup organization finished its interviews on Saturday night, and so, of course, did not pick up this change, but Patrick Caddell, polling for Carter, and Richard Wirthlin, polling for Reagan, did. Caddell was convinced enough of the strength of the trend to inform Carter on Monday that his case was hopeless.

The networks' exit polling, which depends on voters filling out questionnaires as they leave their voting booths, was not sophisticated enough to explain the Sunday-Monday surge. But we do know what dominated the news on those two days: the crisis in Iran. On Sunday, the Iranian parliament set four conditions for the release of the American hostages. Carter administration officials made it clear that they were willing to discuss the Iranians' terms and to send arms to Iran even though it was at war with Iraq. The press speculated that this apparent breakthrough on the hostage issue would help Carter. Apparently it did just the opposite. In the course of the campaign Carter had gained against Reagan in some states by portraying the differences between them on foreign policy as a matter of war versus peace. But on that final weekend the difference between them came to be seen as a matter of strength versus weakness. Carter seemed weak both because he once again proved incapable of bringing the hostages home and because he appeared too willing to make concessions. He may have been operating on the assumption that Americans in their sentimental concern for the hostages would be willing to sacrifice anything to get them back. But Republican polling that week showed that three out of four voters would reject sending arms to Iran even if that were the only solution. It is possible to advance the hypothesis that the hostage issue caused the Sunday-Monday surge for Reagan, the movement that took the election out of the too-close-to-call category and turned it into a landslide.

There was a third reason for the apparent discrepancy between the published polls and the result, and that was the basic underlying attitude toward President Carter's performance. Except for the first month after the taking of the hostages, when his popularity swelled, Carter had a dreadful rating since 1978. During the summer and fall of 1979, no more than 30 percent of those polled rated his performance favorably. Some analysts pointed out as early as February 1980, that Reagan could win if he could convince people that he was reasonably competent and reliable. At times he seemed to be having trouble doing that. But sooner or later, sometime before the end of the campaign, in the debate or in another context, it was inevitable that voters were going to examine him closely and decide whether he was an acceptable alternative to the incumbent they wanted to be rid of. Deeply disappointed by the outcome of the election, some Carter supporters felt that if the events of the last week had gone differently, the President would have been reelected. Perhaps. Given the choice of an incumbent with a poor job rating and a challenger with little experience in the national government, voters will naturally hesitate before making a decision. But if the challenger performs reasonably well, there is little question what that decision will be. It is fair to assume that, even if there had been no debate or no hostage crisis, other events would have helped Reagan in the last week, perhaps too late for the national polls to notice or absorb. The returns on election day were not an accident or a freak response to last-minute events. The outcome of the 1980 presidential election was the logical expression of voters' long-held doubts about Jimmy Carter, and tends to support the view that voters are moved by concern about central and relevant questions of public policy, of governmental performance, and of executive performance.

Carter managed to stir controversy even in his concession speech on election night. When he formally conceded to Reagan from Washington, D.C., it was still more than an hour before polls closed on the West Coast. Election officials reported that many voters left the voting lines when word was passed of Carter's admission of defeat. There were also complaints made about the early call of the election by NBC, more than one hour before Carter formally gave up. Some Democrats blamed Carter's early concession statement for the defeat of several Western Democrats in close contests. March Fong Eu, California's Democratic Secretary of State, estimated that as many as 450,000 citizens in the state decided not to vote after hearing early TV projections and Carter's concession. She threatened to initiate legislation setting polling hours on Monday evenings as well as on Tuesdays, a practice followed in some European countries.[15] But none of the excuses or theories could alter the one overriding fact of the 1980 election: voters had seen all they wanted of Jimmy Carter, and many were equally fed up with a Democratic Congress.

President Carter's early concession and the television networks speedy projections on election night infuriated people, but the *Los Angeles Times* poll found little evidence that it kept large numbers of them from voting. To the contrary, the turnout of registered voters in the Pacific time zone was actually higher than in any other time zone. This was particularly true of registered Democrats, who turned out in proportionately higher numbers in the Pacific states than they did elsewhere in the country. It was just that the Democratic turnout per registered voter was lower almost everywhere than it was among Republicans. This is normal. But the gap between party turnouts was wider in 1980 than in the 1976 election. The *Los Angeles Times* poll found that significant numbers of Democrats did not turn out because they were turned off by the choice of candidates, and it had virtually nothing to do with Carter's concession or the neworks' projections. The survey showed that if all registered voters had turned out, the election would have been as close as most analysts had predicted it would be. People who stayed away from the polls overwhelmingly preferred Carter to Reagan. Among those surveyed, 71 percent said that "even though they knew who had won the presidential election, the news media should not have announced the results until the polls were closed in all parts of the country." People in the Eastern time zone, who had already voted, felt as deeply about this as did those in the West. Likewise, 74 percent said "even though he knew he had lost the election, President Carter should not have publicly admitted defeat until the polls were closed in all parts of the country." Westerners were particularly adamant about this.[16] People who voted were asked whether they still would have gone to the polls if they had heard that Carter already had lost, and 12 percent said they would not have bothered. Among Carter voters, 18 percent felt this way. Only 8 percent of Reagan's did. But it is questionable whether people who did hear actually stayed away from the polls in significant numbers. According to the National Election Service, the official tabulator of the nation's balloting, there was a slightly lower voter turnout in 1980 in California than there was during the 1976 presidential election. But there was a similar dropoff of voting compared to 1976 all across the nation. The *Los Angeles Times* poll found that the turnout among registered voters in the Pacific time zone was seven points higher than it was in any other zone. Among Democrats it was four points higher. Actually, there was a smaller percentage of the adult population that was registered to vote in the Pacific zone than there was in other areas. But a higher proportion of those who were registered in the Pacific states wound up going to the polls. So the end result was that about the same percentage of the eligible voters, 53.95 percent, voted in the Pacific zone as in the rest of the nation. This was the lowest turnout in 32 years. In all, 86,495,678 votes were cast in the 1980 presidential election.[17]

Voting a Minority Habit?

The low voting turnout has generally been attributed to apathy and indifference. The prevailing view seems to be that Americans have an abnormally low interest in the political process. What explanations can one have for the fact that voting in the United States is now a "minority habit?"[18] Why is voter turnout in America anemic in contrast to that in other democratic nations? Who are the people who vote? Who are the non-voters? Does it make a difference that so many Americans fail to vote? Comparing American voting with voting in other free countries, we find Australia with 95 percent, West Germany with 94 percent, Italy with 93 percent, Sweden and Austria with 91 percent, France with 84 percent, Canada and Great Britain both with 77 percent, and so on. Even Switzerland, a country whose constant referenda on matters of public concern apparently overtax its citizenry's interest, manages to have 64 percent voter turnout. It is claimed that American voting turnout exceeds that of only one other democracy, Botswana in Africa.[19] The problem of non-voting in the United States is very serious. Some analysts claim it is reaching epidemic proportions.

The 1980 turnout was the lowest since the 51.1 percent who voted in the 1948 contest between Democratic President Harry S. Truman and Republican Thomas E. Dewey. The highest turnout ever was 62.8 percent in 1960, when Democrat John F. Kennedy defeated Republican Richard M. Nixon by less than one percent of the vote. Just as significant as the declining percentage of the eligible voters in elections is the fact that over the past decade more than fifteen million Americans, many of whom had been regular voters, actually stopped casting their ballots. Consequently, both Jimmy Carter and Ronald Reagan were elected Presidents by about one fourth of their fellow citizens. A similar trend has afflicted local, state, and congressional races in the last decade. Governor Brendan Byrne of New Jersey received a "mandate" of less than 15 percent of the eligible vote in his successful reelection bid in 1977, and Mayor Ed Koch of New York City was the "choice" of less than 12 percent of eligible voters. Curtis Gans of the Committee for the Study of the American Electorate, a bipartisan, nonprofit research group that concentrates on studying voter turnout, has assembled an impressive amount of information concerning the depressingly low level of American political participation. One may disagree with Gans' conclusion that "the decline seems irreversible,"[20] but nobody can deny the seriousness of the situation.

The Non-Voters—Who are They?

The concept of "Non-Voter" party, a term that covers the numbers of people not participating in presidential elections, was introduced by Lance Tarrance. He used government statistics to estimate the number of registered voters in each election from 1928 to 1976. Richard Nixon won a landslide victory in 1972 with the greatest plurality in votes, 19 million, ever recorded in a presidential election. Yet the "Non-Voter" party easily won the election with 62 million votes to Nixon's 47 million. The number of non-voters in the United States has always been substantial. But as the infant nation matured and developed, there was solace in the belief that participation rates seemed to be climbing, slowly to be sure but consistently. Unfortunately this is no longer the case. The rates are falling, and the numbers of nonparticipants are increasing substantially. From the 1950's through 1968, the average percentage of eligible voters not turning out was 39 percent, and the average number of Americans not participating was under 43 million. These figures may be high in cross-national perspective, but they look good when compared to those of the 1970's.

An expanded electorate exacerbated the problem. Turnout rates in the 1970's and in 1980 were a little over one-half of the eligible adult population and, most important, the number of nonvoters now averages between 65 and 75 million.[21] And the figures are still climbing. If the nonvoters had participated in such close elections as 1960, 1968, or 1976, their impact would have been decisive. Even the pluralities in such lopsided contests as in 1972 and 1980 pale in comparison to the numbers who simply do not vote. Any of the election outcomes in the twentieth century could have been reversed through the participation in sufficient numbers of those who have withdrawn from the electorate. The sad fact is that in contrast to most Western democracies no chief executive in the United States has been elected by a majority of the electorate in modern American history. This includes the overwhelming victories of Lyndon Johnson in 1964, Richard Nixon in 1972, and Ronald Reagan in 1980.

Some political analysts claim that Americans who do not vote receive at best minimal representation of their views. According to this view nonvoters' ties to the political system are not likely to be strong. Furthermore, it is asserted that nonvoters provide the potential for a major disruption of the American political scene. In short, nonvoting of this magnitude is considered a very unhealthy condition for a democratic society. Opposed to this interpretation of nonvoting is the view that it does not make much difference that so many Americans fail to vote. Those who find the figures on nonvoting appalling point out that it is easier to vote today than ever. The past decade and a half has seen sweeping reforms specifically designed to encourage voting. The poll tax was outlawed, discrimination at polling places on the basis of race or language was prohibited, 18- to 20-year-olds were enfranchised. During the same period, many states initiated systems of mobile registrars, post-card registration, and election day registration. Yet the percentage of Americans who even bother to register continues to shrink each year.

As of 1980, more than 160 million Americans were eligible to vote. One could call them the potential electorate. Virtually all American citizens over the age of eighteen, except those convicted of major crimes and the mentally ill, are eligible to register and to vote. This constitutes the largest number of American adults eligible to vote in the country's history. With the elimination of literacy tests for federal elections and a sharp reduction in the residency requirements the opportunity to register has never been greater, nor more universal. Congress is considering legislation to enable persons to register by mail rather than, as is now the case, by appearing in person. The relative ease of registration and the eligibility of so many persons are relatively new features of the American political system. The expansion of voting rights has resulted in more Americans than ever before being eligible to vote. In terms of their ability to participate in the political process, Americans have never had greater opportunity to choose their political leaders. And yet, ironically, many Americans do not vote. Forty million Americans failed to register in 1972. In addition, 23 million who were registered failed to vote. Of the 150 million Americans in the potential electorate in 1976, only 80 million voted, the others either failed to register or did not bother to vote after they had registered. In the presidential elections of 1976 and 1980, 45 and 46 percent respectively did not vote. Of the potential electorate of 160 million in 1980, only 86,495,678 Americans voted.[22] Generally congressional and gubernatorial races have an even lower turnout; those not voting usually represent between 55 and 60 percent of the eligible voters. In primaries, 70–80 percent may not vote. This is a far lower turnout than is experienced in the other industrialized democracies in Europe, Canada, Australia, and Japan.

In the 1880's and 1890's, only white adult males were eligible to vote, but a large percentage of those did so. How significant is the fact that along with an expanding electorate has gone a steady decline in participation rates? Who votes and who does not? There have been many studies focusing on voting and voting behavior. There is abundant empirical evidence answering the question, "Who is the nonvoter?" Generally, the nonvoter tends to be young, that is between eighteen and twenty-five years old, or old, over sixty-five. Poorly educated, likely to be from a rural area, more likely to be non-white, the non-voter tends to come from the lowest socioeconomic group of society. In other words, an educated, high-income, white, middle-aged person from a suburb in the North or West is more likely to vote than an uneducated, poor, black youth from the rural South. Or, as Richard Scammon and Ben Wattenberg put it, the typical voter is "unyoung, unpoor, and unblack."[23] In short, we know that different kinds of people participate in voting to different degrees. Such variables as education, age, occupation, income, race, residence, all influence the probability that come election day one will cast a ballot in the voting booth. But how exactly does it work? Do poor people vote less because they are poor, or because they are less educated? Do old people vote less because they are old, or because they are poorer?

In the 1980 presidential election there were two judgments about American politics that had come to be accepted as descriptions of fact: that American electoral politics had undergone a fundamental change in recent years, and that this change was almost entirely for the worse. The evidence cited for these judgments included such things as the declining turnout among, and alienation of, voters; the decline of the parties; the rising importance of television; the increase in the number of primaries; and the growing importance of single issue groups. Each of these developments, which are sometimes described as causes, sometimes as effects, has received considerable attention among political analysts, the press, and politicians. Yet the judgment itself, that there has been deep and negative change, deserves more critical attention.

Those analysts who believe that "the politics of the 1980's is a new, revolutionary politics, almost wholly different from the politics of the 1960's," claim that the key question now and for the future is, "how can I win some non-voters?"[24] Obviously, the phenomenon of non-voting is now central to American elections. In the new politics money and television have replaced issues and parties, and politicians today simply spout whatever the polls tell them people want to hear. As a result, all politicians tend to sound alike, and all of them appeal to the groups, usually middle-of-the-road, most likely to vote. Since few politicians speak to the problems of non-voters, fewer and fewer Americans vote. Among the effects of decreasing turnout is the growing power of small special interest groups which turn out in disproportionate numbers, and therefore "distort" election results. In a low-turnout election such as a primary, the candidate who can get a slightly larger percentage of his supporters to the polls will have a sharp advantage.

A special poll, conducted for E. N. Costikyan's study *How to Win Votes: The Politics of 1980,* reveals that there is no angry majority of the disaffected, the nonvoters and others, who are ready to inundate the political process. The findings of the poll also indicate that there is no wide gulf between voters and nonvoters, no deep-seated ideological schism in the American electorate. If that is so, why, then, does it matter who votes? Is the subject of interest only to campaign managers seeking to squeeze out a victory? Or because only a high turn-out will dilute the power of special interest groups? Does it, in the final analysis, make any difference? Political scientists Raymond Wolfinger of Berkeley and Steven J. Rosenstone of Yale address these questions in a most significant work entitled *Who Votes?*[25] The fascinating study was based on Census Bureau interviews with 88,000 citizens in 1972 and 1974, fifty times the number usually interviewed for polls. Using sophisticated computer analysis, the two political scientists are able to determine which variables, socioeconomic status, age, sex, education, registration laws, political culture, and others, matter and which do not. They are, in fact, able to answer the question of who votes in the American electorate.

Who Votes?

According to Wolfinger and Rosenstone, educated Americans are most likely to vote. Income, sex, and race are not significant independent variables. Education is crucial, and age is second in importance. Both youth and mobility decrease substantially the probability that an individual will vote. White people vote more than blacks, in part because the black population is less educated and younger. Basing their findings on quantitative data, Wolfinger and Rosenstone provide quantitative answers concerning voting behavior. A high school diploma, we are told, increases the probability of voting by 20 percent. Income is far less important than education, and increasing income changes voting probability only up to a point. With college and $10,000 a year, or without college and $15,000, one seems to reach a plateau. Additional education and income make no appreciable difference. In short, voting is a middle-class activity. Wolfinger and Rosenstone demolish some traditional beliefs about voting behavior. Old people, for example, vote less, but only because they are poorer and less educated than the general population. Old age in itself turns out to increase rather than decrease the probability of voting. The two factors having the greatest impact on voter turnout are education and age. While education provides the greatest explanatory power in determining turnout, the life experiences that accompany aging, including exposure to elections and the political system, have a positive impact on voter turnout well into the seventies. Variables that appear to have little or modest impact on voter turnout include income, occupation, and free time. High income, prestigious occupational attainment, and the resource of free time do not effectively raise participation rates in elections. Other myths also fall by the wayside in the two political scientists' analysis of the Census Bureau data set. Farmers, for example, maintain the highest voting turnout after such professionals as medical doctors, dentists, and lawyers. Material possessions, which supposedly motivate a "stake in the system," have virtually no impact on participation rates. Of particular interest is the conclusion of Wolfinger and Rosenstone about the phenomenon of low turnout: on most issues, voters are virtually a carbon copy of the citizen population. Those most likely to be underrepresented are people who lack opinions. The partisan impact of nonvoting is marginal: Democrats are 51.4 percent of citizens and 51.3 percent of voters; Republicans are 36 percent of citizens and 39.7 percent of voters. This small GOP gain is the entire partisan effect on nonvoting. On particular issues, medical insurance, forced busing, crime, welfare, and others, differences are even smaller than this, in percentage terms.

What Wolfinger and Rosenstone cannot do is to explain why voting has decreased since 1960. Their data describe only a pair of consecutive elections; therefore, they cannot ascertain what sorts of people are most responsible for the decline in turnout that has been a notable feature of American civic life over the past decade. They do examine one theory, namely, that what is responsible is the lowering of the voting age to eighteen, since younger citizens always vote in fewer numbers than do older ones. Turnout dropped by 5 percent between 1968 and 1972, but the data indicate that the eighteen-year-old vote only depressed the turnout by 1.2 percent, or one quarter of the whole. Unfortunately they do not estimate the impact on voting of the fact that, due to the baby boom, people eighteen to twenty-four constitute a larger proportion of the population today than they did in 1960 or 1970. It is possible that this would explain an additional portion of low turnout.

Concluding their study, Wolfinger and Rosenstone suggest certain changes in state registration laws that are likely to raise participation rates in the voting process. While the greatest impact would come about by allowing potential voters to register until election day, a projected increase of six percent in the voting population, other reforms might include providing for Saturday and evening registration hours, and permitting absentee registration. Some analysts have even suggested that Election Day should be changed from Tuesday to Sunday or to make it a national holiday, a day when no one has to worry about anything but doing his or her partriotic duty by getting to the polls.[26] If Congress could push the inauguration date from March to January, as it did in 1933, the same body could change Election Day from Tuesday to Sunday at a time in the nation's history when our national elections threaten to become America's number one spectator sport. Voting on Tuesday means getting up earlier to vote before going to work or traipsing over to the polls after a hard day in the factory or the office. It could be argued that Europeans are not much more conscientious than Americans in matters of voting. But they do have one big thing working for them that Americans do not: election day in West European democracies is on Sunday, when people are not working, when there is not much competition for one's patriotism except soccer.

Wolfinger and Rosenstone make clear in their study that the increase in registered voters would not change the nature of the voting population; there would be virtually no change in issue orientations or the demographic, partisan, or ideological characteristics of the voter population. If nonvoters and voters tend to have the same views, and if the age of the voting population explains a portion of the low turnout, one is led to wonder whether too much is not sometimes made of the whole matter. After all, though turnout is down, from 63 percent in 1960 and 62 percent in 1964, to 61 percent in 1968, 56 percent in 1972, 55 percent in 1976, and 54 percent in 1980, it is still above the 52 percent of 1928 and 1932, and the 51 percent of 1952. The downward trend is disturbing, but one could say that in the context of 20th century American experience, present-day turnout is not unusually low. And one wonders whether the issue of voter turnout really deserves all the attention it has been receiving in articles and books. And one similarly wonders whether the recent focus on supposed changes in our political process, more television, more primaries, etc., is not misplaced. If there is anything to be learned from the so-called McGovern "reforms" of Democratic party processes after 1968, it is that they were aimed at capturing power not in order to purify procedures but rather to redirect policy. Only the fact that the policy goals were unpopular made it necessary to cover them with appeals to procedural fair play. Thus, attempts to gain more votes in Democratic party conventions by taking seats away from elected officials and instituting quotas for special groups were described as an effort to end special treatment for "big shots" and discrimination against minorities; what they really represented was a struggle for the power to dictate party policy.

Significance of Low Voter Turnout

To those who deplore the low voter turnout the political significance of the continuing decline in voter participation indicates that the United States is turning into a "minocracy" where a minority of voters with special interests could control the elections. It is asserted that the nonvoters are running the country and vote-dodgers are equated with draft dodgers. One of the festering good deeds that afflict the body politic at regular intervals is the drive to get out the vote. The League of Women Voters, parent-teacher associations, chambers of commerce, labor unions, and other institutions with impeccable reputations for civic righteousness are in the forefront of such efforts. Those who believe that the right to vote includes within it the right not to vote claim that whether either is exercised is an individual decision as personal as whether to wear pajamas to bed.

It is important to know who votes because so many Americans do not. Does that really matter? Many political analysts, including Wolfinger and Rosenstone, feel it does; yet their figures show that voters are politically quite representative of the American population at large. Thus even if everybody voted in presidential elections, instead of only half of those eligible, it would make no difference. The resultant government would be no better than what we are presently getting. No worse either. In fact, the results would be about the same. Wolfinger and Rosenstone have shown that the political preferences of the groups that vote are not substantially different from the views of the entire adult population, so the difference to the American political system is remarkably small. If nothing much would change if everyone went to the polls, what is wrong about political apathy? In answering this crucial question, the finest statistics cannot make up for the absence of normative political theory.

A *New York Times-CBS News* poll following the November 1980 election found that only a fraction of Reagan voters shared his conservative views. Another poll taker, George Gallop, concluded: "Examination of political indicators and the views of voters on key issues shows that the Reagan landslide was not so much the result of an ideological shift to the right among the electorate as dissatisfaction with the leadership of the nation and desire for change."[27] Given the seriousness of the issues facing the American people in the 1980's, it is not important to know exactly who votes, who is from Washington, and how many minority members are on a delegate slate. Instead, we should turn back to some fundamental questions in American politics: How large a government shall we have? How much economic growth? How shall we provide jobs, control inflation and crime? The failures of the 1960's and 1970's were based not so much on our "politics" as on our politicians and their policies. It is these which cry out for attention.

In the 1980's Americans will continue to welcome conservative politicians only if conservatism succeeds where liberalism has failed. How durable Reagan's popularity will be could depend on maintaining a stable economy, the ability of his administration to reestablish America's strategic superiority in the world while preserving the peace, and on Reagan's ability to restore the confidence of the American people in their government. If the answer to these questions is "No," whoever is the GOP's 1988 standard-bearer, will have a hard time convincing voters to perpetuate the new conservative era they seemed to be launching in November 1980.

Notes

1. See especially Gerald Pomper, *Voters' Choice* (N.Y.: Dodd, Mead, & Co., 1975) and W. E. Miller and T. E. Levitin, *Leadership and Change: The New Politics and the American Electorate* (Cambridge, Mass: Winthrop Publishers, 1976).
2. Pomper, *op. cit.,* chapter 8.
3. Angus Campbell et al, *The American Voter* (Chicago: University of Chicago Press, 1960).
4. Quoted in D. B. Hill and N. R. Luttbeg, *Trends in Electoral Voting Behavior* (Itasca, Illinois: F. E. Peacock Publishers, 1980), p. 71.
5. W. J. Crotty and Gary C. Jacobson, *American Parties in Decline* (Little, Brown and Co.: Boston, Toronto, 1980), p. 3.
6. *The CPS American National Election Study,* vol. 1 (Inter-University Consortium for Political and Social Research: Ann Arbor, Michigan, 1977), pp. 288, 410f.
7. See especially Jeff Fishel, ed. *Parties and Elections in an Anti-Party Age* (Indiana University Press: Bloomington, 1978), and Everett Carl Ladd, Jr., "The Polls: The Question of Confidence," in *Public Opinion Quarterly,* vol. 40, No. 4 (Winter 1976–1977).
8. See Table 4.1 in Hill and Luttbeg, *op. cit.,* p. 115.
9. Ibid.
10. Harris Polls, "Trends in Alienation and Powerlessness Felt by Americans, 1966–1977," reprinted in Ibid., p. 117.
11. See David Easton, "A Re-Assessment of the Concept of Political Support," in *British Journal of Political Science,* vol. 5 (October 1975), pp. 435–57.
12. "Times Poll—U.S. Political Process—the Voters Like It," *Los Angeles Times,* January 27, 1980, pp. 1, 29.
13. "Split Dixie Vote Called Anti-Washington Reaction," *Los Angeles Times,* November 22, 1980, Part I, p. 32.
14. "The Mood of the Voter," *Time,* September 15, 1980, p. 8.
15. *U.S. News and World Report,* November 17, 1980, p. 30.
16. *Los Angeles Times,* November 23, 1980, pp. 1 and 8.
17. *Los Angeles Times,* January 6, 1981, p. 13.
18. Martin F. Nolan, "The Off-Year Election Blues," *Boston Globe,* October 15, 1978, p. A 1.
19. Crotty and Jacobson, *op. cit.,* p. 5.
20. Curtis B. Gans, "The Empty Ballot Box: Reflections on Nonvoters in America," *Public Opinion,* September/October 1978, p. 54. See also his "Elections by Default of the Nonvoters,"*Los Angeles Times,* October 8, 1978, p. VI, 5.
21. See "Lowest Voter Turnout Since 1948 Reported," *Los Angeles Times,* January 6, 1981, p. 13.
22. Ibid.
23. Richard Scammon and Ben Wattenberg, *The Real Majority* (New York: Coward-McCann and Geoghegan, 1970).
24. Edward N. Costikyan, *How to Win Votes: The Politics of 1980* (Harcourt, Brace, Jovanovich: New York, 1980).
25. Raymond Wolfinger and Steven J. Rosenstone, *Who Votes?* (Yale University Press: New Haven, Conn., 1980).
26. "U.S. Elections—Always on Sunday?" *San Francisco Sunday Examiner and Chronicle,* May 18, 1980, p. 1.
27. Quoted in "Start of the Reagan Era," *U.S. News and World Report,* January 26, 1981, p. 19.

For Further Reading

Campbell, Angus, et al. *The American Voter.* New York: John Wiley and Sons, Inc., 1966.

Cantril, Albert H., ed. *Polling on the Issues: A Report from the Kettering Foundation.* Cabin John, Maryland, Seven Lock Press, 1981.

Flanigan, William H. and Nancy H. Zingale. *Political Behavior of the American Electorate,* 4th ed. Boston: Allyn and Bacon, 1979.

Scammon, Richard and Ben J. Wattenberg. *The Real Majority: An Examination of the American Electorate.* New York: Coward, McCann and Geoghegan, 1970.

Wolfinger, Raymond and Steven J. Rosenstone. *Who Votes?* New Haven, Conn.: Yale University Press, 1980.

Name _____

Section _____

Date _____

Review Questions for Chapter 10: Voting Behavior

1. *The American Voter* _____

_____

_____

_____

_____

2. "turned off" electorate _____

_____

_____

_____

_____

3. political efficacy _____

_____

_____

_____

_____

4. "crisis of regime" _____

_____

_____

_____

_____

5. "Anti-Washington sentiment" _____

_____

_____

_____

_____

6. Political Polls _____

_____

_____

_____

_____

7. Iranian Hostage Crisis _____

_____

_____

_____

_____

8. Typical non-voter _____

_____

_____

_____

_____

9. *Who votes?* _____

_____

_____

_____

_____

10. Minocracy _____

_____

_____

_____

_____

Essay Study Questions

1. What are the most important changes in voting behavior in the United States in the last two decades?
2. Discuss the relationship between wealth, education and voting.
3. Describe the "average" voter in the United States.
4. Analyze the reasons why many people do not vote and the significance of low voter turnout.

Chapter 11

The United States and the World

The 1970s ended on a rather melancholy note for the United States. It's diplomatic mission was held hostage in Iran. Soviet troops were engaged in a full scale invasion of Afghanistan. America's military, once thought to be the finest and mightiest, appeared weak and wanting when compared with the Soviet Union. America's currency, the dollar, was under heavy attack in all foreign lands and this once proud symbol of fiscal soundness did not fare well against the Japanese yen, the German mark and the French franc. Twice during the 1970s, Americans were sharply jolted by energy crises over which they had no effective control. When the 1970s began, the United States was still involved in the bitterly devisive war in Vietnam. Americans breathed a sigh of relief when their country's participation ended in 1972. After the war, many seemed to yearn for the simpler times of non-involvement and nonconcern that seemed to characterize the United States approach to the world before World War II.

Prior to World War II the United States was seldom directly involved in world politics. Great Britain secured the Atlantic and thereby prevented any threat from Europe. Major power competition in Asia ensured, until a few years prior to the war, that no one country threatened the Pacific Ocean frontier. Latin America had been staked out as a virtual province of the United States and it was secure. In most respects, the United States, prior to the end of World War II, was an observer rather than an active participant in world affairs.

Post World War II

From 1945 through 1950 America's role changed drastically. At the end of World War II the United States was *the* world power. Presidents Franklin D. Roosevelt and Harry S. Truman attempted to create a world wherein governments could cooperate and resolve their differences in a peaceful manner. Their expectations produced the United Nations and the hope that the United States could return to the comfortable and simple times of non-involvement with global affairs. However, the dream quickly turned sour. At Potsdam Truman detected that the Russians were hedging on the Yalta Agreements and soon the dream, of world peace deteriorated into mutual suspicion and hostility. By 1948 the "cold war" between the United States and the Soviet Union was underway and the primary battleground was Europe.

Containment

America's response to the wartime ally which turned into a peacetime rival was to develop the general policy of containment. On the ideological level, this policy was articulated by George F. Kennan.[1] He argued that the Soviet Union should be prevented from spreading its military, political and ideological influence. If successful, containment would force the Russians to be more reasonable and perhaps more democratic. President Truman made containment an official policy when, in 1947, communist activity seemed to threaten both Greece and Turkey. In a speech to Congress, the President made it clear that the United States would do what was necessary on the political, economic and military levels to contain the Soviet Union and the spread of communism. Shortly after Truman proclaimed his doctrine the administration and Congress began to act. Aid and advisors were sent to Greece and Turkey. An ambitious financial aid program of $170 billion, the Marshall Plan, was launched to rebuild the war-shattered economies of Western Europe. NATO, the North Atlantic Treaty Organization, was formed as a result of American leadership in 1949. It is significant to note that for almost two hundred years the United States had avoided military alliances. Similar military-political defense alliances were established in South East Asia, and with Australia and New Zealand. It was clear that the United States regarded the Soviet Union and the ideology of communism as enemies.

America's resolve was tested by the 1948 communist coup in Czechoslovakia and by the Berlin blockade. In 1950, when South Korea was invaded by North Korea, the United States was psychologically and politically ready to respond. The Strategic Air Command encircled the Soviet Union and other communist countries. Foreign aid programs, designed to blunt the appeals of communism in third world countries, were underway and labeled Point Four. It had already been decided to supplement America's nuclear arsenal with thermonuclear weapons.[2] And, domestically, Representative Richard Nixon, Senators Joseph McCarthy and Pat McCarran and convicted spies Ethel and Julius Rosenberg made the public aware of the communist menace. In 1953, the United States agreed to an armistice with its adversaries, North Korea and China. However, America's policy of containment and economic and political non-intercourse with China remained official policy for another twenty years.

After the Korean War, there was a brief thaw in American-Soviet relations. Premier Khrushchev visited the United States and the leaders of the two countries briefly appeared to be on the threshold of a new era of good feelings. However, events during the Eisenhower and Kennedy administrations convinced many Americans that containment was a good policy to pursue with respect to communist countries. Hungary was invaded by the Russian Army, Cuba acquired a marxist government and land based Russian intermediate range ballistic missiles, a wall was erected between West and East Berlin, China acquired nuclear weapons, and Southeast Asia was in turmoil.

America's response to these challenges was to reaffirm the principles of containment with specific policies that were occasionally successful. Eisenhower condemned the Russian invasion of Hungary and allowed quota-free immigration for the "freedom fighters." Eisenhower and his advisors condemned the Cuban government of Fidel Castro and planned the Bay of Pigs invasion. President Kennedy approved of the invasion of Cuba which was launched and failed in a most spectacular and embarrassing fashion. Kennedy's response to the emplacement of Russian missiles in Cuba was more decisive. He blockaded the island and threatened nuclear war and the Russians withdrew their missiles. In addition, President Kennedy condemned the Berlin Wall, attempted to neutralize Laos, and sent American ground troops to Vietnam.

Vietnam

President Johnson, who succeeded the murdered John Kennedy, was also convinced that containment was the best policy for dealing with communist countries. After his 1964 election he quickly committed hundreds of thousands of American troops to fight communists in Vietnam. The very expensive protracted conflict was inconclusive. At the end of his presidency in 1968, Lyndon Johnson was a very confused and bitter man. Relying upon his own instincts and the best and brightest of counsel, he spent billions of dollars, deployed the best of America's fighting men and equipment and endured massive criticism at home and it was all for naught. When he left office, communist forces controlled more of Vietnam than they had in 1964. Johnson's only victory against a perceived communist threat came in 1965. Intelligence information led him to believe that a communist coup was likely to occur in the strife-torn Dominican Republic. He quickly dispatched American military units to the Caribbean island-state and, after a short period of time, a non-communist government was established.

Richard Nixon came into the presidency in 1969 with a firm resolve to end the Vietnam war honorably and to revamp the policy of containment. He was less timid than Johnson in utilizing military options in Vietnam. Nixon ordered the mining of some Vietnamese ports, the bombing of Hanoi and other populated areas and the attacking of enemy installations in Cambodia, which previously were considered out-of-bounds. Nevertheless, in 1972, Richard Nixon agreed to a "peace with honor." The United States would withdraw all of its ground and air forces from the beleaguered land. In return, the North Vietnamese agreed to repatriate American prisoners of war and the remains of those who died in enemy territory. Finally, in 1975 the Vietnamese incident came to a melancholy end. Northern forces, in a series of brilliant strategic maneuvers, quickly overwhelmed the American equipped Southern armies and unified, for the first time in centuries, all of Vietnam. President Gerald Ford had the unhappy fortune of presiding over the first major military-political defeat of the United States since the War of 1812. Containment, it seemed, was moribund, if not dead.

Détente

Richard Nixon and his primary advisor, Henry Kissinger, set the stage for a change in the policy of containment. Détente, an easing of tensions between the two superpowers on the military, economic, and political levels, was put forth as an alternative to containment. Kissinger was convinced that diplomacy and good will could replace the hostility and suspicion that characterized the Cold War.

SALT I

First, the Nixon administration attacked the containment idea of American military superiority. In 1967, the United States decided to unilaterally limit its strategic nuclear forces. It was thought that parity of strategic forces between the superpowers would lessen the fears and suspicion that appeared to fuel the arms race. The Strategic Arms Limitations Talks, SALT, quickly followed. Negotiations, which began in 1967, produced a series of agreements in 1972. First, there was a treaty limiting the number of Anti-Ballistic Missile (ABM) sites to two for each side. Later the number was reduced to one. ABMs are designed to intercept and destroy incoming enemy warheads. The American system, Safeguard, had two missiles. Spartan, a long range missile, was to intercept and destroy targets in the exo-atmosphere; Sprint, a short range missile, was designed to destroy, in the atmosphere, those warheads that penetrated the Spartan shield. After spending a billion dollars on that system, Congress, in 1975, appropriated monies to dismantle Safeguard. Russian MIRV[3] missiles, it was argued, could overwhelm the system by providing too many targets. Others opposed to the system believed it to be too provocative. The Russians, it was thought, might get the impression that the United States was preparing for a first strike by defending its land based Minuteman Inter-Continental Ballistic Missiles ICBM. Russian strategists had greater confidence in their ABM, Galosh. It is located around Moscow. There are sixty-four sites for the two missile system and it can defend a large area of Moscow. Other provisions of SALT included limits on the numbers of ICBMs, Sea Launched Ballistic Missiles SLBM and missiles that could have MIRV capabilities. The Soviet Union was limited to 2,358, and the United States agreed that its strategic force would be limited to 1,710. Both sides were to have no more than 1,320 MIRV missiles.

SALT II

Negotiations that produced SALT II began shortly after SALT I was ratified. The agreements were presented to the United States Senate in 1979 and immediately became embroiled in controversy. SALT II limited both sides to 2,250 strategic missiles of which 1,200 could have MIRV capability with no more than 10 warheads each. The Russian Backfire bomber, a sophisticated and long range airplane was classified as a tactical system and therefore not subject to limitations. The American cruise missile, when mounted on B-52 bombers, was considered a strategic system and therefore subject to the SALT II limits. Cruise missiles are small subsonic guided bombs that travel close to the earth's surface and thereby avoid radar detection. SALT II was silent on throw-weight, which is the lifting capacity of a missile. Russian leaders have opted for large throw-weight missiles such as the SS-18 which can carry one 50 megaton warhead or 6 to 8 MIRV warheads of two megatons each. By contrast, America's heaviest ICBM is a liquid fueled and obsolete Titan II which can throw 10 megatons. SALT II prohibits the United States from acquiring heavy throw-weight missiles. In return, the Soviet negotiators agreed that their country would develop no missiles larger than the SS-18.

During the summer and fall of 1979, hearings on SALT II were conducted by the Senate Armed Forces and Foreign Relations Committees. Conservative and some moderate senators were concerned about the inequality of the agreements. They also felt that SALT II would ensure long-term Russian strategic superiority. Some liberal senators expressed dismay because SALT II provided for increases rather than decreases in strategic arsenals. The treaty was clearly in trouble and many analysts were convinced that the necessary two-thirds ratification vote could not be mustered in the Senate. President Carter faced the probability of being the first chief executive since Woodrow Wilson to have a major treaty rejected by the Senate. The Russian Christmas, 1979, invasion of Afghanistan offered the President a way out of this dilemma. One of the means that he selected to protest the Russian action was to withdraw SALT II from Senate consideration.

Arms Control

Arms control will continue be an issue throughout this century. President Reagan, early in his administration proposed that Strategic Arms Reduction Talks (START) be conducted between the United States and Soviet Union. Indeed the negotiations began but no conclusions were reached and eventually the Soviets walked out. Their ire was raised by the decision of the NATO allies to allow the deployment of American controlled intermediate range missiles, Pershing II and land based cruise missiles in some Western European countries. American missiles were necessary, according to the NATO council, to counter the growing threat posed by the rapid deployment of Soviet SS-20 missiles in Eastern Europe. The SS-20 is a sophisticated 3 MIRV rocket that can strike all major NATO targets. As recently as 1984, Soviet officials refused to resume any arms control talks until the U.S. removes its missiles from Western Europe.

At home, as well as abroad, people were calling upon the United States to do something about the perceived threat of war wherein nuclear weapons would be utilized.

The debate often was very emotional and called for such resolutions as a freeze on nuclear weapons, partial disarmament and a ban on the acquisition of new weapons systems. Results of this concern were seen in Congress. A nuclear freeze resolution was barely defeated and Congress, by a margin of but one vote, decided to fund the acquisition of 10 MX, the first new American ICBM developed in some twenty years. Meanwhile, the Soviet Union continued its relentless acquisition of advanced and large ICBMs. President Reagan clearly viewed arms control as a policy that has rendered the United States inferior to the Soviet Union. His administration asserted that meaningful talks could only be centered on a verifiable reduction of strategic arms while the Soviets want concessions before negotiations. Under the Reagan administration, this aspect of detente was finally discarded.

President Reagan reaffirmed his predecessor's policies, but perhaps under pressure from farm groups, eased up on the exportation of grain. Reagan's successful economic policies at home were reflected in international trade. During his first term, the dollar became increasingly strong against foreign currencies.

During the 1980 campaign, President Reagan expressed allegiance to Taiwan and reservations about the People's Republic. Such concerns carried over into the first part of his administration and resulted in a chill in Sino-American relations. Later, however, while not totally abandoning Taiwan, Reagan, through his trip to China and subsequent trade agreements, managed to heal the rift between the two countries.

Latin America

To many Americans President Carter's policies in this part of the world were flawed. They tended to view his transfer of the canal to Panama as a "give away," his response to a Marxist takeover of Nicaragua was viewed as timid and inconclusive, and his tolerance of a brigade of Soviet troops in Cuba was seen as a lack of resolve. Reagan faced several challenges in the southern hemisphere. It appeared to him that Cuba was using Nicaragua to foment revolution in nearby El Salvador. The president was successful in getting Congress to fund C.I.A. efforts to counter revolutionary forces in El Salvador and to support anti-government forces in Nicaragua. In 1982, Argentina invaded the Falkland Islands, a British colony that formerly belonged to Argentina. The United States decided not to intervene and thereby sided with its NATO ally. Reagan's most decisive move was what some refer to as the liberation of the island of Grenada. In 1983, the island acquired through assassination a radical Marxist leader. Reagan, at the invitation of the governments of nearby islands, dispatched American military forces and put an end to the regime. His hope was to send a stern warning to Cuba and Nicaragua and to reassert America's hegemony in the hemisphere.

Economic Relations

Economically, détente was designed to alter the containment approach of isolating communist countries by lowering trade restrictions which would open American markets to the Russians. A consulate treaty was negotiated and the United States was also prepared to offer Russia most-favored-nation status.[4] On this level, America's first major step along the détente path hurt its own citizens. In 1972, Richard Nixon, by executive agreement, engineered the so-called "wheat deal," wherein, the United States agreed to sell hundreds of thousands of tons to grain to the Soviet Union at premium prices. The deal created food shortages and contributed to inflation at home.

American coporations, eager to exploit the available Russian market, established offices in Moscow and other Russian cities and sold everything from soft drinks to highly sophisticated electronic technology and computers. American marketeers were not impressed with the goods that the Russians were willing to export, although some interest was expressed in automobiles. This aspect of détente suffered considerably in 1978 and 1979. Angered by the Russian refusal to allow free immigration of Jews from their country, Senators such as Henry Jackson of Washington, were able to prevent the granting of most-favored-nation status. Like SALT II, the consulate arrangement was a casualty of the invasion of Afghanistan. In addition, President Carter cut off the sale of grain and all high technology equipment and cancelled America's participation in the 1980 summer Olympic games. Economically, détente did not produce more harmony between the two countries. Furthermore, President Carter's economic sanctions did not effect Russian activities in Afghanistan or elsewhere.

China

A more successful application of détente was launched by Richard Nixon and directed at China. During the Korean War, the United Nations Security Council, following the American lead, branded China an aggressor state and imposed economic sanctions. The idea was to isolate China and to contain its political influence. For twenty years the United States insisted that the legitimate government of China was located in Taiwan. Americans were forbidden from travel in China and they were also prohibited from owning or buying anything that was produced in China. America's posture began to gradually change in 1972 when Henry Kissinger made a secret trip to Peking, which was followed by President Nixon's highly publicized official visit to the Chinese capitol. Shortly thereafter the Republic of China, Taiwan, was removed from the United Nations and replaced by the People's Republic of China. The United States in 1978 recognized the People's Republic of China and withdrew diplomatic recognition from Taiwan. China was granted most-favored-nation status and American business once again discovered the China market.

Mid-East

Throughout the 1970s Americans were made aware of the problems in the Middle East and of its importance to the United States. During the 1973 war between Israel and Egypt, the Organization of Petroleum Exporting Countries OPEC placed an embargo on the sale of crude oil to countries that supported Israel. Shortly thereafter, OPEC doubled the price of its oil. The industrialized nations were hit with shortages, higher prices and inflation. The embargo was lifted in 1974 but members of OPEC continued, on a routine basis, to raise prices. America's response to these challenges was to try to build bridges between Israel and Egypt, thereby preventing future wars, and to strengthen friendly governments in countries such as Iran and Saudi Arabia. Conditions in the area began to unravel towards the end of the decade.

Carter's most significant foreign policy achievement was the Camp David Agreement. Its terms provided for a "peace accord" between Israel and Egypt. The administration hoped that Camp David would be the first step toward a comprehensive solution to the problems that have beset the Middle East since the creation of Israel. Although Egypt and Israel have been the primary antagonists, such problems as occupied lands and Palestinian refugees have long been symbols that have united Middle East Moslems against Israel. Some of the territory that Egypt lost to Israel in the 1967 war was returned and the two sides exchanged ambassadors. But other occupied lands, such as Jerusalem, and the Palestinian refugee situation remain potentially explosive problems.

Camp David, however, did not bring peace to this troubled area. President Carter's response to the Soviet invasion of Afghanistan and the turmoil in Iran was to initiate the Carter Doctrine, which, in effect, extended the policy of containment to the Middle East. His first move was to create the Rapid Deployment Force which was to be highly mobile contingents of Marine, Army, and Air Force units stationed in the United States and able to respond to any Soviet threat to the Middle East. Reagan has reaffirmed this policy and there have been American military exercises in Egypt and in the desert in the south west area of the United States.

Shortly after the change of government in Iran, that country and neighboring Iraq became involved in a war over disputed border areas. The war, which appeared to be one of attrition, threatened the vital shipping lanes of the Persian Gulf. Reagan's response was to extend the Carter Doctrine to the gulf area. He declared that the shipping lanes of the gulf would be kept open by the United States and its allies.

Reagan's biggest challenge and most tragic foreign policy failure was in Lebanon, a country torn by political and religious differences as well as by foreign invasion. In early 1984, it was decided that the only way to bring peace to the beleagured nation was to send in peace keeping forces. Hence, the United States, Italy, and France sent military contingents to Lebanon to attempt to induce some sort of peaceful resolution to the conflict. American Marines were assigned to a vulnerable defensive position near the airport. Fanatics were able to penetrate their defenses with a bomb laden truck that exploded at a barrack and killed more than 200 of the troops. Shortly after that event, the allied units were withdrawn and Lebanon remains a tortured country.

EEK AND MEEK

Reprinted by permission. © 1980 Newspaper Enterprise Association, Inc.

Foreign Policy Goals

Americans have long believed that their foreign policy was unique in that its goals were to realize moral and humanitarian goals. Thomas Jefferson and James Madison were among the first to articulate this point-of-view and their position sparked a debate that has echoed down the corridors of American history. The issue at hand concerned what the United States should do about its first political treaty, a military alliance that was negotiated with the French after the Revolutionary War. Britain and France were at war and according to the treaty, the United States should actively ally itself with France. Jefferson and Madison argued that the country was morally bound to live up to the obligation of the alliance. They felt that foreign policy should not deviate from morality, legality and humanity. After all, these were the hallmarks of decency and civilization.

Alexander Hamilton took the opposite position. He believed that expendiency, not morality, should be the guiding star for foreign policy makers. From this perspective, moral principles and considerations were sometimes out of context in international affairs. Relationships between countries primarily reflected the values of selfish material interest and power. Therefore, according to this approach, foreign policy should reflect only one principle, the national interest. He recommended to President Washington that the United States not abide by the treaty. It would be a policy of national suicide to declare war on England. The British maintained forts on American soil, there was internal dissension at home and the French would not be able to cross the Atlantic to once again help us to fight the British in the Western Hemisphere. President Washington, acting on Hamilton's advice, proclaimed neutrality and, in effect, broke the country's first treaty.

The debate broke out again during the administrations of James K. Polk, William McKinley, Woodrow Wilson, Harry Truman and Lyndon Johnson. Historical circumstances were different but the essence of the issue remained the same, should the purpose of American foreign policy be pragmatism/realism or should it be moralism/idealism. The realist suggests that any given policy may be immoral and possibly illegal but prudent and wise if it either promotes or defends the national interest. On the other hand, the moralist believes that there are certain principles that transcend the nation state; hence, a policy that is immoral or illegal can be neither wise nor prudent.

President Carter made it clear during the campaign of 1976 and during the first part of his term in office that he was going to pursue policies that would be consistent with the goals of human rights and such other moral principles as disarmament. Carter soon discovered the conflict between the demands of national interest and policies of human rights. He was adamant about Soviet policies with respect to dissidents and the immigration of Jews. But, according to his critics he said nothing about the alleged atrocities in Iran when the Shah was in power. In a similar fashion he overlooked domestic conditions in such countries as South Korea and Chile. The tension between moral issues such as human rights and security and political interests will continue throughout the 1980s. A statesman who promotes the interest of his country at the expense of morally desirable goals will surely suffer the slings and arrows of a morally outraged media and public. In the realm of foreign policy it is and will continue to be difficult to serve the interests of one's country and those of humanity simultaneously.

Policy Formulation

President are given little constitutional authority to formulate and conduct security and foreign policy. Most of their authority comes from powers implied in the Constitution and from precedents established during the administration of President Washington. Since independence, the matter of foreign policy formulation has been a subject of contention. Once again, the origins of this debate are to be found in the 1794 clash between Madison, Jefferson and Hamilton. Jefferson and Madison demanded that the Constitution be followed word for word. It did not explicitly give the President authority to proclaim neutrality; therefore, Washington's action was, for them, without foundation. They also extended the argument by contending that the Constitution made Congress the policy making body, and the President's role was to enforce the will of Congress, not to act independently.

Again, Hamilton provided an alternative. Basically, he argued that only the President and not Congress could claim to represent national rather than regional interests. Hamilton also provided the earliest defense of implied powers. Although the Constitution did not grant general policy making powers to the President, the authority for specific actions seemed to be implied in the few enumerated powers. That is, Presidents could act authoritatively in all areas not expressly denied by either the Constitution or by law. Hamilton's view has survived court challenges and congressional criticisms and revolts. The President has been and still is the major mover and shaker, and Congress has grudgingly accepted the role of critic and sometimes consultant. Occasionally, Congress will seek to assert some authority and control over the exercise of foreign policy.

War Powers Resolution

In 1973, Congress, concerned about the war in Southeast Asia, overrode a presidential veto and imposed limitations on the President's power as commander-in-chief of the armed forces. The law requires the President to notify Congress within forty-eight hours if he orders military forces into another country. Furthermore, unless Congress officially approves of the action, the forces must be withdrawn after sixty days. If, during the sixty day period, Congress decides by a simple majority vote against the action, the troops must return and this is not subject to presidential veto. There could be an interesting struggle between the two branches if a future President decides to challenge the constitutionality of this congressional constraint.

Treaties and Executive Agreement

Since the first administration of George Washington, Presidents have formulated and executed foreign policy by means of treaties, executive agreements, executive privilege and executive order.

The Constitution grants the chief executive power to negotiate treaties. However, Congress has a constitutional check; before a treaty is legally binding, it must be ratified by a two-thirds vote in the United States Senate. George Washington established the precedent of executive agreement as a means of excluding the Senate from the treaty-making process. An executive agreement is a commitment between a President and one or more heads of other states. The agreement does not require Senate ratification and technically it is binding only during the incumbent's term of office. The authority for this practice is neither the constitutional nor congressional action but tradition. As such, the executive agreement is part of what is often referred to as the unwritten constitution. In 1937, the Supreme Court, in the case of *United States v. Belmont*, sanctioned executive agreements and granted them the same legal status as treaties. Many executive agreements have been noncontroversial, such as President Franklin D. Roosevelt's tariff-lowering Good Neighbor Policy toward Latin America. Since negotiations and commitments can be made in secret without congressional involvement, the practice has created some disputes.

All of the World War II compacts were executive agreements. The most controversial were those commitments made at Yalta. Congressmen as well as other Americans severely criticized the Yalta Agreements as an abuse of executive power. Also, since continuity in foreign affairs is necessary, executive agreements extend beyond the term of an incumbent. Roosevelt made promises and commitments at Yalta and elsewhere that Truman had to respect. Finally, it was argued that if Congress had been involved, the "mistakes" of Yalta would have been avoided. This criticism led to the introduction of the "Bricker Amendment," which was designed to limit greatly presidential power to make executive agreements. The proposed constitutional amendment missed the necessary two-thirds vote in the Senate by the margin of just one vote.

More recently, the Nixon and Ford administrations committed the United States to wheat deals with the Soviet Union by means of executive agreements. On these occasions Congressmen, foremost among them Senator Henry Jackson of Washington, accused the administrations of creating food shortages and inflationary prices particularly in 1974 by selling so much American grain abroad. Once again, the critics suggested that the mistake would have been avoided if Congress had scrutinized the deals. Critics of the executive agreement maintain that it grants the President far too much power. They also believe that there should be some sort of congressional check. Supporters believe that executive agreements grants the President independence and freedom both of which are indispensable to the successful conduct of foreign affairs. It adds flexibility by enabling the statesman to act in private and with dispatch.

Executive Privilege

Executive privilege is another product of custom and tradition that finds its authority in the early days of the republic. This device provides for a presidential refusal to testify before Congress and the courts in matters that might involve national security. Furthermore, a President may not permit other members of the executive branch to testify, and he can refuse to honor subpoenas for documents in matters that he defines as sensitive to the security of the nation. During the

Watergate scandal the President often invoked executive privilege with respect to releasing taped conversations and other documents. In the summer of 1974, the Supreme Court, for the first time in history, reviewed the practice of executive privilege. It was unanimously ruled in *United States v. Nixon* that executive privilege cannot cover evidence or testimony that has been subpoenaed in criminal proceedings. The court ordered President Nixon to turn over the tapes to the special prosecutor. And so a device that was primarily used in matters of foreign policy and national defense became an instrument in bringing about the first presidential resignation.

Executive Order

The executive order also finds its authority in tradition. More often than not, this device in foreign affairs has been used in conjunction with the President's power as commander-in-chief of the armed forces. A President can, by executive order, send American military forces anywhere in the world without the consent of Congress. In fact, a President need not even consult Congress before he initiates such action. The Constitution clearly states that only Congress has the power to declare war. However, a President can, as commander-in-chief, engage the armed forces in undeclared wars. President Washington established the precedent when he commissioned three military expeditions to fight the Indian Confederation in the Northwest area. President John Adams reaffirmed the policy by engaging the French in an undeclared sea war, and President Jefferson felt that he acted with full constitutional authority when he sent elements of the United States Navy and Marine Corps into the Mediterranean Sea to fight the Barbary Coast Wars.

More recently, President Truman dispatched the armed forces to deter aggression in Korea, and then President Eisenhower, by means of an executive order, accepted the armistice that ended the fighting. Three Presidents used executive orders with respect to American involvement in the Vietnam conflict. President Kennedy started American military involvement, President Johnson continued the policy, and President Nixon ended military participation. President Kennedy ordered a naval blockade of Cuba during the missile crisis, and in 1965, President Johnson ordered United States military involvement during a political crisis and civil war in the Dominican Republic. And, President Reagan ordered the Marines to Lebanon and U.S. military units in Grenada and Libya. Finally, in the arena of foreign affairs, presidents have used the executive order device with respect to matters of diplomatic recognition. The Reagan administration appears to have little faith in the general policy of detente and went back to that of containment. During his first term, the president was very active in the fields of foreign and defense policies.

America's approach to the 1980s will require a good deal of foresight and flexibility. Presidents during this period can expect a variety of challenges on the political, military, and economic levels. The primary antagonist will continue to be the Soviet Union. However, America's leaders must be prepared to deal with potentially explosive issues such as the international energy crisis. Furthermore, revolutionary movements can expect to present challenges in Central and Southern America, Africa and the Middle East. The successful promotion and protection of American interests during what appears to be the troublesome eighties, will require skillful leadership and the cooperation and understanding of Congress and the American people.

Notes

1. George F. Kennan, "X," *Foreign Affairs*, July, 1947, pp. 566–82.
2. Nuclear weapons involve the fissioning of uranium or plutonium atoms. Thermonuclear weapons require the fusion of heavy hydrogen atoms. Nuclear weapons have yields measured in kilotons, or thousands of tons equivalent of TNT. The explosions over Hiroshima and Nagasaki were about 20 kilotons. Thermonuclear weapons have megaton explosive power, or millions of tons equivalent of TNT. Russia tested the largest thermonuclear weapon in the atmosphere in the early sixties. It had a yield in excess of 50 megatons.
3. Missiles that carry clusters of independently targeted warheads. SALT II imposed a limit of 10 MIRV per missile.
4. An agreement wherein Country A (United States) will automatically grant Country B (Soviet Union) trade and tariff concessions that it has granted to other countries.
5. Central Intelligence Agency, *The International Energy Situation: Outlook to 1985*. Washington, D.C.: U.S. Government Printing Office, April, 1977.

For Further Reading

Marshall, Charles B. *The Limits of Foreign Policy*. Baltimore: Johns Hopkins Press, 1958.

Nash, Henry T. *American Foreign Policy: Changing Perspectives on National Security*. Homewood, Illinois: The Dorsey Press, 1978.

Solzhenittsyn, Aleksandr *Detente: Prospects for Democracy and Dictatorship*. New Brunswich, N.J.: Transaction Books, 1976.

Spanier, John *American Foreign Policy Since World War II* 8th ed. New York: Holt, Rinehart and Winston, 1980.

Waltz, Kenneth N. *Man, the State and War: A Theoretical Analysis*. New York: Columbia University Press, 1959.

Name _____

Section _____

Date _____

Review Questions for Chapter 11: The United States in the World

1. Truman Doctrine _____

_____

_____

_____

_____

2. Carter Doctrine _____

_____

_____

_____

_____

3. Executive Agreement _____

_____

_____

_____

_____

4. Detente _____

_____

_____

_____

_____

5. SALT _____

_____

_____

_____

_____

6. *U.S. v. Nixon* (1974) _____

_____

_____

_____

_____

7. Camp David Agreement _____

_____

_____

_____

_____

8. NATO _____

_____

_____

_____

_____

9. *U.S. v. Belmont* (1937) _____

_____

_____

_____

_____

10. Executive Order _____

_____

_____

_____

_____

Essay Study Questions

1. Discuss the War Powers Resolution.
2. Do you agree or disagree with U.S. Policy in Latin America? Why?
3. Is containment a bad or good policy? Why?
4. What is the best way to control nuclear weapons and prevent their use?

Chapter 12

State and Local Government

In recent years increasing attention has been given to the role of "the average citizen" in the affairs of government. Twenty years ago the galvanizing issues were civil rights and the war in Vietnam; today they are energy and the economy. Citizen participation is the new watchword and we are told that it is at the state and local levels that the person on the street can make his views best known. These are the governmental units closest to us, and thus people who were "dropping out" with Dr. Timothy Leary in the late 1960s are today seeking elective and appointive offices in statehouses and city halls across the land. Just a few years ago Tom Hayden (the husband of actress Jane Fonda) was one of the leaders of this nation's anti-Vietnam movement. Today, he is an elected member of the California State Legislature.

Proposition 13

In terms of citizen participation, perhaps the most significant happening in the last ten years has been the movement to limit the taxing and spending powers of local government. The most famous such effort was California's Proposition 13—a 1978 initiative passed by the citizens of that state which slashed local property taxes.

In the years since that initial shot was fired numerous tax-policy changes for state and local government have been instituted throughout the land. A sampling:

—The amounts collectable through the property tax were frozen in Virginia, Kentucky and New Mexico.
—The state income tax was lowered in Kansas, Maryland, Indiana, Arkansas, Mississippi and Vermont.
—Spending limits were placed on state and/or local governments in Arizona, Utah, Nevada, Hawaii, Michigan and Texas.
—A property tax cut program almost identical to California's Proposition 13 was passed in Idaho.
—Nevada cut its local property taxes in half and made up the difference by raising the sales tax.

This national, citizen-based movement to lower taxes is often referred to as "Proposition 13 Fever."

At the state and local levels, "power to the people" may be a movement whose time has come, but it may also be just an empty slogan. The extent of its reality depends upon circumstances in each individual situation. It depends upon the state of public opinion, upon individual commitment and upon how open or closed the power structures happen to be in any given jurisdiction. In order to understand the ability—or inability—of citizens to have a real impact on their state and local governments the most important thing to consider is the structure of those governments. Such structures, or legal arrangements, give power to some and limit it for others. For example, if a state constitution gives overwhelming power to the governor at the expense of the legislature then it is likely that citizen input and access will be severely reduced. Because this is so this chapter will focus on how power is organized at the state and local levels.

We will first examine the main forms of city government since these bear very heavily on whether power will rest with the mayor, the city council, the city manager or someone else. The type of voting procedure used also has an impact on the possibility of "people power" and control and thus we will assess the major electoral plans in use in local government today.

Regarding the operation of the fifty states we will look first at the legislatures. Our focus will be upon the extent to which power is either centralized within a power elite or dispersed to as many participants as possible. A similar perspective will guide our analysis of the roles of the fifty governors.

There Are Four Forms of Local Government

Over the years politicians and reformers have argued about the best way to run local government. Some have emphasized the officials' direct accountability to the local citizens while others have claimed that the primary value ought to be efficiency. In response to these debates different systems of local government have been developed and implemented. Thus not all local governments are organized the same way. They do things one way in Chicago and another in Las Vegas.

Currently there are four main forms of municipal government; four ways in which local government may be organized to carry out its functions. Whether a locality has one form or another depends upon such things as its size, its geographic location and the nature of the services it offers to its citizens. Let us briefly examine these four types of local government.

The Strong Mayor-Council Plan

The form of local government most widely found in the eastern part of the United States is known as the Strong Mayor-Council plan. Here the idea of separation of powers is applied at the municipal level with the popularly elected council serving as the legislative branch and the mayor as the chief executive. Remembering how the national government in Washington, D.C. is organized, you should see some definite similarities with this type of local government. In terms of an analogy it might be said that the mayor is to the council as the President is to Congress.

In fact the similarities are very real. Congress passes laws and the administrative branch executes them. The council enacts ordinances and the mayor's staff carries them out. For example, the council may decide that a certain act is a misdemeanor. It is then up to the Police Department, which reports to the Mayor, to enforce this law. The president also makes numerous proposals to Congress concerning what new laws are needed. A mayor does the same thing with his council.

The mayor is said to be "strong" because of his leadership of the council and for two other reasons, as well. First, it is the mayor who appoints most of the other executive officials: assessor, controller, city clerk, etc. In Washington the president appoints his own Cabinet—the men and women who will run the executive branch of government. In city halls across the land, the strong mayor also appoints the individuals who make up what is essentially his or her cabinet. Remember that if you appoint someone to office you can give them orders and ultimately can ask for their resignation if they don't conform. This fact gives you power.

The other factor generating power for the strong mayor is the executive budget. Under this form of local government the annual operating budget is prepared, not by the council, but by the mayor. It is he who makes the initial—and most important—decisions about how a city will spend its money. And money is power. Thus we may conclude that there are three main criteria by which to distinguish a strong mayor: leadership of the council, an effective appointment power and the presence of an executive budget.

Weak Mayor-Council Plan

A second, but less widely used, form of local government is known as the Weak Mayor-Council Plan. This system enjoyed its heyday in the last century, for it championed the concepts of Jacksonian Democracy. That is, it was based on the idea that as many executive officials as possible—and not just the mayor—should be directly elected by the people. Theoretically more direct accountability would mean better representation. In the strong-mayor system the people *elect* the mayor who then *appoints* all the other executive officials. By contrast, under the weak mayor system the mayor is merely one of a number of executive officials all of whom are directly elected by the citizenry. The treasurer, superintendent of streets, controller and others thus may all owe their holding of office directly to the voters, not to the mayor. He did not appoint them; he cannot remove them or give them orders.

It should be clear why this approach is called the "weak mayor" system. Although theoretically the mayor is the chief executive officer, in reality he possesses insufficient tools to direct the executive branch of city government. Other executive officials may not share his sense of priorities and are likely to belong to the rival policial party. If one is to control even a small municipal organization it must be through a series of key appointees, but the weak mayor lacks these. He may also lack the strong mayor's budget-formulation power, for in many cities of this type the annual spending plan is drawn up not by the mayor but by the council or by a special commission. Face it: if he can't tell subordinates what to do and if he can't determine how the money is going to be spent, he has to be called "weak." Since there can be little coordination of effort the system is said to opt for accountability rather than efficiency.

The Council Manager Plan

The third form of municipal government, and the one most widely used in the western states, is known as the Council-Manager Plan. It shares with the two forms already examined a vesting of legislative authority in an elected council. The representatives who make up the council pass the laws and set the policies. But they also do something else that they do not do under either of the other plans: they select the chief administrative officer. This individual is the city manager, a public management professional, not a local politician. The chief administrative officer serves "at the pleasure" of the council, and his job is to carry out their laws; to manage their town.

This system emphasizes efficiency, for it seeks to turn questions of day-to-day administration over to a technically trained expert. The city manager then appoints all of the various department heads. They are responsible to him and he, in turn, is responsible to the elected city council.

To say that he "serves at their pleasure" and that he "carries out their laws" does not mean, however, that the city manager has little power. Although technically subservient to the council, he usually has substantial influence given the fact that the council is made up of part-time political amateurs, while he is a full-time professional. He is looked to by the council for advice on new policies, or policy changes, to be enacted. He is an on-going source of information to elected decision makers who lack his ready access to the workaday routines and workaday data of the operating departments. He, like the strong mayor, is also the one who formulates the municipal budget each year.

All of these factors tend to make the city manager a powerful force in those cities which have adopted this plan. Still "when push comes to shove" the council, as the democratically elected representative body, has the right to fire the manager when his views differ with theirs. And it is this "final authority" that guarantees their control of the local government.

The Commission Plan

The fourth form of municipal organization is known as the Commission Plan. Just to keep things clear, it should be noted that many local governments, like the City of Las Vegas and Clark County in Nevada, call their legislative bodies commissions, although the governments themselves have been set up along the lines of the city manager model.

The Commission Plan differs from the other systems primarily in its elimination of the idea of separation of powers. Instead of having a directly elected legislative branch counterbalancing the executive, the Commission Plan does away with the independent executive altogether.

The commission is composed of elected representatives. They carry on the legislative function by passing ordinances and making the basic decisions about the kinds of services that the municipality will offer. This is how the members operate as a group, but singly they carry things one step further. Each commissioner, and there will usually be anywhere from three to seven, also serves as the head of a city departments such as fire, sanitation, or recreation. Thus instead of following traditional American principles, this system of government combines legislative and executive power in one set of hands.

Since the ideas of separation of powers and checks and balances were designed as safeguards against corruption and tyranny, it may not be too surprising for the student to learn that this system has been plagued with charges of graft and special favors, vote trading and log rolling. The typical scenario finds the commissioners rather uninterested in playing the watchdog role over the administration, since they are the administration. Thus instead of working together to root out problems, they work together to increase each others' appropriations and stay out of each others' business. "I won't make trouble for your department, if you don't make trouble for mine," is the refrain often heard. Because of such problems, the Commission Plan is the least used of the four forms of local government.

Electoral Systems Differ

It is often said that "there is no Republican or Democratic way to pave a street." That is, it is widely agreed that local government is concerned primarily with technical and service matters that are thoroughly routine in nature. If this is true, it means that partisan politics have no place in the making of many local government decisions. If, indeed, there is "one best way" to run a fire station or a recreation program, then "politics" can make no real contribution.

The action taken as a result of such thinking has been a movement to substitute non-partisan for partisan ballots. Under the non-partisan system candidates run as individuals only and without the aide of such labels as "Republican" or "Democrat." We are told that the voters should be deprived of the "crutch" of party labels to help them in making election decisions. When this happens they will have to examine the records of the individual candidates. The result will be more rational voting. Other arguments on behalf of non-partisan elections include the idea that the absence of labels will limit the effect of state and national trends on local choices. Finally, we are told that the insulation of government from the political parties will cause a higher caliber of candidate to offer himself for office.

None of these ideas have ever been proven, but that has not stopped them from being extremely popular. This has been especially true in the western states where approximately ninety percent of all local elections bar national party labels from the ballot.[1] By way of contrast we should note that the comparable figure for the northeast is only twenty-five percent.

The other main variations in how local councilmembers are elected involves whether the contests are staged at-large or by wards. In a ward system the city is geographically divided into a series of districts and each district has one representative on the council. The election campaign thus takes place within each district with two or more candidates competing for the one seat. The winner then becomes the spokesperson for his or her ward. Under this system power is scattered; it is based in the neighborhoods and in numerous "ward organizations." Chicago is one of the best examples of a ward system in the country. There the power of each of the fifty aldermen rests on a "back-home" district base.

The alternative system for selecting a council is known as the at-large election. Here each member of the council stands for election before the entire city. To keep the number of candidates from becoming unwieldy the terms of office are staggered. Thus usually no more than two positions, thus four candidates, will be before the voters in any given year.

Like non-partisan voting, the at-large system has been presented to Americans as a way of reforming local government. If non-partisanship was going to take the politics out of local decision-making then the addition of at-large elections was going to guarantee that those elected would take a "city-wide" perspective in problem solving. Since they would no longer be "messenger boys" and "bargaining agents" for individual sections of the city the council members would be able to look instead to the overall good and promote such good-government goals as comprehensive planning and the city-wide forecasting of needs. This does appear to have been the outcome in many cities that have instituted the plan, but such results are by no means universal.

One very real problem with at-large voting is that it tends to dilute the strength of various minority groups. These groups may be sizeable and have enough voters to carry one or more wards where most of their members reside. However, when they are mixed into a single, city-wide district their members will be swallowed up by the majority. Under a five-seat ward system a minority group with twenty percent of the population will most likely be able to control at least one council seat. If the same city switches to an at-large system that twenty percent then has to stand against the eighty percent majority. The result is likely to be the winning of no seats by the minority group.

Local Government: Conclusion

A major theme in local government organization and reorganization during the twentieth century has been efficiency. Services should be provided in a less costly manner; politics should be removed and rationality restored. Innovators have offered three reforms: the city manager system with elections held on a non-partisan and at-large basis. Reformers have been fairly effective in reaching their goals, but they have also endangered local stability by ignoring such very real conflicts as those based on race, ethnicity and socio-economic class. It may be true that there is no Republican or Democratic way to build a street, but it is equally true that the decision about *where* to build the new street is often basically a political one.

State Governments

State governments are sometimes referred to as the "forgotten men" of American government. Large numbers of citizens follow the daily news from Washington and tend to be aware of what local governments are doing simply because they are so close. That leaves the states in a middle-ground of non-attention, yet they are a critical link in the federal system. They have major responsibilities in such areas as police service, pollution control, income security programs, health and education. They administer numerous grant programs for the national government and they pass the laws specifying what local governments can and cannot do.

Generally speaking the most important actors in the fifty state governments are the governors and the legislators. In each of the fifty jurisdictions these actors set the basic goals and policies. They decide what is to be done, and how. Sometimes this kind of decision making is undertaken in an atmosphere of ongoing cooperation between the two branches—as frequently happens when the capitol and the governor's mansion are controlled by the same political party. In other states and at other times conflict and deadlock are likely to characterize the normal state of affairs. To understand what this means for the chances for effective government each of these institutions needs to be examined individually.

It is a little-known fact that in most state legislatures power is more highly concentrated than it is in the United States Congress. Congress is based on a system of fragmented power in which most of the "clout" rests with the standing committees. While state legislatures do use committees, they do not generally grant them nearly as much independent power. Instead, power is centralized and rests with the leadership—officials like the Speaker of the House and the President of the Senate. The authority of the legislative leaders generally rests upon the holding of certain key powers which will now be examined in detail.[2]

Committee Appointments

First of all, it is frequently their job to appoint the members of standing committees such as Commerce, Agriculture, and Natural Resources. This power generates political muscle in two ways. First of all, it allows the leadership to put its most trusted people on the key committees. If the leadership knows ahead of time that two or three committees will get most of the 'action' this term they can assign to those committees people they trust; people who see the world in the same way they do. A second political angle to the seat assignment job is the ability to reward friends and punish enemies. If you control the distribution of posts, you control other people's careers. You can award the 'plums' and the sought-after seats to those who have been most cooperative with you in the past. Similarly, you can place uncooperative members on committees that will do them no good at all. This power, then, is a source of political muscle because other legislators know what the leader can do to, or for, them, and they shape their behavior accordingly.

Committee Chairmanships

A second critical power enjoyed by the leadership in many states is the right to appoint committee chairpersons. Each committee must have a chairman and if the leadership has not selected him or her it may be very difficult for that leadership to enlist cooperation. For example, in Congress the committee chairpersons are selected either by seniority, (the member of the majority party with the longest continuous record of service on a committee is automatically its chairperson as in the Senate) or by election by fellow committee members, as in the House of Representatives. In either case the chair holds his position independently of the leadership. If he doesn't owe his position to the leader he doesn't have to obey him, but in many states he does owe his appointment to those above him. The result? A greater centralization of influence and an increased risk that some kind of elite power structure will emerge.

Bill Assignment

The third critical leadership power involves what is known as bill assignment. When a bill is introduced in a state legislature it does not automatically go to the floor for a vote. First it must be referred to a committee that will examine it, perhaps hold public hearings on it and then recommend either passage or defeat to the entire chamber. Because the committee's recommendations are usually followed, the committee stage is a critical one for any bill. Thus, what does it mean if we know ahead of time that one committee favors a particular bill while another one opposes it? Obviously it means that if we want to see the bill passed we will want it referred to the committee that is already favorably disposed toward it; and vice versa.

The key point in all of this is that it is the legislative leadership that makes these decisions. It is true that usually there are by-laws setting forth the jurisdiction of each committee and that therefore the leader may have little choice about where to assign a bill. However, in many instances the boundaries will be vague, and he will have substantial discretion. Should a particular labor bill go to the Commerce Committee or to the Labor Committee? Should a bill regulating insecticides used by farmers go to the Agriculture Committee or the Environmental Affairs Committee? Farm interests are more likely to be represented on the former than on the latter body and thus the simple, seemingly neutral, decisions about where to send the bill for investigation can influence and even pre-determine the outcome.

Parliamentary Procedure

A fourth source of clout is the leader's control over parliamentary procedure. He can hasten or delay certain bills through his control of the calendar, his power of recognition and his authority to entertain particular motions. He controls debate; he usually decides when to call for a vote and he is responsible for declaring the results of that vote. This latter function is not just a simple score-keeping activity since the leader also decides when a vote is to be declared closed.

Conference Committees

Lastly, the legislative leadership is usually in charge of making appointments to conference committees. These are government bodies whose job is to iron out any differences that may exist in upper and lower house versions of bills that have been passed. Generally conference committee reports tend to be accepted by both houses. Since their views normally prevail it means that the makeup of these committees is critical to the outcome. And who controls this last important step? Normally, the leadership.

The legislatures are essential components of the fifty state governments. They make policy decisions affecting millions of people, yet in most jurisdictions their powers are concentrated in just a few sets of hands. This fact has profound implications for democracy, for it means that we may have government "for the people," but it is at least questionable whether it is government "of the people and by the people."

The Governor

In most states there is one other central figure: the governor. He occupies the key policy-making position and he can normally rally sufficient support for his programs given his standing in the state political party. Increasingly, the governor's mansion is also serving as a recruiting ground for presidential candidates.

Still, not all governors are equally powerful. Some states give them very wide-ranging authority while others specifically limit what they can do. When we analyze and compare the governorships in all fifty states it becomes possible to construct a list of "power attributes." These represent an attempt to answer the question of what makes for a strong governor?

The Four-Year Term

The first critical component of gubernatorial strength is a four-year term of office. When a new governor is inaugurated to a two-year term his incumbency is half over by the time he finally gets all of his appointments made and his administration fully consolidated. The four-year governor, on the other hand, has a reasonable amount of time—the same that the Constitution gives to the president—to establish meaningful priorities and undertake the implentation of his programs. It is presumptuous to hold a chief executive responsible for certain tasks if he is not also given enough time to carry them out.

Governors from states with a two-year term—states like New Mexico and New Hampshire—are frequently heard to say that they cannot spend enough time on the job. Instead they have to devote much of their time just to running for office.

Reelection

The ability to run for office again points to the second characteristic of a strong governor. He is one who is allowed by state law to succeed himself in office. Throughout much of our history many states have limited their governors to a single term—an impulse apparently based on a deep-seated distrust of the executive. Such a provision puts him at an extreme disadvantage in his dealings with the legislature. State senators and representatives are not similarly limited, and this means that, especially with regard to the legislative leadership, these denizens of the capitol can usually count on being around long after any current governor is gone. Under such circumstances, why look to the chief executive for advice and guidance, programs and priorities? This means that when there are differences of opinion between the two branches the legislature will feel very little incentive to bargain and compromise; and why should it? If its members will but wait patiently, the source of their problems will be forced by law to leave office soon enough. Of course, such a way of looking at legislative/executive relations often results in "government by stalemate."

Appointment Power

The third criterion for a strong governor is an effective appointment power; the ability to select the other members of the administrative team. It should be recalled that this was also one of the ways in which we distinguished between weak and strong mayors. In most states numerous other executive branch officials—Secretary of State, Attorney General, Controller, etc.—are directly elected by the citizens. This means, of course, that the governor has little or no control over them. Such a system is said to be characterized by "executive fragmentation," because authority is so divided as to make it nearly impossible for the governor to provide central coordination.

The theory behind such an arrangement is a noble one—that in a democracy these other executive officials should be directly accountable to the people. This will mean the appointment of fewer political hacks and less "government by cronyism." Officials presumably will respond more quickly to people's needs if it is the people—and not the governor—who put them in office.

The trouble with such a theory unfortunately is that it assumes citizen attentiveness to, and knowledge about, these other positions and their incumbents. Voters can hold their officials responsible for their acts only if they are familiar with their records, yet voting surveys indicate that an alarming percentage of the voting age population cannot even provide such basic information as the names of the executive officials currently in office. (Take a quick quiz. Who is the present attorney general in your state?) Hence the general accountability theory does not work very well in practice. Instead what we frequently have is attention to the needs of certain key interest groups that watch the operations of the agency in question. The average voter may not know much about the candidates for a state board of regents, but you may rest assured that the education community is very knowledgeable on this subject.

While executive fragmentation does not generally result in enhanced accountability it does operate to the detriment of governmental efficiency. When a governor's power is diminished by having to share it with others he cannot set priorities and give direction to the executive branch. Setting goals and measuring attainment becomes problematical since in a fragmented system the governor has to depend upon the whims of others. Hawaii and New Jersey are the two states least hindered by executive fragmentation, while Texas and South Carolina limit their governors' appointment powers the most.

Budget

The fourth component of gubernatorial power is the executive budget. Today most states give their chief executive the authority to draw up the annual spending plan. As it does for the strong mayor and the city manager, this prerogative gives the governor the very real ability to direct the executive branch and coordinate programs. The governor can reduce or expand departmental budget requests at will before they get to the legislature. In such undertakings he is assisted by a special budget bureau composed of trained fiscal experts. This pool of technical competence is matched by few legislatures and thus serves as an important power base for the governor.

Veto Power

The fifth, and last, item in our enumeration of power capabilities is the type of veto power. The veto, of course, is the act by which a chief executive rejects a bill which has been passed by the legislature. If the veto is not overridden the effect is to kill the bill. Most people know how this works as far as the President is concerned, but what few realize is that most governors have stronger veto powers than does the President.

In addition to the "regular" veto just described most states give their governors a tool called the item veto to be used on appropriations bills. As its name implies the item veto gives the governor considerable flexibility since he is not required to either sign or reject an entire bill. It is not uncommon for an appropriations bill to pass the legislature and be ninety-nine percent acceptable to the governor. Still, there is a section to which he objects. With the item veto he can reject the offending provisions and leave the remainder of the bill intact; not even a president can do that.

A third kind of veto, the reduction veto, adds yet more power and flexibility. Like the item veto it applies only to appropriations bills, and like it, it also allows a governor to target individual provisions. The "item veto" is somewhat constricting, however, in that the governor must "take or leave" the whole item. As its name implies, the reduction veto allows the governor to keep certain expenditures but at a reduced level. It may be unrealistic to speak of the governor item vetoing, for example, one whole program within mental health. But if he can use his reduction veto to lessen it by ten percent this will heighten his power over both his own executive branch and with the legislature when it comes to bargaining and making compromises.

Finally, a handful of states—like Illinois—give their chief executive a fourth type of veto power—the so-called amendatory veto. This is a device enabling the governor to make certain kinds of minor changes in a bill when he signs it. If the legislature does not respond by overruling the amendment then the bill, together with the governor's changes, becomes law.

To reiterate, we have been examining the five key factors that make for a strong governor. These are relevant to a basic understanding of state government since the governor is generally the most important political figure in the state. When we analyze what he can and cannot do, we are able to assess his ability to effectively administer an executive branch employing thousands of persons and his clout in dealing with a legislature frequently enjoying a centralized leadership structure.

Conclusion

At the beginning of this chapter we spoke of "people power," citizen input and direct democracy. Such concepts have been part of our political culture for two hundred years, but one thing that should be clear now is that they operate at the state and local levels more as slogans than as reality. The drive for increased efficiency and governmental effectiveness has meant that more and more power is being centralized and being placed in the hands of experienced, professional leaders. The cry to "get things done," at the same time that a tax revolt is in full swing, has meant that efficiency, rather than accountability, has become the key energizing and organizing principle for state and local government. The use of the city manager form of government may lead to more cost-effective government, but it will not necessarily guarantee more citizen participation. Strong governors who appoint their own "cabinets" and wield strong veto powers may make state government more rational and better coordinated, but they will not necessarily facilitate increased voter input. Our systems of state and local government are definitely becoming more and more efficient and this is all to the good. The other side of this coin, however, is the realization that we are accepting more and more "government for the people" and less and less "government by the people."

Notes

1. *National Municipal Review*, 1968, Washington, D.C.: International City Manager's Association, p. 58.
2. Malcolm Jewell, *The State Legislatures* (New York: Random House, 1962), Chapter 5.
3. Joseph Schlesinger, "The Politics of the Executive," in Jacob and Vines, (eds.), *Politics in the American States*, (Boston: Little, Brown and Co., 1965) pp. 207–238.

For Further Reading

Bollens, John and Schmandt, *The Metropolis*. (New York: Harper and Row, Publishers, 1982).
Dye, Thomas, *Politics in States and Communities*. (Englewood Cliffs, New Jersey, 1981).
Harrigan, John, *Politics and Policy in States and Communities*. (Boston, Mass: Little, Brown and Co., 1984).
Henry, Nicholas, *Governing At The Grassroots*. (Englewood Cliffs, New Jersey: Prentice-Hall, 1980).
Maddox, R. and Fuquay, R., *State and Local Government*. (New York: Van Nostrand Co., 1981).

Name _____

Section _____

Date _____

Review Questions for Chapter 12: State and Local Government

1. List the four main forms of local government used in the U.S. today.

_____

_____

_____

_____

2. Which of these four plans is used by the City of Las Vegas, NV?

_____

3. Local government electoral systems vary. In some, the city is divided up geographically into a series of districts and each district is given representation on the council. Such an arrangement is called a (an) _____ system.

4. In the other type of electoral system each member of the council stands for election before the entire city. This approach is called a (an) _____ system.

5. One big problem with at-large voting is that it tends to _____ the electoral strength of minority groups.

6. In most state legislatures power is more _____ than it is in the U.S. Congress.

7. There are five key powers held by the leadership in the majority of our state legislatures. One of these is the power to make committee appointments. What are the other four?

   _____

   _____

   _____

   _____

8. What are the "power attributes" of a state governor that give him real authority?

   _____

   _____

   _____

   _____

   _____

9. List the four different types of gubernatorial vetoes.

   _____

   _____

   _____

   _____

10. "_____ Fever" is the name frequently given to the national, citizen-based movement to lower state and local taxes.

Essay Study Questions

1. Discuss the powers of local administrators (mayors and city managers) through which they are given the authority to hire people for jobs and to prepare municipal budgets.

2. Compare and contrast the U.S. Congress and a "typical" state legislature in terms of the concept of "fragmentation of power."

Chapter 13

Issues for the Eighties and Beyond

The 1960s and early 1970s was a period of political and social ferment in the United States. Practices and traditions were challenged, institutions were attacked, and reforms were demanded in all areas. It was a time when many Americans believed that social ills could be overcome. In an atmosphere of unbridled enthusiasm, planners created programs, spent money, and developed agencies and bureaus to deal with the perceived problems. Poverty, hunger, and discrimination were outlawed. Education was promised to all Americans. And one of the last frontiers, space, was conquered. Experimentation in everything from drugs to social programs was the vogue.

By 1973, this "can do" mood was replaced with one of skepticism. The soaring sixties evolved into the sedentary seventies. Americans ran out of breath and the spirit became reflective and somewhat pessimistic. Government, viewed as the great healer and provider in the 1960s, became an enemy by the late 1970s and early 1980s. In many respects, the 1980 campaign, as articulated by most of the candidates, was antigovernment. More than anything else, the campaign reflected the current desire of many Americans to be left alone. President Reagan sensed this mood and promised to get government off the backs of the people. A similar attitude was expressed by Mr. Reagan in 1984. He spoke of traditional values and a vision of the future that would provide happiness for all with little government interference.

Students, professing altruism in the 1960s, were concerned about participatory democracy, the war in Viet Nam, the military establishment, environmental pollution, and the plight of the underprivileged. Students in the late 1970s and early 1980s, like those thirty years earlier, were more concerned about grades, admission to professional schools, and employment. Demonstrations on campuses, or anywhere else for that matter, became rare. The "do your own thing" attitude of the 1960s has evolved into a "don't bother me" and "don't get involved" sentiment.

In the 1960s Americans were busily programming an optimistic future. In the 1970s Americans took refuge in the past. The mood of the country was less confident and less self-righteous. Two events in the transitional period are important. The first were the 1974 and 1979 energy crises and the second was the inflation-recession cycle that has plagued the economy.

Energy Shortages

Long accustomed to cheap and abundant supplies of gasoline, Americans were shocked in 1974 when they were forced to wait in long lines for a few gallons. But the immediate crisis passed, the economy improved, and Americans were once more able to purchase sufficient gasoline, albeit at higher prices. Some felt that shortages had been contrived by the oil companies so that they might reap higher prices and Congress launched an investigation. But, by and large, Americans in the mid-1970s acted as though energy sources were once again inexhaustible. Consumption continued to increase as did the imports of foreign oil. Energy was not a major issue during the 1976 campaign however, shortly after his inauguration, President Carter presented Congress with a proposed comprehensive energy plan. Carter was impressed with a February, 1977 Central Intelligence Agency report on the world's dwindling oil supplies.[1] The report forecast that by 1985, the major powers would become net energy importers competing over scarce supplies in various parts of the world. Such competition could produce another world war, runaway inflation, disastrous depressions and civil wars. Carter's plan was to try to make America less dependent upon foreign oil. He emphasized a shift to coal for the production of electricity. Deregulation of the price controls imposed on the oil and natural gas industries was also advocated. Such action would provide the oil and natural gas companies with the profit incentive to explore and develop hitherto undeveloped and in some cases remote fields. Carter's plan also emphasized conservation and the development of synthetic fuels.

In a series of televised fireside chats, Carter tried to convince Congress and the American people that there was a genuine and dangerous energy crisis. Apparently, Congressmen sensed that Americans were in no mood to make additional sacrifices with respect to energy and beyond creating the Department of Energy, they gave the President little of what he had requested. Once again the country developed a feeling of euphoria with respect to energy.

Iran

During 1978, domestic problems in Iran, a major oil exporter, were building toward a crisis. Oil workers in that country went on strike and reduced Iran's flow to a trickle. In early 1979, the government of the Shah collapsed and leadership shifted to a religious leader, Aytollah Khomenii. The Aytollah was intent upon creating an Islamic republic that was violently anti-American and anti-Communist. The impact on the United States was immediate and dramatic. By the spring of 1979 Americans were once again waiting in long lines for limited amounts of gasoline. In addition, they watched gasoline and other fuel prices soar to one dollar a gallon and beyond. This time Congress and the President responded to the mounting crisis. A windfall profit tax was instituted against the oil companies. Its purpose was to return excess industry profits to segments of society that were most damaged by the soaring prices.

Iran and Iraq were at war during the 1980s. During the middle part of the decade, their dispute spilled into the Persian Gulf. Ships were damaged and sunk by missiles and mines. President Reagan, in a forceful speech, let it be known that the United States would take the responsibility for keeping the Gulf open and secure. American involvement in that part of the world will continue to spark controversy and concern throughout the decade.

Conservation

President Carter again came up with an energy program. The centerpiece of his plan was conservation. Tax credits were made available for citizens who insulated their homes or invested in other energy-saving investments. Thermostats in public buildings were ordered to be set at no higher than 65° in the winter and no lower than 75° in the summer. In July, 1980 Congress passed the Energy Security Act. The purpose of the law was to make America more energy independent by developing synthetic fuels. The act created a public corporation, the Synthetic Fuels Corporation, which was empowered to make direct loans for shale oil extraction and coal gasification projects. A target production rate equal to 500,000 barrels of oil per day was set for 1987 and 2 million barrels per day by 1992. In addition the act appropriated additional monies for the development of solar and geothermal energy and alcohol fuels. A rider to the Act provided that at least 100,000 barrels of oil a day be added to the strategic petroleum reserve, which was originally authorized in 1975. Most of the reserves are being stored in salt dome caverns in Louisiana and Texas. Such goals of synthetic fuel production are likely not to be achieved. In February 1981, President Reagan recommended a major reduction in the Synthetic Fuels Corporation's budget.

Shortly after his inauguration, President Reagan completely decontrolled the price of oil and consumer prices jumped. Nevertheless, it became clear by 1981 that conservation and higher fuel prices were beginning to slow consumption. By 1984, supply had so exceeded demand that gasoline, in some areas, was priced below one dollar per gallon. Americans were not as inconvenienced by high prices and shortages as they were in the 1970s. Nevertheless, eventually the piper must be paid. Fossil fuels are finite resources that will become more and more scarce. The Reagan administration, apparently having faith in the market place as a solution to depleting world wide energy reserves, has not developed a comprehensive energy program.

Mass Rapid Transit

Higher energy costs have had their greatest impact on low income families and the elderly. Governments have been slow to respond to their plight. Rapid transit in most major and mid-size American communities is, for the most part, woefully inadequate, in disrepair, and dangerous. Hence, many Americans are forced to rely upon the automobile as their primary means of transportation. Furthermore, many aged and most disadvantaged Americans cannot afford to purchase energy efficient vehicles. The Bay Area Rapid Transit project in the San Francisco area is an admirable example of intergovernmental cooperation in providing a very efficient, modern and relatively inexpensive transportation system. Similarly, the Metro system in the Washington D.C. area is an excellent example of a modern system that intergovernmental efforts can provide. Unfortunately, there are few other examples of such progress. Such endeavors are very costly and difficult to initiate. Again, the Reagan administration has recommended a major reduction in federal subsidies to mass rapid transit. Mass rapid transit will likely be as plagued with underfunding and official disinterest for the remainder of the decade. Government officials in Washington and in the state houses seem reluctant to change the *status quo.*

Nuclear Power

The most controversial alternative energy source is nuclear. The Three Mile Island, Pennsylvania reactor accident in 1979 proved that power generating reactors are vulnerable to accidents. A nuclear explosion in a reactor is impossible. But, accidents such as those at the Three Mile Island facility can cause damage to nearby areas and potential threats to human life. Despite rigid licensing and operating procedures and series of redundant safety systems, no power generating reactor is absolutely safe. Nevertheless, nuclear power remains an attractive method of generating electricity because it is relatively cheap and clean. Furthermore, with the advent of breeder reactors, it is possible to create more plutonium fuel than was originally consumed. There is a breeder reactor facility in Clinch River, Tennessee. President Carter, concerned about the spread of plutonium, which may also be used to produce nuclear weapons, decided to shut down the facility. He hoped that this gesture would have a non-proliferation (of nuclear weapons) effect. President Reagan, however, has decided to go ahead with the breeder program. He apparently believes that the country needs nuclear power to supplement oil, natural gas and coal.

Reactors, like other energy sources, pose some environmental problems. Most of them require large quantities of water to keep the core cool so that the heat generated by the process of fissioning atoms does not melt the facility. Furthermore, like other power generating plants, water is converted to steam in order to power the turbines which produce electricity. If the heated water is pumped back into a nearby river or ocean it can create thermal pollution and thereby harmfully effect aquatic life. This problem has been minimized by cooling the water in holding ponds or towers before its release into rivers or oceans. Waste disposal presents a greater challenge. When the uranium or plutonium fuel is exhausted, there remain quantities of highly radioactive by-products. Some of these materials retain their radioactive poison for tens of thousands of years. Much of the waste is stored in containers and then either buried in the earth or placed in abandoned salt mines. Leaks, and several have occurred, could cause major damage. The Department of Energy is looking at safer methods for waste storage. Currently, above ground disposal in reinforced concrete bunkers is being studied.

The development of nuclear energy has, because of construction overruns and complicated licensing and regulatory procedures, become prohibitive. In 1983 several utilities, including Long Island Lighting were almost forced into bankruptcy because of their involvements with nuclear energy.

Solar Energy

President Carter was a strong advocate of solar energy as a means of generating electricity. In order to promote this alternate energy source, he had a solar system installed in the White House. During the late seventies, solar energy became somewhat of a fad. Home owners installed solar units to heat their swimming pools and household water. Some systems are quite elaborate while others are relatively simple and inexpensive. Commercial exploitation of solar energy was inaugurated on October 30, 1980, when Solar One was dedicated. Located in the Mojave desert near Daggett, California, it is the largest single solar energy project in the world. Eventually, it will produce as much as 10 megawatts of electricity, enough to power a town of about 8,000 people. Other, more exotic methods of producing electricity, such as fusion, wind, tides and geothermal are being explored. However, research and development efforts in these areas has not progressed very rapidly.

Growth

The economic hard times of the seventies were probably triggered by the oil embargo. But the foundations were laid in the hectic sixties. Overproduction of commodities from automobiles to college graduates glutted the market. Many Americans were unemployed, underemployed, or employed, but not in professions for which they had been trained. The American economy has always been geared towards rapid production and growth. Economic prosperity is measured in terms of the number of houses, automobiles, and other commodities that are produced and sold. The future may change. A trend toward limited growth can be observed in some communities. In Sonoma County, California, attempts were made to restrict the construction industries. The county lost its case. But, San Diego and San Jose, California are examples of where further growth and expansion are being resisted more successfully. However, concerns about growth and its related problems were not as pronounced in the eighties. Environmental groups expressed outrage at some of former Secretary of the Interior Watt's policies with respect to public lands. But by and large, most Americans appeared to be more concerned with lower inflation and interest rates and higher levels of economic growth. Problems associated with rapid growth will continue to impact upon America's urban and rural environments. Smog, congestion, acid rain, and other associated problems are certain to be heightened in the future. Perhaps one of the greatest challenges for decision makers during the remainder of the 1980s and beyond will be controlling the detrimental aspects of economic growth.

People and Food

The relationship between people and food will certainly continue to be a major issue in the future. Malthus was probably right when he put forth his axiom that people reproduce geometrically while food sources only increase arithmetically. That is, eventually people will outstrip their food supplies and widespread famines will be common. In the 1960s many felt that the food aspect of the Malthusian axiom had been overcome. Those were the days of the so-called "green revolution." Advances in agricultural technology, such as potent insecticides and hybrid plants, greatly increased the yield per acre. Nevertheless, contemporary demographers are certain that starvation will inevitably make food a highly political tool.[2] From this perspective, the food producing nations are likely to become more powerful in the future. Famine has already plagued India, Bangladesh, and parts of Africa, and the future does not look very bright for other areas.

By the middle of 1975 the population of the world passed the four billion mark. By the year 2010 it is estimated that this figure may double. There are many reasons for such rapid growth. Medical and other technological advances have controlled most of the diseases that once served as natural checks on population growth. War, another traditional check on population, has not appreciably reduced the numbers of people that must be fed. And modern birth control techniques, for one reason or another, are unacceptable to many inhabitants of underdeveloped countries. Therefore, famine will likely be the primary handmaiden of the Grim Reaper in the future.

In 1976, the Central Intelligence Agency, after years of study, predicted that soon there will be a major shift in the earth's climate. If this expectation is accurate or even nearly accurate, then there will be a dramatic decline in the production of food. Citizens of the United States will probably not be severely affected by this change. Chances are they will continue to eat junk food, pop vitamin pills, and be concerned about overweight problems. On the other hand, America will no longer be the granary of the world. In the future, policymakers may have to use political expediency or economic advantage as standards to employ when deciding which of the world's starving people are worth saving.

Social Welfare

Social welfare programs are likely to continue to be controversial. Originally, such programs were designed to aid citizens who were unable to fend for themselves, such as the physically and mentally handicapped and orphans. After World War II, there was a belief that the state was responsible for providing its citizens with a life of dignity and self-respect. This movement produced welfare payments, medicare and medicaid programs, food stamps, and a host of other related programs. Critics of this approach invariably point to welfare cheating and other abuses as reasons for terminating or severely curtailing programs. How much social welfare can the country and its taxpayers afford? President Reagan obviously believes that the taxpayers cannot afford as much in the eighties as they supported in the seventies. He recommended cuts in virtually all social welfare programs. A matter that must be considered is just how much are citizens entitled to get from their governments. President Reagan opened the debate and the issue will be discussed in Congress and statehouses for many years to come.

Illegal Aliens

During the late seventies and early eighties a good deal of attention was focused on illegal immigration. Most of these people enter the United States in search of employment and a better way of life. Many come from Mexico and their presence has posed a real problem in the border states of Texas, Arizona, New Mexico and California. Indeed, the Commissioner of the Immigration and Naturalization Service observed that "We're facing a vast army that is carrying out a silent invasion of the United States."[3] Many of these people are hired by unscrupulous employers at wages much below minimum levels, thereby depriving some Americans of employment. This problem was compounded in the late seventies and early eighties by a tide of refugees from Southeast Asia, Cuba and Haiti. Assimilation of these people in times of economic uncertainty is difficult. Should America continue its open door policy with respect to refugees? Representatives of the Immigration and Naturalization Service believe that they are underfunded and understaffed and therefore unable to stem the tide of illegal aliens or properly screen refugees. There is no penalty for illegally entering the United States and only in California and New Hampshire is it against the law to hire illegal aliens. When President Carter opened the gates to the Cubans who left that island from the part of Mariel he opened a pandora's box of problems. While many of the "Marielitos" proved to be good citizens, others were hardened criminals and mentally ill. Hence, they presented a challenge to America's social welfare and criminal justice systems.

Congress, in response to these problems considered the Simpson-Mazolli bill, which among other things would impone fines on employers that hire illegal aliens and grant amnesty to those who have lived in this country illegally since 1981. The controversial bill, if passed, probably will not appreciably stem the influx of illegal aliens. Their numbers and the problems that are thereby created will continue to plague decision makers for the remainder of this century.

Senior Citizens

Problems of the aged will be a continuing concern. Sometimes characterized as the silent or forgotten Americans, senior citizens are emerging as a significant pressure group. Government has responded to their plight by providing such programs as medicare, meals on wheels and public housing. Many older Americans live on fixed incomes which are ravished by spiraling fuel and food bills. Cost of living adjustments by social security and other retirement programs are simply not adequate. Life expectancy has increased steadily because of better nutrition and advancements in medicine. The number of senior citizens increases every year, as do their problems. Pressures on such systems as social security and medicare are enormous. President Reagan has promised not to cut into senior citizen's social security benefits, but under consideration for reduction have been "minimum" social security retirement benefits and payments to children surviving an insured parent. Some have suggested that unless the system is reformed, it may collapse into bankruptcy.

Taxes

Americans consider themselves to be a heavily taxed people. Every year most pay a federal income tax. Most pay state income taxes, and quite a few are also required to pay city and county taxes on their incomes. Property is taxed, so are automobiles, gasoline, food, tobacco products, alcoholic beverages, and telephone calls. However, some Americans pay little or no taxes. They are either the very wealthy who can take advantage of write-offs and loopholes or they have acquired money by illegal means and do not declare it as taxable income. America has what is known as a progressive tax system. That is, a system wherein everyone is supposed to contribute his or her fair share. But most of that burden is being shouldered by the middle class. Attempts to institute meaningful reforms, for the most part, have been unsuccessful. However, in 1978, the taxpayers in California overwhelmingly passed Proposition 13, a property tax-cutting measure. Citizens in other states initiated similar tax-cutting referendums. Perhaps the most ambitious measure was Proposition 2½ which was enacted by the voters in Massachusetts in 1980. Tax money is used to provide general and specific services and to pay the salaries of government employees. Many communities faced with reluctant taxpayers and programs that were deemed to be indispensable have tried to balance their budgets by eliminating the positions of policemen, firemen, and street sweepers. Such measures are probably temporary expedients at best. It seems that in the future taxpayers must either pay more of their money to governments, or that governments must begin eliminating programs and services that are not absolutely indispensable.

The Deficit

The national debt, in the amount of over $156 billion, was a key issue in the 1984 presidential campaign. Walter Mondale charged that President Reagan was actually planning to increase federal taxes in the event he would win the election, in order to reduce the national debt. Reagan repeatedly denied that he had a "secret" plan to raise taxes. The Reagan administration's position is that "supply side" economics and greater growth in high technology would allow the country to "grow out" the deficit. The Democrats took the position that only by raising taxes would the debt be eliminated or at least substantially reduced. Despite the Democrats' attacks on Reagan's "no more taxes" policy, most Americans felt that the Republicans had been very successful in lowering inflation and reducing interest rates. By mid-summer of 1984, the Republicans could even claim that they are making headway in the battle to reduce unemployment. These successes, they argued, were the result of the administrations hard-nosed policy of favoring business at the expense of "wasteful" governmental programs. The only problem it seems is the deficit.

Crime

Crime in the streets of large cities seemed to be relentlessly increasing. Many law enforcement officers were convinced that the rising crime tide was tied to what was believed to be lax judges and an increasingly permissive society. Some of the lawbreakers who patrol the streets engage in what has been labeled victimless crimes. More often than not, such practitioners are prostitutes. A national prostitute organization, Call Off Your Old Tired Ethics (COYOTE) believes that hired sex should be decriminalized. Perhaps practices of this sort should be legalized and regulated. Venereal disease, exploitation by pimps, and crimes such as extortion and thievery could be better controlled. Another so-called victimless crime is indulgence in soft narcotics such as marijuana. Such states as Oregon and California have, for all practical purposes, decriminalized the use of marijuana. Gambling, another ancient vice, has been proscribed in some forms by many states and communities. Twenty-nine of the states have some legalized gambling, and some have state operated lotteries. For years, people have bet their money on horse races, wheels of fortune, dice, sporting events, and political races.

Legalizing such activities as prostitution, soft drugs, and gambling may make these activities less attractive and less dangerous. Legalization could provide strict licensing and regulation rules which might inhibit associated unsavory activities. Furthermore, decriminalization would enable more time for law enforcement officers to police thugs, rapists, murderers, and others who present real threats to public safety.

Some of the more heinous and infamous acts suggest that many criminals have absolutely no regard for human life and human dignity. It has been asserted that most judges bend over backwards to protect the rights of criminals. But what of the rights of their victims? If they survive, victims of violent crimes are usually scarred physically or psychologically for life. In contemporary America, punishment does not seem to be much of a deterrent because there seems to be very little of it. Judges sentence criminals to prison, perhaps for a life sentence, but due to parole practices the culprits are soon back on the streets seeking new victims. However, by the mid-eighties crimes against property and persons took a sharp decline. Analysts believe that the economic recovery and such programs as secret witness and neighborhood watch are probably responsible. President Reagan has focused on the illegal drug traffic as a measure to reduce crime even further. Drugs, while they may provide a temporary pleasure, create problems for individuals and society. Drugs and their trafficing are probably implicated in a large percentage of felony crimes in the United States. Those who favor legalizing recreational drugs argue that such action would, for the most part, decriminalize their activity and provide additional tax revenues for government. A similar argument is made for such other forms of criminal activity as prostitution and gambling. In states and communities where such practices are legal and strictly controlled, there appears to be not as much related criminal activity.

Volunteer Army

In the late 1960s it was decided that the selective service system, for the most part, was unfair. Hence the draft was replaced with an all volunteer armed force. At first, the military had to lower its admission standards in order to fill enlistment quotas. There was fear that the American military would degenerate into a raucous bunch of unreliable mercenaries. In the early days of this transition there was evidence that seemed to confirm these fears. The American Army, particularly those elements stationed in Western Europe, was riven with drug addiction and racial dissension. But the end of American involvement in Viet Nam and the depressed economy suddenly made the military an attractive occupational option. From 1974 through 1978 quotas were easily attained and standards were raised. Nevertheless, the move away from the draft is a significant departure from tradition. Citizen soldiers, people who filled the ranks and then returned to civilian occupations, were the backbone of the military. Their primary commitment was to their country, not to the military establishment. An all volunteer military establishment, as has happened in other countries, could become an elitist group that yearns for political power. Furthermore, recent studies by the Department of Defense and private individuals have viewed the volunteer army with a certain degree of alarm. Many believe that the military is undermanned and in a sorry state of readiness. President Carter responded to this concern in 1979 and asked Congress to reinstitute mandatory draft registration. It may be that the eighties will require the reinstitution of a peacetime draft. The Supreme Court decided that the 1964 civil rights act did not require young women to register and be subjected to involuntary military service.

Inflation

During the campaign of 1980 and in speeches since his inauguration, President Reagan has stressed the instability of the economy. The culprit, according to the President, is inflation, a trend that has eroded the value of the dollar since the end of World War II. During the fifties and sixties inflationary pressures were modest. But, during the seventies the spiral seemed out of control. Double digit inflation was a common news report. Presidents Ford and Carter seemed helpless to control the trend. Americans watched as inflationary trends chewed away at their savings, hiked prices on everything, and made the promise of a family home become, for many, financially impossible. Public employees and others on fixed income were hit especially hard. President Reagan is certain that government and deficit spending is primarily responsible for the state of the economy. To redress the situation he imposed a freeze on federal agency employment and promised an overall reduction of federal employees. He also proposed the elimination of the Departments of Energy and Education, which he considered to be unnecessary. Finally, he ordered major reductions in all department budgets except that of the Department of Defense, which was increased.

President Reagan's former budget director, David Stockman, believed that such action would cut inflation in half by the mid-eighties and increase employment and industrial production. Is government primarily responsible for cycles of inflation, unemployment and recession that seem to have become all too frequent? Deficit spending on the part of government agencies does tend to drive prices upward. However, these are external factors that are not affected by the reduction of services and budgets. Future O.P.E.C. price increases will continue to have an inevitable impact on the American economy as will the policies of deregulation of the energy and other industries.

President Reagan's plans to reduce federal income taxes by 30 percent over a three year period could also be inflationary. The President may well whip inflation by painting an austere and perhaps even recessionary picture for the late eighties.

Reapportionment

The Constitution requires that a national census be conducted every ten years so that the House of Representatives can be reapportioned to reflect shifts in population. The 1980 census revealed that the nation's population had increased by eleven percent since 1970. States in the West and the so-called sunbelt region scored the most significant gains. Nevada, Arizona, Wyoming, Utah, Idaho, Colorado, New Mexico and Texas showed large percentage increases, while the Mid-Western and Northern industrial states showed either declines or slight growth. Since 1970, such population shifts have been reflected in the electoral college, states in the West and South have gained representation in Congress and electoral votes at the expense of the industrial and colder areas of the country. For example, the 1980 head count indicated increases in the following states: California, Nevada and Arizona and decreases in such states as Illinois, Indiana and New York. It is significant to note that gains have been made in states that, for the most part, since 1972 have been in the Republican Party's column in presidential elections. If the trend continues the Democratic Party may find it increasingly difficult to elevate a member of its ranks to the presidency.

1980 Census and Changes in the Electoral College

State	Number of Senators	Number of Representatives	Net Change
Alabama	2	7	0
Alaska	2	1	0
Arizona	2	5	+1
Arkansas	2	4	0
California	2	45	+2
Colorado	2	6	+1
Connecticut	2	6	0
Delaware	2	1	0
*D.C.	0	0	0
Florida	2	19	+4
Georgia	2	10	0
Hawaii	2	2	0
Idaho	2	2	0
Illinois	2	22	−2
Indiana	2	10	−1
Iowa	2	6	0
Kansas	2	5	0

*the 23rd Amendment granted the District of Columbia three electoral votes.

1980 Census and Changes in the Electoral College—*Continued*

State	Number of Senators	Number of Representatives	Net Change
Kentucky	2	7	0
Louisiana	2	8	0
Maine	2	2	0
Maryland	2	8	0
Massachusetts	2	11	−1
Michigan	2	18	−1
Minnesota	2	8	0
Mississippi	2	5	0
Missouri	2	9	−1
Montana	2	2	0
Nebraska	2	3	0
Nevada	2	2	+1
New Hampshire	2	2	0
New Jersey	2	14	−1
New Mexico	2	3	+1
New York	2	34	−5
North Carolina	2	11	0
North Dakota	2	1	0
Ohio	2	21	−2
Oklahoma	2	6	0
Oregon	2	5	+1
Pennsylvania	2	23	−2
Rhode Island	2	2	0
South Carolina	2	6	0
South Dakota	2	1	−1
Tennessee	2	9	+1
Texas	2	27	+3
Utah	2	3	+1
Vermont	2	1	0
Virginia	2	10	0
Washington	2	8	+1
West Virginia	2	4	0
Wisconsin	2	9	0
Wyoming	2	1	0

Planning

America's traditional, laissez faire, free enterprise system will continue to be molded and shaped by more planning on the national level. Perhaps even its traditional concern with self-interest may have to be adjusted, more than in the past, to concerns with the interests of the community. Education and college degrees no longer mean straight avenues to jobs and positions. In this age of transition and uncertainty, people yearn for at least a minimum of predictability. Political, social, and intellectual alienation grow from the sense of insecurity, uncertainty, and of powerlessness over one's own life and future.

Alcohol and Drugs

Since the end of the Civil War, alcohol has been a concern of many Americans. Abolition was the first battle cry and this drive eventually led to the adoption of the eighteenth amendment which outlawed the possession and sale of alcoholic beverages. Recently, concerns about alcohol abuse have turned to those who drive while intoxicated. Mothers Against Drunk Drivers was organized to prevent the carnage on American highways that is caused by those who drive under the influence of alcohol or drugs. Many states responded to their pressure and passed tough drunk driving laws. On the national level, Congress passed a law that recommended to the states a national legal drinking age of 21. Congress decided to tie such a raising of age to a states access to federal highway monies.

Alienation

Alienation is a concept that has been used throughout the twentieth century to describe a negative relationship between man and his society, especially his government. Basically, it is a feeling of powerlessness and a recognition that change is impossible. Governments and bureaucracies are perceived as being impersonal and uncontrollable. "You can't fight City Hall" is an old American adage that has been used to describe this feeling of frustration. A promise of American society has long been that of a government for the people. But there seems to be a wide discrepancy between promise and reality. Citizens are confronted frequently with unresponsive public officials at all levels. Also, they are routinely tangled up in red tape and shuttled from one office to another in search of solutions to their problems.

Political scientists for many years have urged students and others to vote and also to become more knowledgeable about government. Despite their exhortations, Americans remain politically apathetic. Voting turnouts are often low, and attendance at public meetings is usually limited to the participants and members of the press. General knowledge among citizens at large about governmental matters and procedures is low. Education, it has been argued, is a way to bring about change. But it has not worked. The era of mass man has also produced the era of the mass voter. Perhaps many Americans perceive their individual vote as being insignificant. It is difficult, except in the smallest of communities, to make a convincing case for the importance of an individual vote. Furthermore, a lack of substance in most elections might also explain nonparticipation. Americans are usually asked to vote for a personality rather than a program. Seldom do they get the opportunity to vote on a specific issue such as salaries of congressmen, state legislators, and city councilmen. Perhaps many Americans stay away from public meetings because they are convinced that their voices will not be heard and their opinions will be discounted. Many view government as terribly complex, insensitive, indifferent, and impersonal. In fact the sentiment might be summed up in the questions, "why learn about something I cannot change? Why be aware of a process in which I cannot participate? And who the hell cares anyway." It is possible that future complexities and problems will produce even bigger and more unresponsive governments, which will probably increase the individual's sense of helplessness and frustration. Such trends are potentially dangerous because they tend to produce a lack of commitment to the political system. In an atmosphere of extreme alienation people are likely either to turn inward and cast a pox on everyone else's house or accept a Messiah who promises deliverance, which is the way Mussolini, Hitler, and other demagogues came to power.

Education

Another vital concern confronting the nation is the quality of education. Study after study reported the bad news that many of our children can't read, write, or perform simple mathematical problems. Student scores on national tests have been declining for several decades. Teachers complain that they are underpaid and that there are too many students in the classroom. Moreover, studies indicate that the brightest college graduates no longer choose to enter the teaching profession, but are now opting other, better-paying professions.

There is no consensus as to why the quality of education in American schools has deteriorated so badly. Some critics blame poor student performance on television and the other electronic forms of entertainment, while others charge that the fault lies with inattentive and/or working parents. Some say low teacher pay is a factor or that a general decline in educational standards coupled with a spread of permissiveness is the true cause of the mediocrity in education.

Most observers argue, however, that poorly educated generations of students will have difficulty in fulfilling the needs of a competitive "high-technology" economy. Our national defense and security needs are such that we will continue to require students trained in science, mathematics, foreign languages and policy expertise. The question is, how best to rectify the situation? One trend is now clear: Elementary and secondary schools, along with colleges and universities, are beginning to hold students to higher standards—higher reading scores, more mathematics and science, and additional courses in English, foreign languages and computer sciences. Nonetheless, most states are reluctant to raise taxes to pay for better teachers. President Reagan suggested during the 1984 presidential campaign that a school teacher be launched into orbit aboard the space shuttle to publicize the importance of teachers in our society. Whether the Reagan administration intends to go beyond this symbolic gesture and announce a program for upgrading education is open to question. Otherwise, improvements will have to come about as a result of the uncoordinated efforts of the states and local school districts.

Gramm—Rudman—Hollings

During the early 1980's, the federal deficit expanded by leaps and bounds. By 1985, the deficit was well over 200 billion dollars and climbing rapidly towards the half trillion dollar mark. Unwilling to deal with the problem and unwilling or unable to pass a budget, Congress, in a 1985 rush to adjourn for Christmas, enacted the Gramm—Rudman—Hollings deficit reduction plan. The measure is designed to balance the budget by fiscal year 1991 by establishing a time table, that must be met by either reductions in government spending or increased taxation. According to the legislation, mandatory cuts imposed in any year must be fifty percent from defense and fifty percent from domestic programs. Although the responsibility of meeting the Gramm—Rudman—Hollings demands is remaining with Congress, the executive branch will also play a role in the deficit reduction process. The agencies of the executive branch that are involved in reviewing the deficit and making proposed cuts are the General Accounting Office and the Office of Management and budget. The Congressional Budget Office is also involved in reporting on the deficit. Based on their reports, the President will impose across the board cuts if Congress does not enact a budget that meets the specified deficit reduction goals.

In the domestic area, Congress exempted certain programs from the Gramm—Rudman Act. Such programs include Social Security, veterans compensation and pensions, food stamps and interest on the National Debt. Programs such as medicare and veteran and Indian health programs received special protection from deep mandatory cuts. Such programs could only be cut by one percent in 1986 and two percent in later years regardless of the size of the total cut needed to reach the deficit reduction target.

Gramm—Rudman—Hollings is a reaction to the federal government's spending far more on programs that it has received in revenues. Economists and politicians have long warned that such a practice would inevitably lead to a fiscal disaster. The legislation has stirred a great deal of concern and criticism. President Reagan is determined not to raise any taxes which means that all adjustments will have to come from existing federal programs. The impact will effect every American directly or indirectly. Some federal programs will be eliminated and others will be curtailed. It is clear that one result of the legislation is that the federal government will become less of a provider and partner. State and local governmental units, which have long benefited from federal trough, will have to become more independent.

Like most legislation, Gramm—Rudman—Hollings was challenged in court. A group of congressmen initiated a federal lawsuit claiming that the bill is unconstitutional. Their belief is based on the fact that the bill, by delegating the congressional authority to appropriate funds to the President, violates the separation of powers doctrine.

The Problem of Terrorism in the Late 1980's

In response to a new series of terrorist attacks in 1985 and 1986 in which a number of Americans were killed and injured, the Reagan Administration decided to counter the growing threat of terrorist violence with countermeasures of its own and urgent appeals to the international community to join in combating the menace. Already in 1984, after nine employees were killed in a truck bomb attack on the American Embassy in Beirut, Secretary of State George Shultz announced the anti-terrorist doctrine of "active prevention." In announcing the doctrine, Mr. Shultz declared that the United States reserved the right to launch retaliatory and preemptive strikes, even without proof of who committed particular acts of terror, even at the cost of innocent lives. Though the United States did not launch such strikes, it appeared to have authorized Israel to do so in its behalf.

The new series of terrorist attacks began with the murder of three Israelis in Cyprus on September 1985. Although Cyprus convicted the killers, Israel unleashed a devastating raid on Palestine Liberation Organization headquarters in Tunis, killing some sixty Palestinians and a dozen Tunisians. President Reagan called the raid a "legitimate response" to terrorism, apparently forgetting that Tunisia is a faithful friend, that it had long opposed Arab radicalism, that it had no involvement in Middle East wars, and that he himself had endorsed the P.L.O.'s move from Lebanon to Tunisia. Furthermore, the P.L.O.'s official body, as against dissidents outside Tunis, claimed it had nothing to do with the Cyprus murders, an assertion not disproved.

Far from being intimidating, the Israeli bombing incited terrorists to commit new outrages: seizure of the Italian cruise ship Achille Lauro and the Killing of a Jewish American; then the Egyptair hijacking to Malta; finally the savage airport massacres in Rome and Vienna in late December 1985, killing nineteen innocent people, including five Americans.

In a televised press conference in January 1986, President Reagan announced measures to punish the "criminal outrages by an outlaw regime," referring to Libyan leader Muammar Gaddafi's government. The President accused Gaddafi of providing sanctuary for the terrorists responsible for the outrages, and of engaging "in armed aggression against the United States." And finally Reagan called for swift retribution: the United States and the rest of the world must "act decisively and in concert to exact from Gaddafi a high price." Discussing the Libyan leader's threat to send suicide squads to the U.S., the President dared the flamboyant and erratic Libyan to come himself and declared disdainfully, "I find he is not only a barbarian but he is flakey."

Having delivered his verbal attacks on Gaddafi, the President proceeded to announce a set of reprisals that fell short of "active prevention." The United States severed all economic ties with Libya and made it illegal for Americans to travel or live in that country, a measure aimed at forcing about 1,500 United States citizens residing there to leave. Reagan also ordered the freezing of several hundred million dollars in Libyan governmental assets held by U.S. banks. But he found no suitable way to take immediate military aim at the elusive shadow of terrorism. The closest the President got to mentioning an armed reprisal was to promise "further steps" if those sanctions proved ineffective.

Whatever limited effect the sanctions might have had was rendered largely toothless by the failure of America's allies to join in them. Not a single NATO government followed Reagan's request to sever trade. And while Canada announced that it would stop government help to any firm engaged in transactions with Libya and Italy suspended arms shipments, most European leaders, protecting their self-interest, expressed doubts that economic policies could be an effective political weapon.

Dealing with the problem of terrorism President Reagan ran into the same frustrating limits to American power that doomed earlier efforts to failure. For Reagan, the wrist-slap image that emerged was partly the result of his own earlier rhetoric that promised much more. In 1981, he vowed "swift and effective retribution" for terrorist acts. And in October 1984, the President boasted that "you can run but you can't hide" after U.S. warplanes successfully intercepted and forced down an Egyptian airliner carrying the hijackers of the cruise ship Achille Lauro.

It is clear that strong forces curb the effective use of the immense power of the American presidency, even against targets with as little world stature as Gaddafi. Some of these are based on moral considerations and others are basic American constitutional and traditional barriers against employing unbridled military force or tactics, such as assassination, restrictions supported by civilian as well as military leaders alike.

The United States probably will not use the same methods as Israel. The Israelis consider such reprisals as the bombing and shelling of P.L.O. bases in Lebanon and Tunis political statements not part of their anti-terrorist strategy. Israeli leaders don't claim that retaliation stops terror. Israel's greatest success has consisted of sealing its borders, tightening airline and embassy security and infiltrating terrorist organizations. It is a common perception in the Middle East and even in Europe that the United States sets a higher priority on punishing a handful of terrorist killers than on making peace, all the while refusing to see a relationship between terrorism and peace. Moderate Arab regimes, long courted by Washington, have been estranged by what they see as American complicity in the Tunisia raid. Egypt, our most valued Arab friend, was alienated over the Achille Lauro affair. American obsession with terrorism at the expense of concern for peacemaking has invited a resurgence of Soviet influence, in retreat since 1972. Syria, the Soviet Union's closest ally in the Middle East, has become the dominant force in Lebanon, and its influence is growing stronger in moderate Jordan. For the first time, Soviet diplomats move around easily in the Persian Gulf and are welcome even in Saudi Arabia. The Sudan, once safely in America's orbit, is tilting toward Libya, a Soviet client.

The chief beneficiaries of American policy concerning terrorism are the Arab "rejectionists." They use acts of terrorism precisely to thwart any Arab drift toward peace with Israel and friendship with the United States. If the United States wants to defeat Middle East terrorism, it must press to get Arabs and Israelis to the negotiating table. "Active prevention" simply presents terrorists with a platform. It is not just a matter of punishing the perpetrators of individual terrorist acts and their supporters. To get to the core of the matter, the United States must use its immense influence to bring about a negotiated peace which, hopefully, would greatly lessen the threat of terrorism. To completely eliminate individual terrorist acts by fanatics and deranged individuals may be beyond the power of any government.

However, in April of 1986, the Reagan Administration signaled an end to its vacillation with an air strike against terrorist targets in Libya. Reagan apparently believes that military action will succeed because reason, diplomacy and economic sanctions have not.

Notes

1. Central Intelligence Agency, *The International Energy Situation: Outlook to 1985*. Washington, D.C.: Government Printing Office, April 1977.
2. See for example, William and Paul Paddock. *Famine 1975: America's Decision Who Will Survive*. (Boston: Little, Brown and Company, 1967).
3. Holger Jensen, "Illegal Aliens Getting the Jobs." *The Associated Press* reprinted in the *Las Vegas Review Journal*. (June 27, 1976), p. 24.

For Further Reading

Amory B. Lovings, *World Energy Strategies: Facts, Issues, and Options*. New York: Harper and Row Publishers, 1975.

Nathan Glazer, *Affirmative Discrimination*. New York: Basic Books, 1976.

Kay L. Schlozman and Sidney Verba, *Injury to Insult: Unemployment, Class and Political Response*. Cambridge, Mass.: Harvard University Press, 1979.

Janet Boles, *The Politics of the Equal Rights Amendment: Conflict and the Decision Process*. New York: Longman, 1979.

Gary Orfield, *Must We Bus? Segregated Schools and National Policy*. Washington, D.C.: The Brookings Institution, 1978.

Name _____

Section _____

Date _____

Essay Study Questions for Chapter 13: Issues for the Eighties and Beyond

1. Should the nation develop long range plans in order to meet possible energy shortage? What should these plans be? _____

_____

_____

_____

_____

2. How best to deal with the problem of illegal immigration _____

_____

_____

_____

_____

3. To what extent is the drop in crime related to a healthy economy? Are there other factors involved in a lower crime rate? _____

_____

_____

_____

_____

4. In what ways are large deficits detrimental to the economy? _____

_____

_____

_____

_____

5. What are the major criticisms of the state of education in America today? What are some of the putative causes of the alleged decline in education? What are some of the proposals to rectify the situation? _____

_____

_____

_____

_____

6. What is meant by political alienation? How potentially dangerous is it? _____

_____

_____

_____

_____

7. How best can terrorism be prevented? _____

_____

_____

_____

_____

_____

_____

_____

_____

_____

_____

The Declaration of Independence

As It Reads in the Parchment Copy

The Unanimous Declaration of the Thirteen United States of America

When in the Course of human events, it becomes necessary for one people to dissolve the political bands, which have connected them with another, and to assume among the powers of the earth, the separate and equal station to which the Laws of Nature and of Nature's God entitle them, a decent respect to the opinions of mankind requires that they should declare the causes which impel them to the separation.—We hold these truths to be self-evident, that all men are created equal, that they are endowed by their Creator with certain unalienable Rights, that among these are Life, Liberty and the pursuit of Happiness.—That to secure these rights, Governments are instituted among Men, deriving their just powers from the consent of the governed,—That whenever any Form of Government becomes destructive of these ends, it is the Right of the People to alter or to abolish it, and to institute new Government, laying its foundation on such principles and organizing its powers in such form, as to them shall seem most likely to effect their Safety and Happiness. Prudence, indeed, will dictate that Governments long established should not be changed for light and transient causes; and accordingly all experience hath shewn, that mankind are more disposed to suffer, while evils are sufferable, than to right themselves by abolishing the forms to which they are accustomed. But when a long train of abuses and usurpations, pursuing invariably the same Object evinces a design to reduce them under absolute Despotism, it is their right, it is their duty, to throw off such Government, and to provide new Guards for their future security.—Such has been the patient sufferance of these Colonies; and such is now the necessity which constrains them to alter their former Systems of Government. The history of the present King of Great Britain is a history of repeated injuries and usurpations, all having in direct object the establishment of an absolute Tyranny over these States. To prove this, let Facts be submitted to a candid world.—He has refused his Assent to Laws, the most wholesome and necessary for the public good.—He has forbidden his Governors to pass Laws of immediate and pressing importance, unless suspended in their operation till his Assent should be obtained; and when so suspended, he has utterly neglected to attend to them.—He has refused to pass other Laws for the accommodation of large districts of people, unless those people would relinquish the right of Representation in the Legislature, a right inestimable to them and formidable to tyrants only.— He has called together legislative bodies at places unusual, uncomfortable, and distant from the depository of their public Records, for the sole purpose of fatiguing them into compliance with his measures.—He has dissolved Representative Houses repeatedly, for opposing with manly firmness his invasions on the rights of the people.—He has refused for a long time, after such dissolutions, to cause others to be elected; whereby the Legislative powers, incapable of Annihilation, have returned to the People at large for their exercise; the State remaining in the meantime exposed to all the dangers of invasion from without, and convulsions within.—He has endeavoured to prevent the population of these States; for that purpose obstructing the Laws for Naturalization of Foreigners; refusing to pass others to encourage their migrations hither, and raising the conditions of new Appropriations of Lands.—He has obstructed the Administration of Justice, by refusing his Assent to Laws for establishing Judiciary powers.—He has made Judges dependent on his Will alone, for the tenure of their offices, and the amount and payment of their salaries.— He has erected a multitude of New Offices, and sent hither swarms of Officers to harrass our people, and eat out their substance.—He has kept among us, in times of peace, Standing Armies without the Consent of our legislatures.—He has affected to render the Military independent of and superior to the Civil power.—He has combined with others to subject us to a jurisdiction foreign to our constitution, and unacknowledged by our laws; giving his Assent to their Acts of pretended Legislation.—For quartering large bodies of armed troops among us:—For protecting them, by a mock Trial, from punishment for any Murders which they should commit on the Inhabitants of these States:—For cutting off our Trade with all parts of the world:—For imposing Taxes on us without our Consent:—For depriving us in many cases, of the benefits of Trial by Jury:—For transporting us beyond Seas to be tried for pretended offenses:—For abolishing the free System of English Laws in a neighboring Province, establishing therein an Arbitrary government, and enlarging its Boundaries so as to render it at once an example and fit instrument for introducing the same absolute rule into these Colonies:—For taking away our Charters, abolishing our most valuable Laws, and altering fundamentally the Forms of our Governments:—For suspending our own Legislatures, and declaring themselves invested with power to legislate for us in all cases whatsoever.—He has abdicated Government here, by declaring us out of his Protection and waging War against us.—He has plundered our seas, ravaged our Coasts, burnt our towns, and destroyed the lives of our people.—He is at this time transporting large Armies of foreign Mercenaries to compleat the works of death, desolation and tyranny, already begun with circumstances of Cruelty & perfidy, scarcely paralleled in the most barbarous ages, and totally unworthy the Head of a civilized nation.—He has constrained our fellow Citizens taken Captive on the High Seas to bear Arms against their Country, to become the executioners of their friends and Brethren, or to fall themselves by their hands.—He has excited domestic insurrections amongst us, and has endeavoured to bring on the inhabitants of our frontiers, the merciless Indian Savages, whose known rule of warfare, is an undistinguished destruction of all ages, sexes and conditions. In every stage of these Oppressions We have Petitioned for Redress in the most humble terms: Our repeated Petitions have been answered only by repeated injury. A Prince whose character is thus marked by every act which may define a Tyrant, is unfit to be the ruler of a free people. Nor have We been wanting in attentions to our British brethren. We have warned them from time to time of attempts by their legislature to extend an unwarrantable jurisdiction over us. We have reminded them of the circumstances of our emigration and settlement here. We have appealed to their native justice and magnanimity, and we have conjured them by the ties of our common kindred to disavow these usurpations, which would inevitably interrupt our connections and correspondence. They too have been deaf to the voice of justice and of consanguinity. We must, therefore, acquiesce in the necessity, which denounces our Separation, and hold them, as we hold the rest of mankind, Enemies in War, in Peace Friends.—

We, therefore, the Representatives of the United States of America, in General Congress, Assembled, appealing to the Supreme Judge of the world for the rectitude of our intentions do, in the Name, and by the Authority of the good People of these Colonies, solemnly publish and declare, That these United Colonies are, and of Right ought to be Free and Independent States; that they are Absolved from all Allegiance to the British Crown, and that all political connection between them and the State of Great Britain, is and ought to be totally dissolved; and that as Free and Independent States, they have full Power to levy War, conclude Peace, contract Alliances, establish Commerce, and to do all other Acts and Things which Independent States may of right do.—And for the support of this Declaration, with a firm reliance on the protection of divine Providence, we mutually pledge to each other our Lives, our Fortunes and our sacred Honor.

The Constitution of the United States of America

We the People of the United States, in Order to form a more perfect Union, establish Justice, insure domestic Tranquility, provide for the common defence, promote the general Welfare, and secure the Blessings of Liberty to ourselves and our Posterity, do ordain and establish this Constitution for the United States of America.

Article. I.

Section. 1. All legislative Powers herein granted shall be vested in a Congress of the United States, which shall consist of a Senate and House of Representatives.

Section. 2. The House of Representatives shall be composed of Members chosen every second Year by the People of the several States, and the Electors in each State shall have the Qualifications requisite for Electors of the most numerous Branch of the State Legislature.

No Person shall be a Representative who shall not have attained to the age of twenty five Years, and been seven Years a Citizen of the United States, and who shall not, when elected, be an Inhabitant of that State in which he shall be chosen.

Representatives and direct Taxes shall be apportioned among the several States which may be included within this Union, according to their respective Numbers, which shall be determined by adding to the whole Number of free Persons, including those bound to Service for a Term of Years, and excluding Indians not taxed, three fifths of all other Persons. The actual Enumeration shall be made within three Years after the first Meeting of the Congress of the United States, and within every subsequent Term of ten Years, in such Manner as they shall by Law direct. The Number of Representatives shall not exceed one for every thirty Thousand, but each State shall have at Least one Representative; and until such enumeration shall be made, the State of New Hampshire shall be entitled to chuse three, Massachusetts eight, Rhode-Island and Providence Plantations one, Connecticut five, New-York six, New Jersey four, Pennsylvania eight, Delaware one, Maryland six, Virginia ten, North Carolina five, South Carolina five, and Georgia three.

When vacancies happen in the Representation from any State, the Executive Authority thereof shall issue Writs of Election to fill such Vacancies.

The House of Representatives shall chuse their Speaker and other Officers; and shall have the sole Power of Impeachment.

Section. 3. The Senate of the United States shall be composed of two Senators from each State, chosen by the Legislature thereof, for six Years; and each Senator shall have one Vote.

Immediately after they shall be assembled in Consequence of the first Election, they shall be divided as equally as may be into three Classes. The Seats of the Senators of the first Class shall be vacated at the Expiration of the second Year, of the second Class at the Expiration of the fourth Year, and of the third Class at the Expiration of the sixth Year, so that one third may be chosen every second Year; and if Vacancies happen by Resignation, or otherwise, during the Recess of the Legislature of any State, the Executive thereof may make temporary Appointments until the next Meeting of the Legislature, which shall then fill such Vacancies.

No Person shall be a Senator who shall not have attained to the Age of thirty Years, and been nine Years a Citizen of the United States, and who shall not, when elected, be an Inhabitant of that State for which he shall be chosen.

The Vice President of the United States shall be President of the Senate, but shall have no Vote, unless they be equally divided.

The Senate shall chuse their other Officers, and also a President pro tempore, in the Absence of the Vice President, or when he shall exercise the Office of President of the United States.

The Senate shall have the sole Power to try all Impeachments. When sitting for that Purpose, they shall be on Oath or Affirmation. When the President of the United States is tried the Chief Justice shall preside: And no Person shall be convicted without the Concurrence of two thirds of the Members present.

Judgment in Cases of Impeachment shall not extend further than to removal from Office, and disqualification to hold and enjoy any Office of honor, Trust or Profit under the United States: but the Party convicted shall nevertheless be liable and subject to Indictment, Trial, Judgment and Punishment, according to Law.

Section. 4. The Times, Places and Manner of holding Elections for Senators and Representatives, shall be prescribed in each State by the Legislature thereof; but the Congress may at any time by Law make or alter such Regulations, except as the Places of chusing Senators.

The Congress shall assemble at least once in every Year, and such Meeting shall be on the first Monday in December, unless they shall by Law appoint a different Day.

Section. 5. Each House shall be the Judge of the Elections, Returns and Qualifications of its own Members, and a Majority of each shall constitute a Quorum to do Business; but a smaller Number may adjourn from day to day, and may be authorized to compel the Attendance of absent Members, in such Manner, and under such Penalties as each House may provide.

Each House may determine the Rules of its Proceedings, punish its Members for disorderly Behaviour, and, with the Concurrence of two thirds, expel a Member.

Each House shall keep a Journal of its Proceedings, and from time to time publish the same, excepting such Parts as may in their Judgment require Secrecy; and the Yeas and Nays of the Members of either House on any question shall, at the Desire of one fifth of those Present, be entered on the Journal.

Neither House, during the Session of Congress, shall, without the Consent of the other, adjourn for more than three days, nor to any other Place than that in which the two Houses shall be sitting.

Section. 6. The Senators and Representatives shall receive a Compensation for their Services, to be ascertained by Law, and paid out of the Treasury of the United States. They shall in all Cases, except Treason, Felony and Breach of the Peace, be privileged from Arrest during their Attendance at the Session of their respective Houses, and in going to and returning from the same; and for any Speech or Debate in either House, they shall not be questioned in any other Place.

No Senator or Representative shall, during the Time for which he was elected, be appointed to any civil Office under the Authority of the United States, which shall have been created, or the Emoluments whereof shall have been encreased during such time; and no Person holding any Office under the United States, shall be a Member of either House during his Continuance in Office.

Section. 7. All Bills for raising Revenue shall originate in the House of Representatives; but the Senate may propose or concur with amendments as on other Bills.

Every Bill which shall have passed the House of Representatives and the Senate, shall, before it become a Law, be presented to the President of the United States; If he approve he shall sign it, but if not he shall return it, with his Objections to that House in which it shall have originated, who shall enter the Objections at large on their Journal, and proceed to reconsider it. If after such Reconsideration two thirds of that House shall agree to pass the Bill, it shall be sent, together with the Objections, to the other House, by which it shall likewise be reconsidered, and if approved by two thirds of that House, it shall become a Law. But in all such Cases the Votes of both Houses shall be determined by yeas and Nays, and the Names of the Persons voting for and against the Bill shall be entered on the Journal of each House respectively. If any Bill shall not be returned by the President within ten Days (Sunday excepted) after it shall have been presented to him, the Same shall be a Law, in like Manner as if he had signed it, unless the Congress by their Adjournment prevent its Return, in which Case it shall not be a Law.

Every Order, Resolution, or Vote to which the Concurrence of the Senate and House of Representatives may be necessary (except on a question of Adjournment) shall be presented to the President of the United States; and before the Same shall take Effect, shall be approved by him, or being disapproved by him, shall be repassed by two thirds of the Senate and House of Representatives, according to the Rules and Limitations prescribed in the Case of a Bill.

Section. 8. The Congress shall have Power To lay and collect Taxes, Duties, Imposts and Excises, to pay the Debts and provide for the common Defence and general Welfare of the United States; but all Duties, Imposts and Excises shall be uniform throughout the United States;

To borrow Money on the credit of the United States;

To regulate Commerce with foreign Nations, and among the several States, and with the Indian Tribes;

To establish an uniform Rule of Naturalization, and uniform Laws on the subject of Bankruptcies throughout the United States;

To coin Money, regulate the Value thereof, and of foreign Coin, and fix the Standard of Weights and Measures;

To provide for the Punishment of counterfeiting the Securities and current Coin of the United States;

To establish Post Offices and post Roads;

To promote the Progress of Science and useful Arts, by securing for limited Times to Authors and Inventors the exclusive Right to their respective Writings and Discoveries;

To constitute Tribunals inferior to the supreme Court;

To define and punish Piracies and Felonies committed on the high Seas, and Offences against the Law of Nations;

To declare War, grant Letters of Marque and Reprisal, and make Rules concerning Captures on Land and Water;

To raise and support Armies, but no Appropriation of Money to that Use shall be for a longer Term than two Years;

To provide and maintain a Navy;

To make Rules for the Government and Regulation of the land and naval Forces;

To provide for calling forth the Militia to execute the Laws of the Union, suppress Insurrections and repel Invasions;

To provide for organizing, arming, and disciplining, the Militia, and for governing such Part of them as may be employed in the Service of the United States, reserving to the States respectively, the Appointment of the Officers, and the Authority of training the Militia according to the discipline prescribed by Congress;

To exercise exclusive Legislation in all Cases whatsoever, over such District (not exceeding ten Miles square) as may, by Cession of Particular States, and the Acceptance of Congress, become the Seat of the Government of the United States, and to exercise like Authority over all Places purchased by the Consent of the Legislature of the State in which the Same shall be, for the Erection of Forts, Magazines, Arsenals, dock-Yards, and other needful Buildings;—And

To make all Laws which shall be necessary and proper for carrying into Execution the foregoing Powers, and all other Powers vested by this Constitution in the Government of the United States, or in any Department or Officer thereof.

Section. 9. The Migration or Importation of such Persons as any of the States now existing shall think proper to admit, shall not be prohibited by the Congress prior to the Year one thousand eight hundred and eight, but a Tax or duty may be imposed on such Importation, not exceeding ten dollars for each Person.

The Privilege of the Writ of Habeas Corpus shall not be suspended, unless when in Cases of Rebellion or Invasion the public Safety may require it.

No Bill of Attainder or ex post facto Law shall be passed.

No Capitation, or other direct, Tax shall be laid, unless in Proportion to the Census of Enumeration herein before directed to be taken.

No Tax or Duty shall be laid on Articles exported from any State.

No Preference shall be given by any Regulation of Commerce or Revenue to the Ports of one State over those of another; nor shall Vessels bound to, or from, one State, be obliged to enter, clear or pay Duties in another.

No Money shall be drawn from the Treasury, but in Consequence of Appropriations made by Law; and a regular Statement and Account of the Receipts and Expenditures of all public Money shall be published from time to time.

No Title of Nobility shall be granted by the United States; And no Person holding any Office of Profit or Trust under them, shall, without the Consent of the Congress, accept of any present, Emolument, Office, or Title, of any kind whatever, from any King, Prince or foreign State.

Section. 10. No State shall enter into any Treaty, Alliance, or Confederation; grant Letters of Marque and Reprisal; coin Money; emit Bills of Credit; make any Thing but gold and silver Coin a Tender in Payment of Debts; pass any Bill of Attainder, ex post facto Law, or Law impairing the Obligation of Contracts, or grant and Title of Nobility.

No State shall, without the Consent of the Congress, lay any Imposts or Duties on Imports or Exports, except what may be absolutely necessary for executing its inspection Laws: and the net Produce of all Duties and Imposts, laid by any State on Imports or Exports, shall be for the Use of the Treasury of the United States; and all such Laws shall be subject to the Revision and Controul of the Congress.

No State shall, without the Consent of Congress, lay any Duty of Tonnage, keep Troops, or Ships of War in time of Peace, enter into any Agreement or Compact with another State, or with a foreign Power or engage in War, unless actually invaded, or in such imminent Danger as will not admit of delay.

Article. II.

Section. 1. The executive Power shall be vested in a President of the United States of America. He shall hold his Office during the Term of four Years, and, together with the Vice President, chosen for the same Term, be elected, as follows:

Each State shall appoint, in such Manner as the Legislature thereof may direct, a Number of Electors, equal to the whole Number of Senators and Representatives to which the State may be entitled in the Congress: but no Senator or Representative, or Person holding an Office of Trust or Profit under the United States, shall be appointed an Elector.

The Electors shall meet in their respective States, and vote by Ballot for two Persons, of whom one at least shall not be an Inhabitant of the same State with themselves. And they shall make a List of all the Persons voted for, and of the Number of Votes for each; which List they shall sign and certify and transmit sealed to the Seat of the Government of the United States, directed to the President of the Senate. The President of the Senate shall, in the Presence of the Senate and House of Representatives, open all the Certificates, and the Votes shall then be counted. The Person having the greatest Number of Votes shall be the President, if such Number be a Majority of the whole Number of Electors appointed; and if there be more than one who have such Majority, and have an equal Number of Votes, then the House of Representatives shall immediately chuse by Ballot one of them for President; and if no Person have a Majority, then from the five highest on the List the said House shall in like Manner chuse the President. But in chusing the President, the Votes shall be taken by States, the Representation from each State having one Vote; a quorum for this Purpose shall consist of a Member or Members from two thirds of the States, and a Majority of all the States shall be necessary to a Choice. In every Case, after the Choice of the President, the Person having the greatest Number of Votes of the Electors shall be the Vice President. But if there should remain two or more who have equal Votes, the Senate shall chose from them by Ballot the Vice President.

The Congress may determine the Time of chusing the Electors, and the Day on which they shall give their votes; which Day shall be the same throughout the United States.

No Person except a natural born Citizen, or a Citizen of the United States, at the time of the Adoption of this Constitution, shall be eligible to the Office of President; neither shall any person be eligible to that Office who shall not have attained to the Age of thirty five Years, and been fourteen Years a Resident within the United States.

In Case of the Removal of the President from Office, or of his Death, Resignation, or Inability to discharge the Powers and Duties of the said Office, the Same shall devolve on the Vice President, and the Congress may by Law provide for the Case of Removal, Death, Resignation or Inability, both of the President and Vice President, declaring what Officer shall then act as President, and such Officer shall act accordingly, until the Disability be removed, or a President shall be elected.

The President shall, at stated Times, receive for his Services, a Compensation, which shall neither be encreased nor diminished during the Period for which he shall have been elected, and he shall not receive within that Period any other Emolument from the United States, or any of them.

Before he enter on the Execution of his Office, he shall take the following Oath or Affirmation:— "I do solemnly swear (or affirm) that I will faithfully execute the Office of President of the United States, and will to the best of my Ability, preserve, protect and defend the Constitution of the United States."

Section. 2. The President shall be Commander in Chief of the Army and Navy of the United States, and of the Militia of the several States, when called into the actual Service of the United States; he may require the Opinion, in writing, of the principal Officer in each of the executive Departments, upon any Subject relating to the Duties of their respective Offices, and he shall have Power to grant Reprieves and Pardons for Offenses against the United States, except in Cases of Impeachment.

He shall have Power, by and with the Advice and Consent of the Senate, to make Treaties provided two thirds of the Senators present concur; and he shall nominate, and by and with the Advice and Consent of the Senate, shall appoint Ambassadors, other public Ministers and Consuls, Judges of the supreme Court, and all other Officers of the United States, whose Appointments are not herein otherwise provided for, and which shall be established by Law; but the Congress may by Law vest the Appointment of such inferior Officers, as they think proper, in the President alone, in the Courts of Law, or in the Heads of Departments.

The President shall have Power to fill up all Vacancies that may happen during the Recess of the Senate, by granting Commissions which shall expire at the End of their next Session.

Section. 3. He shall from time to time give to the Congress Information of the State of the Union, and recommend to their Consideration such Measures as he shall judge necessary and expedient; he may, on extraordinary Occasions, convene both Houses, or either of them, and in Case of Disagreement between them, with Respect to the Time of Adjournment, he may adjourn them to such Time as he shall think proper; he shall receive Ambassadors and other public Ministers; he shall take Care that the Laws be faithfully executed, and shall Commission all the Officers of the United States.

Section. 4. The President, Vice President and all Civil Officers of the United States, shall be removed from Office on Impeachment for, and Conviction of, Treason, Bribery, or other high Crimes and Misdemeanors.

Article. III.

Section. 1. The judicial Power of the United States, shall be vested in one supreme Court, and in such inferior Courts as the Congress may from time to time ordain and establish. The Judges, both of the supreme and inferior Courts, shall hold their Offices during good Behaviour, and shall, at stated Times, receive for their Services, a Compensation, which shall not be diminished during their Continuance in Office.

Section. 2. The judicial Power shall extend to all Cases, in Law and Equity, arising under this Constitution, the Laws of the United States, and Treaties made, or which shall be made, under their Authority;—to all Cases affecting Ambassadors, other Public Ministers and Consuls;—to all Cases of admiralty and maritime Jurisdiction;—to Controversies to which the United States shall be a Party;—to Controversies between two or more States;—between a State and Citizens of another State;—between Citizens of different States;—between Citizens of the same State claiming Lands under Grants of different States, and between a State, or the Citizens thereof, and foreign States, Citizens or Subjects.

In all Cases affecting Ambassadors, other public Ministers and Consuls, and those in which a State shall be Party, the supreme Court shall have original Jurisdiction. In all the other Cases before mentioned, the supreme Court shall have appellate Jurisdiction, both as to Law and Fact, with such Exceptions, and under such Regulations as the Congress shall make.

The Trial of all Crimes, except in Cases of Impeachnent, shall be by Jury; and such Trial shall be held in the State where the said Crimes shall have been committed; but when not committed within any State, the Trial shall be at such Place or Places as the Congress may by Law have directed.

Section. 3. Treason against the United States, shall consist only in levying War against them, or in adhering to their Enemies, giving them Aid and Comfort. No Person shall be convicted of Treason unless on the Testimony of two Witnesses to the same overt Act, or on Confession in open Court.

The Congress shall have Power to declare the Punishment of Treason, but no Attainder of Treason shall work Corruption of Blood, or Forfeiture except during the Life of the Person attainted.

Article. IV.

Section. 1. Full Faith and Credit shall be given in each State to the public Acts, Records, and judicial Proceedings of every other State. And the Congress may by general Laws prescribe the Manner in which such Acts, Records and Proceedings shall be proved, and the Effect thereof.

Section. 2. The Citizens of each State shall be entitled to all Privileges and Immunities of Citizens in the several States.

A Person charged in any State with Treason, Felony, or other Crime, who shall flee from Justice, and be found in another State, shall on Demand of the executive Authority of the State from which he fled, be delivered up, to be removed to the State having Jurisdiction of the Crime.

No Person held to Service or Labour in one State, under the Laws thereof, escaping into another, shall, in Consequence of any Law or Regulation therein, be discharged from such Service or Labour, but shall be delivered up on Claim of the Party to whom such Service or Labour may be due.

Section. 3. New States may be admitted by the Congress into this Union; but no new State shall be formed or erected within the Jurisdiction of any other State; nor any State be formed by the Junction of two or more States, or Parts of States, without the Consent of the Legislatures of the States concerned as well as of the Congress.

The Congress shall have Power to dispose of and make all needful Rules and Regulations respecting the Territory or other Property belonging to the United States; and nothing in this Constitution shall be so construed as to Prejudice any Claims of the United States, or of any particular State.

Section. 4. The United States shall guarantee to every State in this Union a Republican Form of Government, and shall protect each of them against Invasion; and on Application of the Legislature, or of the Executive (when the Legislature cannot be convened) against domestic Violence.

Article. V.

The Congress, whenever two thirds of both Houses shall deem it necessary, shall propose Amendments to this Constitution, or, on the Application of the Legislatures of two thirds of the several States, shall call a Convention for proposing Amendments, which, in either Case, shall be valid to all Intents and Purposes; as Part of this Constitution, when ratified by the Legislatures of three fourths of the several States, or by Conventions in three fourths thereof, as the one or the other Mode of Ratification may be proposed by the Congress; Provided that no Amendment which may be made prior to the Year One thousand eight hundred and eight shall in any Manner affect the first and fourth Clauses in the Ninth Section of the first Article; and that no State, without its Consent, shall be deprived of it's equal Suffrage in the Senate.

Article. VI.

All Debts contracted and Engagements entered into, before the Adoption of this Constitution, shall be as valid against the United States under this Constitution, as under the Confederation.

This Constitution, and the Laws of the United States which shall be made in Pursuance thereof; and all Treaties made, or which shall be made, under the Authority of the United States, shall be the supreme Law of the Land; and the Judges in every State shall be bound thereby, any Thing the Constitution or Laws of any State to the Contrary notwithstanding.

The Senators and Representatives before mentioned, and the Members of the several State Legislatures, and all executive and judicial Officers, both of the United States and of the several States, shall be bound by Oath or Affirmation, to support this Constitution; but no religious Test shall ever be required as a Qualification to any Office or public Trust under the United States.

Article. VII.

The Ratification of the Conventions of nine States, shall be sufficient for the Establishment of this Constitution between the States so ratifying the Same, done in Convention by the Unanimous Consent of the States present the Seventeenth Day of September in the Year of our Lord one thousand seven hundred and Eighty seven and of the Independence of the United States of America the Twelfth In witness whereof We have hereunto subscribed our Names,

GO. WASHINGTON—PRESIDT.

and deputy from Virginia

AMENDMENTS TO THE CONSTITUTION

Amendment [I.]*

Congress shall make no law respecting an establishment of religion, or prohibiting the free exercise thereof; or abridging the freedom of speech, or of the press; or the right of the People peaceably to assemble, and to petition the Government for a redress of grievances.

Amendment [II.]

A well regulated Militia, being necessary to the security of a free State, the right of the people to keep and bear Arms, shall not be infringed.

Amendment [III.]

No Soldier shall, in time of peace be quartered in any house, without the consent of the Owner, nor in time of war, but in a manner to be prescribed by law.

Amendment [IV.]

The right of the people to be secure in their persons, houses, papers, and effects, against unreasonable searches and seizures, shall not be violated, and no Warrants shall issue, but upon probable cause, supported by Oath or affirmation, and particularly describing the place to be searched, and the persons or things to be seized.

Amendment [V.]

No person shall be held to answer for a capital, or otherwise infamous crime, unless on a presentment or indictment of a Grand Jury, except in cases arising in the land or naval forces, or in the Militia, when in actual service in time of War or public danger; nor shall any person be subject for the same offence to be twice put in jeopardy of life or limb; nor shall be compelled in any criminal case to be a witness against himself, nor be deprived of life, liberty, or property, without due process of law; nor shall private property be taken for public use, without just compensation.

Amendment [VI.]

In all criminal prosecutions, the accused shall enjoy the right to a speedy and public trial, by an impartial jury of the State and district wherein the crime shall have been committed, which district shall have been previously ascertained by law, and to be informed of the nature and cause of the accusation; to be confronted with the witnesses against him; to have compulsory process for obtaining witnesses in his favor, and to have the Assistance of Counsel for his defence.

Amendment [VII.]

In Suits at common law, where the value in controversy shall exceed twenty dollars, the right of trial by jury shall be preserved, and no fact tried by a jury, shall be otherwise re-examined in any Court of the United States, than according to the rules of the common law.

---

*Brackets enclosing an amendment number indicate that the number was not specifically assigned in the resolution proposing the amendment.

Amendment [VIII.]

Excessive bail shall not be required, nor excessive fines imposed, nor cruel and unusual punishments inflicted.

Amendment [IX.]

The enumeration in the Constitution, of certain rights, shall not be construed to deny or disparage others retained by the people.

Amendment [X.]

The powers not delegated to the United States by the Constitution, nor prohibited by it to the States, are reserved to the States respectively, or to the people.

Amendment [XI.]

The Judicial power of the United States shall not be construed to extend to any suit in law or equity, commenced or prosecuted against one of the United States by Citizens of another State, or by Citizens or Subjects of any Foreign State.

Amendment [XII.]

The Electors shall meet in their respective states and vote by ballot for President and Vice-President, one of whom, at least, shall not be an inhabitant of the same state with themselves; they shall name in their ballots the person voted for as President, and in distinct ballots the person voted for as Vice-President, and they shall make distinct lists of all persons voted for as President, and of all persons voted for as Vice-President, and of the number of votes for each, which lists they shall sign and certify, and transmit sealed to the seat of the government of the United States, directed to the President of the Senate;—The President of the Senate shall, in the presence of the Senate and House of Representatives, open all the certificates and the votes shall then be counted;—The person having the greatest number of votes for President, shall be the President, if such number be a majority of the whole number of Electors appointed; and if no person have such majority, then from the persons having the highest numbers not exceeding three on the list of those voted for as President, the House of Representatives shall choose immediately, by ballot, the President. But in choosing the President, the votes shall be taken by states, the representation from each state having one vote; a quorum for this purpose shall consist of a member or members from two-thirds of the states, and a majority of all the states shall be necessary to a choice. And if the House of Representatives shall not choose a President whenever the right of choice shall devolve upon them, before the fourth day of March next following, then the Vice-President shall act as President, as in the case of the death or other constitutional disability of the President— The person having the greatest number of votes as Vice-President, shall be the Vice-President, if such number be a majority of the whole number of Electors appointed, and if no person have a majority, then from the two highest numbers on the list, the Senate shall choose the Vice-President; a quorum for the purpose shall consist of two-thirds of the whole number of Senators, and a majority of the whole number shall be necessary to a choice. But no person constitutionally ineligible to the office of President shall be eligible to that of Vice-President of the United States.

Amendment [XIII.]

Section 1. Neither slavery nor involuntary servitude, except as a punishment for crime whereof the party shall have been duly convicted, shall exist within the United States, or any place subject to their jurisdiction.

Section 2. Congress shall have power to enforce this article by appropriate legislation.

Amendment [XIV.]

Section 1. All persons born or naturalized in the United States and subject to the jurisdiction thereof, are citizens of the United States and of the State wherein they reside. No State shall make or enforce any law which shall abridge the privileges or immunities of citizens of the United States; nor shall any State deprive any person of life liberty, or property, without due process of law; nor deny to any person within its jurisdiction the equal protection of the laws.

Section 2. Representatives shall be apportioned among the several States according to their respective numbers, counting the whole number of persons in each State, excluding Indians not taxed. But when the right to vote at any election for the choice of electors for President and Vice President of the United States, Representatives in Congress, the Executive and Judicial officers of a State, or the members of the Legislature thereof, is denied to any of the male inhabitants of such State, being twenty-one years of age, and citizens of the United States, or in any way abridged, except for participation in rebellion, or other crime, the basis of representation therein shall be reduced in the proportion which the number of such male citizens shall bear to the whole number of male citizens twenty-one years of age in such State.

Section 3. No person shall be a Senator or Representative in Congress, or elector of President and Vice President, or hold any office, civil or military, under the United States, or under any State, who, having previously taken an oath, as a member of Congress, or as an officer of the United States, or as a member of any State legislature, or as an executive or judicial officer of any State, to support the Constitution of the United States, shall have engaged in insurrection or rebellion against the same, or given aid or comfort to the enemies thereof. But Congress may by a vote of two-thirds of each House, remove such disability.

Section 4. The validity of the public debt of the United States, authorized by law, including debts incurred for payment of pensions and bounties for services in suppressing insurrection or rebellion, shall not be questioned. But neither the United States nor any State shall assume or pay any debt or obligation incurred in aid of insurrection or rebellion against the United States, or any claim for the loss or emancipation of any slave; but all such debts, obligations and claims shall be held illegal and void.

Section 5. The Congress shall have power to enforce, by appropriate legislation, the provisions of this article.

Amendment [XV.]

Section 1. The right of citizens of the United States to vote shall not be denied or abridged by the United States or by any State on account of race, color, or previous condition of servitude.

Section 2. The Congress shall have power to enforce this article by appropriate legislation.

Amendment [XVI.]

The Congress shall have power to lay and collect taxes on incomes, from whatever source derived, without apportionment among the several States, and without regard to any census or enumeration.

Amendment [XVII.]

The Senate of the United States shall be composed of two Senators from each State, elected by the people thereof, for six years; and each Senator shall have one vote. The electors in each State shall have the qualifications requisite for electors of the most numerous branch of the State legislatures.

When vacancies happen in the representation of any State in the Senate, the executive authority of such State shall issue writs of election to fill such vacancies; *Provided,* That the legislature of any state may empower the executive thereof to make temporary appointments until the people fill the vacancies by election as the legislature may direct.

This amendment shall not be so construed as to affect the election or term of any Senator chosen before it becomes valid as part of the Constitution.

Amendment [XVIII.]

Section 1. After one year from the ratification of this article the manufacture, sale, or transportation of intoxicating liquors within, the importation thereof into, or the exportation thereof from the United States and all territory subject to the jurisdiction thereof for beverage purposes is hereby prohibited.

Sec. 2. The Congress and the several States shall have concurrent power to enforce this article by appropriate legislation.

Sec. 3. This article shall be inoperative unless it shall have been ratified as an amendment to the Constitution by the legislatures of the several States, as provided in the Constitution, within seven years from the date of the submission hereof to the States by the Congress.

Amendment [XIX.]

The right of citizens of the United States to vote shall not be denied or abridged by the United States or by any State on account of sex.

Congress shall have power to enforce this article by appropriate legislation.

Amendment [XX.]

Section 1. The terms of the President and Vice President shall end at noon on the 20th day of January, and the terms of Senators and Representatives at noon on the 3d day of January, of the years in which such terms would have ended if this article had not been ratified; and the terms of their successors shall then begin.

Sec. 2. The Congress shall assemble at least once in every year, and such meeting shall begin at noon on the 3d day of January, unless they shall by law appoint a different day.

Sec. 3. If, at the time fixed for the beginning of the term of the President, the President elect shall have died, the Vice President elect shall become President. If a President shall not have been chosen before the time fixed for the beginning of his term, or if the President elect shall have failed to qualify, then the Vice President elect shall act as President until a President shall have qualified; and the Congress may by law provide for the case wherein neither a President elect nor a Vice-President elect shall have qualified, declaring who shall then act as President, or the manner in which one who is to act shall be selected, and such person shall act accordingly until a President or Vice President shall have qualified.

Sec. 4. The Congress may by law provide for the case of the death of any of the persons from whom the House of Representatives may choose a President whenever the right of choice shall have devolved upon them, and for the case of the death of any of the persons from whom the Senate may choose a Vice President whenever the right of choice shall have devolved upon them.

Sec. 5. Sections 1 and 2 shall take effect on the 15th day of October following the ratification of this article.

Sec. 6. This article shall be inoperative unless it shall have been ratified as an amendment to the Constitution by the legislatures of three-fourths of the several States within seven years from the date of its submission.

Amendment [XXI.]

Section 1. The eighteenth article of amendment to the Constitution of the United States is hereby repealed.

Sec. 2. The transportation or importation into any State, Territory or possession of the United States for delivery or use therein of intoxicating liquors, in violation of the laws thereof, is hereby prohibited.

Sec. 3. This article shall be inoperative unless it shall have been ratified as an amendment to the Constitution by conventions in the several States, as provided in the Constitution, within seven years from the date of the submission thereof to the States by the Congress.

Amendment [XXII.]

Section 1. No person shall be elected to the office of the President more than twice, and no person who has held the office of President, or acted as President, for more than two years of a term to which some other person was elected President shall be elected to the office of the President more than once. But this Article shall not apply to any person holding the office of President when this Article was proposed by the Congress, and shall not prevent any person who may be holding the office of President, or acting as President, during the term within which this Article becomes operative from holding the office of President or acting as President during the remainder of such term.

Sec. 2. This Article shall be inoperative unless it shall have been ratified as an amendment to the Constitution by the legislatures of three-fourths of the several States within seven years from the date of its submission to the States by the Congress.

Amendment [XXIII.]

Section 1. The District constituting the seat of Government of the United States shall appoint in such manner as the Congress may direct:

A number of electors of President and Vice President equal to the whole number of Senators and Representatives in Congress to which the District would be entitled if it were a State, but in no event more than the least populous State; they shall be in addition to those appointed by the States, but they shall be considered, for the purposes of the election of President and Vice President, to be electors appointed by a State; and they shall meet in the District and perform such duties as provided by the twelfth article of amendment.

Sec. 2. The Congress shall have power to enforce this article by appropriate legislation.

Amendment [XXIV.]

Section. 1. The right of citizens of the United States to vote in any primary or other election for President or Vice President, for electors for President or Vice President, or for Senator or Representative in Congress, shall not be denied or abridged by the United States or any State by reason of failure to pay any poll tax or other tax.

Section 2. The Congress shall have power to enforce this article by appropriate legislation.

Amendment [XXV.]

Section 1. In case of the removal of the President from office or his death or resignation, the Vice President shall become President.

Sec. 2. Whenever there is a vacancy in the office of the Vice President, the President shall nominate a Vice President who shall take office upon confirmation by a majority vote of both houses of Congress.

Sec. 3. Whenever the President transmits to the President pro tempore of the Senate and the Speaker of the House of Representatives his written declaration that he is unable to discharge the powers and duties of his office, and until he transmits to them a written declaration to the contrary, such powers and duties shall be discharged by the Vice President as Acting President.

Sec. 4. Whenever the Vice President and a majority of either the principal officers of the executive department or of such other body as Congress may by law provide, transmit to the President pro tempore of the Senate and the Speaker of the House of Representatives their written declaration that the President is unable to discharge the powers and duties of his office, the Vice President shall immediately assume the powers and duties of the office as Acting President.

Thereafter, when the President transmits to the President pro tempore of the Senate and the Speaker of the House of Representatives his written declaration that no inability exists, he shall resume the powers and duties of his office unless the Vice President and a majority of either the principal officers of the executive department or of such other body as Congress may by law provide, transmit within four days to the President pro tempore of the Senate and the Speaker of the House of Representatives their written declaration that the President is unable to discharge the powers and duties of his office. Thereupon Congress shall decide the issue, assembling within 48 hours for that purpose if not in session. If the Congress, within 21 days after receipt of the latter written declaration, or, if Congress is not in session, within 21 days after Congress is required to assemble, determines by two-thirds vote of both houses that the President is unable to discharge the powers and duties of his office, the Vice President shall continue to discharge the same as Acting President; otherwise, the President shall resume the powers and duties of his office.

Amendment [XXVI.]

Section 1. The right of citizens of the United States, who are 18 years of age or older, to vote shall not be denied or abridged by the United States or any state on account of age.

Sec. 2. The Congress shall have the power to enforce this article by appropriate legislation.

Index

Abortion, 51
ABSCAM, 66
Acton, Lord, 14
Adams, Henry, 14
Adams, John, 38
Ad Hoc committees, 60
Advise and consent, 63
Affirmative action, 49, 51
Agnew, Spiro, 64
Alien and Sedition Acts, 38
Alienation, 230
Amending the Constitution, 62
25th Amendment, 63
American Civil Liberties Union, 47
Armstrong, Scott, 27
Assistant President Pro Tem, 60
At-large elections, 211

Bail, 45
Barber, James D., 84, 85, 86, 87
Barron v. *Baltimore,* 38
Bentham, Jeremy, 4
Benton v. *Maryland,* 45
Betts v. *Brady,* 46
Bills of attainder, 65
Black, Hugo, 27, 39
Brandeis, Louis D., 28
Brennan, William, 50
Brown v. *Board of Education of Topeka, Kansas,* 31, 49, 117
Buckley v. *Valeo,* 116
Budget and Accounting Act of 1921, 79, 84
Bureaucracy, 93, 101, 103
Burger, Warren, 27, 29, 43, 50
Busing, 49, 50

Campaign Finance Reform Law, 115
Camp David Agreement, 199
Carswell, G. Harrold, 63
Carter, Jimmy, 50, 71, 72, 78, 80, 84, 85, 86, 196, 198, 199, 201, 220, 222
Change of venue, 46
Chase, Margaret, 74
Chase, Salmon, 27
Chief diplomat, 80, 81
Chief executive, 74, 80

Chief executive, functions and roles of, 78, 79, 80, 81, 82, 83, 84, 85
Chief legislator, 82
Chief of party, 83
Chief of state, 79
City manager, 209, 210
Civil Rights Act of 1957, 62
Civil Rights Act of 1964, 49, 51
Clark, Tom, 31
Cloture, 62
Coleman, James, 50
Commander-in-chief, 81
Commission Plan, 210
Commonwealth, 5, 6
Communist Party, 39, 40
Community Development Block Grants Program, 96
Competitive individualism, 12, 13, 14
Concurring opinion, 28
Conference committee, 60, 214
Congressional oversight, 101
Congress of the U.S., 103, 118, 212
Connecticut Compromise, 59
Constitutionalism, 14
Constitutional theory, 74, 75
Containment, 193
Coolidge, Calvin, 85, 87
Corwin, Edward S., 5
Craig v. *Boren,* 50
Cruel and unusual punishment, 47
Culture, 1, 2

Defense Department, 94, 106
Delegated authority, 99
Dennis v. *United States,* 39
Detente, 195
Distributive policy, 109
Double jeopardy, 44, 45
Douglas, William O., 23, 27

Egalitarianism, 8, 9
Eisenhower, Dwight D., 27, 86, 194
Elazar, Daniel J., 3, 4
Engel v. *Vitale,* 42
Equal Rights Amendment, 51, 52, 63
Ethics, 66

Exclusionary rule, 43, 44
Executive agreement, 202
Executive order, 202
Executive privilege, 202
Ex post facto laws, 65

Falwell, Jerry, 43
Federalism, 117
Federalist, 7, 72, 78
Federal Trade Commission, 99, 110
Filibuster, 61
Floor leaders, 60
Ford, Gerald, 72, 86
Fortas, Abe, 23, 29
Free exercise of religion, 42
Frontiero v. *Richardson,* 50
Full Employment Act, 84
Furman v. *Georgia,* 47

Galileo, 9
Gay rights, 52
General Accounting Office, 102
Gideon v. *Wainwright,* 46
Goldwater, Barry, 72
Gramm-Rudman-Hollings, 231
Great Compromise, 59
Gregg v. *Georgia,* 47

Hamilton, Alexander, 77, 78, 81, 200, 201
Harding, Warren, 86
Harvey, William, 9
Haynsworth, Clement F., 63
Hays, Wayne, 66
Hobbes, Thomas, 4, 6, 8, 9, 10, 11, 12
Holmes, Oliver Wendell, 28
Hoover, Herbert, 80, 84, 86
Hopper, 61
Human nature, 8, 9
Humphrey, Hubert, 72

Impeachment and removal, 64
Independent Regulatory Commission, 98
Interstate Commerce Commission, 100
Item veto, 62

Jacobellis v. *Ohio,* 41
Jaffa, Harry, 3
Jefferson, Thomas, 1, 6, 37, 42, 77, 78, 81, 83, 200, 201
Jenkins v. *Georgia,* 41
Johnson, Andrew, 64
Johnson, Lyndon, 29, 72, 80, 85, 86, 195
Joint committees, 60

Judicial review, 19, 26, 105
Judicial self-restraint, 19, 32
Judiciary Act of 1789, 26

Kaddafi, Muammar, 233
Kennan, George F., 193
Kennedy, John F., 72, 86, 194
Khrushchev, Nikita, 194
Kissinger, Henry, 195
Koenig, Louis W., 80

Laetrile, 106, 107
Las Vegas, NV, 210
Lebanon, 199
Liberalism, 4, 5, 6, 7, 8, 9, 10, 11, 12, 13, 14
Lincoln, Abraham, 6, 27, 75, 80, 81
Lobbying, 111
Local government, 208, 209, 210, 211, 212
Locke, John, 4, 7, 8, 75

Machiavelli, Niccolo, 9
Madison, James, 78, 200, 201
Mapp v. *Ohio,* 43
Marbury v. *Madison,* 19, 26
Marketplace, 4, 5, 14
Marshall, John, 19, 26, 29, 38
Marshall Plan, 194
Massachusetts v. *Shepherd,* 44
Mayor Council Plan, 208, 209
McCarthy, Joseph, 39
McGovern, George, 72
McRae v. *Harris,* 51
Meier, Kenneth, 110
Merit system, 20, 21
Miller v. *California,* 41
Miller, Henry, 41
Mill, John Stuart, 4
Mills, Wilbur, 66
Minor v. *Happersett,* 50
Miranda v. *Arizona,* 44
Missouri Plan, 20
Mondale, Walter, 225
Moral Majority, 43
Muller v. *Oregon,* 50
Murray v. *Curlett,* 42

NAACP, 30
National Conservative Political Action
    Committee, 113
NATO, 194
Natural law, 11, 12
Near v. *Minnesota,* 46
Necessary and proper clause, 61
New Jersey Plan, 59

Nixon, Richard, 29, 72, 84, 86, 194, 198
Non-partisan elections, 211

Obscenity, 41
O'Connor, Sandra Day, 23
Office of Management and Budget, 103, 105
O'Hare, Madeline Murray, 42
Omnibus Judgeship Act of 1978, 25
OPEC, 199

Parliamentary procedure, 214
Patterson Plan, 59
Plessy v. *Ferguson,* 48
Pocket veto, 62
Political action committees, 116
Political culture, 2, 3, 4, 5, 6, 7, 8, 9, 10, 11, 12,
    13, 14
Prerogative theory, 75
Presidential character, 84, 85
Presidential leadership, 76, 77, 78
Presidential Powers, Theories of, 74, 75, 76
President Pro Tem, 60
Property, 13, 14
Proposition, 13, 207
Protector of peace, 83
Protestantism, 4

Qualifications for Presidency, 71, 72
Quid pro quo, 112

Racial equality, 48, 49, 50, 51
Randolph Plan, 49
Reagan, Ronald, 23, 72, 78, 82, 86, 96, 102, 103,
    197, 219, 221, 225, 227
Reed v. *Reed,* 50
Regents of the University of California v. *Bakke,*
    49
Regulatory policy, 109
Religion, 41, 42, 43
Reorganization Acts, 79
Reynolds v. *United States,* 41
Ricardo, David, 4
Right to counsel, 46, 47
Right to die, 52, 53
Right to vote, 47, 48
Roelefs, H. Mark, 6, 8
Roe v. *Wade,* 51
Roosevelt, Franklin D., 23, 27, 31, 38, 74, 80, 82,
    86, 193
Rossiter, Clinton, 78, 79, 80
Rostker v. *Goldberg,* 50
Roth v. *United States,* 41
Rousseau, Jean Jacques, 7
Rules Committee, 61

SALT, 195, 196
SALT II, 80
Selection of judges, 20, 21, 23
Senatorial courtesy, 65
Seniority, 66
Separate But Equal Doctrine, 48
Separation of powers, 99
Sheppard v. *Maxwell,* 46
Sherbert v. *Verner,* 41
Smith Act, 39
Smith, Adam, 4
Smith, Alfred E., 74
Speaker of the House, 60
Speedy Trial Act, 45
Standing committees, 60
Standing to sue, 30
Stare decisis, 24
START, 197
State Department, 94
State government, 212, 213, 214, 215, 216
State of nature, 10, 11
Stewardship theory, 75
Subsidy, 110
Sunbelt, 72
Sutherland, George, 80

Taft, William Howard, 74, 86
Taney, Roger, 29
Thurmond, Strom, 62
Tocqueville, Alexis de, 12
Tongsun Park, 66
Total incorporation, 39
Trial by jury, 45, 46
Truman, Harry S., 31, 81, 86, 193, 194
Tylor, Edward B., 1

U.S. Army Corps of Engineers, 110
U.S. Department of Education, 95
U.S. Department of Energy, 95
U.S. Department of Housing and Urban
    Development, 96, 102
U.S. Department of Justice, 97
U.S. Department of the Interior, 95, 117
U.S. Department of Transportation, 96
U.S. Environmental Protection Agency, 101
U.S. Food and Drug Administration, 106, 107
U.S. Forest Service, 95
U.S. Treasury Department, 98
U.S. v. *Leon,* 44
U.S. v. *Nixon,* 31
United States v. *Nixon,* 203
United Steel Workers v. *Weber,* 49

Veblen, Thorstein, 13
Veto, 216
Vietnam, 195
Virginia Plan, 59
Voice of people, 83
Voting Rights Act of 1965, 48

Wall of separation, 42
War Powers Act, 64, 201
Warren, Earl, 27, 29, 31, 42
Washington, George, 74, 79, 200, 201, 202

Watergate, 71
Whips, 60
Wilson, Woodrow, 80, 81, 82, 83, 86
Women's rights, 50, 51, 52
Woodward, Bob, 27
Woody v. *People,* 42
Writ of certiorari, 24, 25
Writ of habeas corpus, 65

Yates v. *United States,* 39
Young v. *American Mini-Theatres,* 41